D0051135

SMART ALECK

Books by Howard Teichmann
Smart Aleck: The Wit, World, and Life of Alexander Woollcott
George S. Kaufman: An Intimate Portrait

SMART ALECK

the wit
world
and life
of Alexander Woollcott

by Howard Teichmann

WILLIAM MORROW AND COMPANY, INC.
NEW YORK   1976

Grateful acknowledgment is made to the following for permission to reprint material:

To *The New Yorker*, for excerpts from various columns.

To the Estate of Samuel H. Adams, for excerpts from A. WOOLLCOTT:
HIS LIFE, AND HIS WORLD by Samuel H. Adams.

To The Viking Press, Inc., for excerpts from THE LETTERS OF
ALEXANDER WOOLLCOTT, edited by Beatrice Kaufman and Joseph
Hennessey, copyright 1944 by Beatrice Kaufman and Joseph Hennessey,
renewed 1972 by Joseph Hennessey.

To Bernard Geis Associates, for excerpts from HARPO SPEAKS, by
Harpo Marx with Rowland Barber, copyright © 1961 by Harpo Marx
and Rowland Barber.

To the Estate of Alexander Woollcott, for excerpts from Woollcott's
radio broadcasts.

PICTURE CREDITS:

Illustrations courtesy of the following:

1, 2: Aleck's nieces, Mrs. Joan Jennings, Mrs. Polly Murphy, and Mrs.
Nancy Smith; 3: Mr. Rex O'Malley; 4, 5: Hamilton College Library; 6:
Miss Margalo Gillmore; 7, 10, 15, 16, 18, 20, 21, 24, 25, 26, 28, 30, 31,
32, 33, 34, 35: Mr. Richard Carver Wood; 17, Mr. Paul H. Bonner,
Jr.; 9: Miss Katharine Cornell; 11, 12, 13: Columbia Broadcasting
System; 19: Mr. Joseph Hennessey; 22: Mr. Francis Robinson; 23:
Lincoln Center Library; 27: *Vogue;* 29: Miss Helen Hayes.

Printed in the United States of America.

1 2 3 4 5 80 79 78 77 76

Library of Congress Cataloging in Publication Data

Teichmann, Howard.
 Smart Aleck: the wit, world, and life of Alexander Woollcott.

 Bibliography: p.
 Includes index.
 1. Woollcott, Alexander, 1887–1943–Biography. I. Title.
PS3545.O77Z9   818'.5'209 [B]   75-40129
ISBN 0-688-03034-3

BOOK DESIGN: HELEN ROBERTS

This Book Is for
JUDY

with love and devotion

Contents

Contents

Author's Note

SOME YEARS AGO I WAS SITTING IN AN OFFICE AT a television station in San Francisco. The swirling fog, driven by the wind and illuminated by the office light, shot upward wildly. The fog reminded me of the blizzards in my own Middle West where gales swept the snow from the ground and sent it streaking into the sky.

A young man with a pleasant face and too much blond hair asked me to follow him into the studio. En route to the cameras and hot lamps we struck up a brief conversation about *The Man Who Came to Dinner.*

"What do *you* know about *The Man Who Came to Dinner?*" I asked. After all, it was a play that had been written some thirty-five years ago.

"I played Sheridan Whiteside," the young man replied.

"I was under the impression that Monte Woolley had played Sheridan Whiteside," I said facetiously.

"Not in the Alameda High School production two years ago, he didn't," my young guide answered. "Tell me, was Alexander Woollcott *really* the one Kaufman and Hart were writing about?"

"He was," I said.

Just as I spoke, he swung open the door to the television studio and held a cautioning finger to his lips. Then he whispered that a commercial was being shown and that I should slip into the chair across from my host. I did as I was instructed. After acknowledging the host's kind introduction, I was expected to discuss a variety of subjects. Instead I talked for the full half-hour about Alexander Woollcott. I discussed Alexander Woollcott the newspaperman, the drama critic of *The New York Times,* the Master of the Hounds at the Algonquin Round Table, the wit, the actor, the playwright, the world traveler, the radio broadcaster, the last remaining man in an ever-maddening world who could make a success of a play or a book he thought worthy.

The half-hour, with four commercial interruptions, slipped by before I was aware of it. My host formally thanked me, and the young man with the pleasant face who had played Sheridan Whiteside guided me out of the studio and into a taxi.

"Good-bye," he said. "It was just marvelous hearing about Mr. Woollcott. How is he?"

"Woollcott?" I screamed as the cab pulled away. "He's been dead for years!"

"Who's dead?" inquired the cab driver.

"Nobody you'd know."

Back at the hotel, my wife was waiting for me.

"Very interesting listening to you go on about Woollcott," she said.

"Thank you," I answered.

"Considering that you never met him, don't you think you ought to know more about him? Suppose it wasn't a half-hour show, but an hour program, what would you have done?"

That's how I came to write this book.

It is astonishing to hear young people talk with such zest about Woollcott. I had expected—and rightly—that their parents or grandparents would remember Aleck. But to listen to youngsters no older than my guide in San Francisco chatter away excitedly about Aleck stimulated my curiosity.

Immediately upon my return to New York I began my own

form of literary archaeology. Never had there been a conversation-alist, a jester, a storyteller, a critic of theater and literature such as he. Nor has there been anyone to succeed him in the thirty-odd years since his death. During the period I researched George S. Kaufman, I frequently wondered who had shaped his razor wit. By the time I finished that happy task, I realized the model for young Kaufman had been Woollcott. Aleck, who had no model, greatly influenced the humor not only of his own time but of today.

Money was not Woollcott's goal. Recognition, fame, and glory were what he wanted. And that's what he got. He had a small talent, but he used it brilliantly. He tried to fool the world, and he succeeded. He strove to fashion a character that would be remembered. And he did.

Precisely for these reasons I write that Woollcott was an American Original. He created a style for himself which stemmed from his own shame and inferiorities. The acrimonious remarks unleashed by his tongue came from being the object of crude and insulting jokes made by thoughtless cousins or fellow students. These people were so much like one another and yet so different from Aleck that he had to find a way of becoming immune to their barbs.

This is not to excuse the bitterness distilled within Woollcott in the long years before he could begin to strike back.

It would be easy to write a puff piece about him, but sometimes Aleck exuded so much pure malevolence in his speech that an analysis had to be made to determine its cause. Research on Woollcott revealed that pain lay at the bottom of his rancor, sorrow caused cruelty, humiliation brought about his pettiness. Aleck's audacity, however, came from his own inner courage.

To compensate, he had an enthusiasm that led to excitement, which in turn induced passion that created a following for whatever he spoke of or wrote about. Aleck's boundless encouragement of his friends, their words, and their works made them consider him a life enhancer.

❁　❁　❁

Doing a biography must be very much like mining for precious stones. I read once that the first diamonds in the South African fields were found lying on the ground or at least close enough to the surface so that a stick might turn them over. Today many of the mines go down five miles beneath the earth, where the heat from this planet's molten core makes the digging strenuous and debilitating.

Digging for the truth may become equally arduous. Fear that Woollcott might be unmasked as a homosexual caused many of his friends to bring great pressure to bear on his first biographer, Samuel Hopkins Adams. The resultant work vacillated from portraying Woollcott as a kind of eunuch to implying he was a closet queen. His second biographer, writing under the pseudonym Philistina, pictured Aleck as a man hopelessly in love with a pre-teen girl, thus preceding Nabokov's masterpiece, *Lolita,* by twenty years. His third biographer, Edwin P. Hoyt, briefly employed the mumps theory as a crutch and then purposely hurried away from the subject.

I cannot subscribe to any of these deceits. Our times have changed so rapidly, and with them our mores, that homosexuality is no longer a matter for the closet but for parades.

Prospecting in the biographical field has uncovered the fact that while he might have been many things, Alexander Woollcott was *not* a practicing homosexual—even though he did have urges in that direction. In his youth there were many signs that point to transvestism. Letters, interviews, scraps of paper, and photographs have convinced modern medicine and me on that point.

During my years of excavating Woollcott, I came upon many remarkable, hitherto unknown gems of knowledge. Dead since 1943, Woollcott has remained magically alive. Certainly the many performances of *The Man Who Came to Dinner* given annually throughout the world account for a portion of the interest in Aleck. Other elements contribute to the recurrence of Woollcott as a present-day personality.

The post-World War II motion picture *Laura* has its most interesting character, Waldo Lydecker, based entirely upon the traits
of Alexander Woollcott. Clifton Webb, who played Lydecker,
appeared as the Woollcottian character, Sheridan Whiteside, in
the Chicago company of *The Man Who Came to Dinner*. Waldo
Lydecker is urbane, arrogant, witty, a gourmet with a syndicated
column, a radio program of his own, and a table at the Algonquin
Hotel's restaurant. He is lonely, demanding, slightly effeminate,
and he writes for fifty cents a word. Like Woollcott, he holds court
in a bathtub, insults or praises whomever he chooses, and admits
readily to being a most "bizarre" fellow. With *Laura* appearing
on the tube half a dozen times a year, how can Woollcott be forgotten?

Last year a character in a television drama, overweight, mus-
tached, and bespectacled, was introduced as "Alexander."

"Oh?" inquired the actor playing opposite him. "Alexander the
Great, the cocktail, or Woollcott?"

This year in *Publishers Weekly*, John J. Delaney, a senior editor
at Doubleday, stated in an article called "Bookselling in New
York: 1930s–1970s":

> But nobody before, during, or since that era ever affected
> book sales as did Alexander Woollcott. Every bookseller in
> the country gathered before the radio on Sunday night to
> hear what books Woollcott would talk about or even men-
> tion. Just a mention by Woollcott was enough to sell thou-
> sands of copies. Possibly Walter Winchell, during the war
> years, was able to have such influence. With Winchell, it
> was only certain books that took off, but with Woollcott,
> it was anything he mentioned. His charm and the enthusi-
> asm he generated were contagious and were country-wide
> in the effect they provided on book sales.

That describes his influence on the literary world. In the theater
Alexander Woollcott singly raised the place of the drama critic in

America from the role of the harlot to the profession of the journalist.

In the past sixty years *The New York Times* has had eight men in the position of drama critic. Of the eight, John Corbin served merely as a standby until Woollcott returned from the war in France. Then Corbin went back to the editorial board and Woollcott picked up where he had left off prior to the commencement of hostilities.

After his departure, Woollcott was followed by Stark Young, who wrote well, meant well, but lasted only a short time.

Brooks Atkinson made the job of drama critic into the post of a high judge sitting on the loftiest bench in the court of last resort. Cool where Woollcott had been effusive, reserved where Woollcott had waxed ecstatic, Atkinson brought to his position an erudite dignity. If any one man may be credited with establishing Off Broadway and Off Off Broadway, Atkinson is the man.

Howard Taubman had given the *Times* twenty-five years as its music critic and, as he neared retirement, found himself hustled into the drama spot. He was honest, faithful to his newspaper and his readers, well liked, and a moving force in securing the return of repertory to New York.

Stanley Kauffmann is a motion-picture critic and a good one, too. His tenure at the *Times* was not long enough to prove himself in dramatic criticism.

Walter Kerr is the equal of any American drama critic at any time. After fifteen years of stimulating the readers of the *Herald Tribune* he moved to Forty-third Street. At his own request his stint at daily reviewing on the *Times* lasted one season. Now he holds forth wittily and wisely on Sundays only.

Clive Barnes is the incumbent. In style and influence he thus far appears to be closer to Woollcott than Atkinson. He is friendly, he is warm; press him and he can sting just as quickly as Aleck. His interest in and encouragement of ballet have done for the dance what Woollcott fifty years ago did for the drama. Although his jowls cannot compete with Aleck's, and his chins number two rather than three, read him. He rivals Woollcott.

Of the eight men, only four have had great significance in the *Times* drama pages: Woollcott, Atkinson, Kerr, and Barnes. The first three have left their distinctive marks on the American theater. As for the fourth, he is presently running far ahead of the field, but the final precincts are yet to be heard from.

Although Woollcott wrote books or compiled anthologies that numbered more than twenty, magazine articles counted in the high hundreds, and radio programs and theatrical reviews listed in the thousands, he is not remembered for any large body of work. Rather, the memory of Alexander Woollcott remains alive and vital today not for what he did but for what he was.

His ability to assess talent was on a par with his ability to surround himself with people who sparkled in the mirrors he held up for them. And remember, please, that while he was holding up those mirrors, he kept the center of the stage for himself.

Aleck enjoyed greatly the enormous gift he had for bringing out the best in his friends and the worst in his enemies.

As the "Notes and Comment" in *The New Yorker* read following his death, "We are glad we knew him well, for he was a most uncomfortable man to know slightly."

I have taken the fiat of referring to Woollcott as Aleck. Harold Ross called him Alex on paper, Alec to his face, and Lord knows what behind his back. Friends wrote to him utilizing Alec without the *k* and Aleck with it. I have chosen Aleck not only because he signed the bulk of his personal letters that way, but also because among the corrective notes on *The New Yorker* profile of him Woollcott scribbled, "My name is Aleck, not Alec."

Of such small information biographies are made. They are written, however, with the aid of many individuals. What follows is a list of most of the people who were kind enough to allow themselves to be interviewed, to speak with me on the telephone, or to put down on paper their recollections of Aleck Woollcott. Their patience, guidance, and information are greatly appreciated.

George Abbott
David Abrahamsen, M.D.
Lord (Jeffrey) Amherst
Andrew A. Anspach
Shepard Aronson, M.D.
George Backer
C. LeRoy Baldridge
Lucinda Ballard
Nathaniel Benchley
Jack Benny
Irving Berlin
Paul Bonner
Charles Brackett
Irving Caesar
Marc Connelly
Katharine Cornell
Russel Crouse
Mina Curtiss
Ruth J. Dean
Howard Dietz
Ruth Dubonnet
Weyland Echols
Morris Ernst
Clifton Fadiman
Janet Flanner
Bramwell Fletcher
Edna Ferber
Geraldine Fitzgerald
Janet Fox
Vinton Freedley

Margalo Gillmore
Lillian Gish
Ruth Goetz
Dan Golenpaul
Ruth Gordon
Edith Grafton
Samuel Grafton
Alice Guinzburg
Margaret Hamilton
William Harbach
Averell Harriman
Jed Harris
William Harris
Helen Hayes
Lillian Hellman
Helen Hennessey
Joseph Hennessey
Albert Hirschfeld
Ann Honeycutt
John Hutchens
Joan Jennings
Camille Jensen
Frode Jensen, M.D.
Nunnally Johnson
Alexander King
Arthur Kober
Charles Lederer
Leo Lerman
Oscar Levant
Howard Lindsay

Anita Loos	Dorothy Schiff
Henry Lowenfeld, M.D.	Irma Selz
Yela Lowenfeld, M.D.	Mortimer Shapiro, M.D.
Clare Boothe Luce	William Shawn
Alfred Lunt	Toots Shor
Phyllis McGinley	Herman Shumlin
Leueen MacGrath	Daniel Silberberg
Irving Mansfield	Leonard Sillman
Armina Marshall	Murray Yale Silver, M.D.
Groucho Marx	Cornelia Otis Skinner
Harpo Marx	Walter Slezak
Helen Kirkpatrick Milbank	Nancy Smith
Claudia Morgan	Paul Stewart
Theresa Morse	Rex Stout
Kathleen Harriman Mortimer	Frank Sullivan
Polly Murphy	Iphigene Ochs Sulzberger
Natalia Murray	Pratt Williams Swanke
Adolph Shelby Ochs	Althea Truax
Rex O'Malley	Hawley Truax
William S. Paley	DeWitt Wallace
Murdock Pemberton	Richard Watts
Herbert Porter, M.D.	A. H. Weiler
Margaret Leech Pulitzer	Lael Wertenbaker
Paul Robeson, Jr.	Dame Rebecca West
Francis Robinson	Katherine White
Samuel Rosenberg	Isobel Wilder
Harry Ruby	Thornton Wilder
Melvin Ryder	Herschel Williams
Morrie Ryskind	Peggy Wood
Dore Schary	Richard Carver Wood
Stuart Scheftel	Sam Zolotow

In terms of further gratitude, I must thank Lawrence Hughes, president of the house that is publishing this book, for his patience in granting me an extra year for research and writing. My deepest thanks must go to Hillel Black for his confidence, encouragement, and editorial guidance. Wholehearted gratitude goes to Candida Donadio for her devotion and counsel. Still more gratitude goes to my colleagues of thirty years in the English Department of Barnard College, Columbia University—Dr. Eleanor Tilton, Dr. David Robertson, and Dr. Remington Patterson—for their scholarly inquiries and guidance.

I am indebted to William Shawn, managing editor of *The New Yorker* magazine, for generously providing me with every word written by or about Alexander Woollcott in his periodical. Additional thanks are due to Helen Stark, editorial librarian of *The New Yorker*, for the vast amount of detailed research she graciously amassed for me.

Those repositories of knowledge, the libraries, have earned a large share of my gratitude: the Library of Congress in Washington, D.C.; the Wollman Library of Barnard College; the Butler Library and the Low Library of Columbia University. Much gratitude goes to Sylvia Hilton, head librarian, and Helen Ruskell, assistant head librarian, of the New York Society Library; Frank K. Lorenz, reference librarian, at the Burke Library of the Hamilton and Kirkland Colleges; Paul Myers, curator, Theatre Collection, New York Public Library; Paul Rugen, keeper of manuscripts, New York Public Library; Joseph Viola, ranking assistant, Newspaper Collection, Michael H. Nash, library archivist, Joseph Phalen and Richard Salvato, technical assistants—all of the New York Public Library.

Additional thanks must go to Leo Lerman for granting me permission to see the sealed letters of Eleanora von Mendelsohn, presently stored in the Annex of the New York Public Library. They are not due to be made public for another twelve years, and a day spent with those letters equals a month of talking with people who remember Aleck and the baroness. To Charles Lyle and his associates at the Monmouth County (New Jersey) Historical Society, I am in debt for information of the early days of Woollcott's family and of the commune in which they lived.

As for Aleck's immediate family, gratitude must go to his three nieces, Polly Murphy, Joan Jennings, and Nancy Smith, for presenting me with a verbal family album. To Mrs. Smith I give added thanks for allowing me to read and run portions of Woollcott's childhood diary.

Helen Hayes, who showed the forbearance of a martyr in our three lengthy interviews and countless telephone calls, I can only applaud in the same way audiences have been cheering her throughout her life. I am deep in the debt of Katherine White, who insisted on applying to me the same high standards she forced upon Woollcott when she was his editor.

Aleck had no dearer friend than Joseph Hennessey, and his gentle tolerance toward my constant inquiries has won him a special place in my heart. To Richard Carver Wood goes not only my gratitude for his many fine photographs of Aleck and his cronies but also for sharing with me the flavor of the times in which they lived. Equal thanks must go to Constance Bessie of *Newsweek* and John Fink, formerly of the *Chicago Tribune*, for contributions over and above the call of friendship.

Judith Steckler carefully and, in my opinion, superbly researched this book. I cannot provide her with enough thanks. Eileen Kelly transcribed the hundred-odd taped interviews that one day will be deposited in the Wisconsin State Historical Society's Mass Communications Center. She, too, has my thanks.

Finally, my everlasting gratitude goes to my wife, Evelyn, without whose creative encouragement, editorial advice, and critical aid this book would not have been written.

H. T.

1 Stepping Out

*I*N THE EARLY EVENING OF OCTOBER 5, 1925, A young actress, beautiful and talented, walked nervously back and forth in her bedroom at 15 Park Avenue in New York. Her bobbed hair bounced as she paced and the beads on her evening gown clicked softly.

Each time she passed her mirror she checked herself. She wanted to look right. She *had* to look right, for tonight she was going to do something she had never done before.

Helen Hayes was going to an opening with a drama critic.

This was no ordinary critic. This was a haughty and urbane man, whose tongue and typewriter could pour forth invective as easily as adulation. This was the man who had discovered Katharine Cornell, Ruth Gordon, Lynn Fontanne, Alfred Lunt, Paul Robeson, and Fred and Adele Astaire. He could take credit for turning W. C. Fields from a juggler to a comic, for changing Will Rogers from a comedian to a writer. He had started as a fifteen-dollar-a-week reporter on *The New York Times* and had gone on to become the youngest and most powerful drama critic since Edgar Allan Poe. His wit ranged from impish to devastating, his friends from the Marx Brothers to the Prince of Wales, his interests varied from Charles Dickens to Dorothy Parker. He could and did hold his own with Presidents, publishers, and panjandrums of the stage.

This was Alexander Woollcott, clearly a man with whom no one dared trifle.

The doorbell to the apartment that Helen Hayes shared with her mother, Constance Hayes Brown, rang loudly. Miss Hayes's mother opened the door and Alexander Woollcott entered with nothing less than a flourish.

Mrs. Brown was horrified. The man who swept into the living room was monstrous. Although he stood a shade over 5 feet, 7 inches in height and his hands and feet were tiny, he weighed well over 250 pounds. Above his triple chins sat a face dominated by a pair of spectacles of such magnifying thickness that his eyes appeared to be fierce even when he said nothing. Under a small, beaklike nose was a seemingly villainous moustache.

His attire included white tie, tails, a voluminous cape, a huge black hat with a wide brim, and a cane with a large ivory head. He looked so debauched to Helen Hayes's mother that the poor woman excused herself, flew into her daughter's bedroom, and begged her not to go out with that man.

"He doesn't look like the kind of person you could *ever* become friendly with," she said. "Let me go back out and tell him you're not feeling well."

To her mother's dismay, Helen Hayes shook her head. Miss Hayes had been acting since early childhood. She was still very young, petite, and innocent, but even then her knowledge of the theater was vast. She knew how important the right contacts were, even to the very best of actresses. And there, standing impatiently in her living room, was the most influential drama critic in the country.

Ignoring her mother's pleas, she put on her best coat and her warmest smile and proceeded to take Mr. Woollcott's arm. Helen Hayes was off for an evening she would never forget.

In those days New York taxis were large, limousinelike vehicles with glass partitions that could be rolled up to separate the driver from his passengers.

"Maxine Elliott's Theatre," Woollcott told the cabbie after he and Miss Hayes had settled back. "Thirty-ninth Street between—"

"I know, I know," the cabbie interrupted scornfully in the fashion of his profession.

Conversation was the most important item in Woollcott's life. Writing and eating ran a close second and third, but talk always came first. He spoke easily and well. His voice may have been a trifle high but he made up for that by the force with which he expressed himself.

Did Miss Hayes like the ivory-headed cane he was carrying?

Oh my, yes.

It belonged to Coquelin.

The great French actor?

He starred in Rostand's plays, you know.

Did he?

The cane was given to him by mutual friends.

How very thoughtful.

Did Miss Hayes care for Harold Ross's new magazine, *The New Yorker?*

Indeed she did.

A good thing, too, because Woollcott and Ross and Ross's wife, Jane Grant, and Woollcott's college classmate, Hawley Truax, all lived together on West Forty-seventh Street.

So Miss Hayes understood.

Did she like the new play she was rehearsing?

She did.

What was it called?

Young Blood.

Uninspired, but then so was Calvin Coolidge and look where he wound up. Would Miss Hayes care to come to the luncheon club Woollcott had founded at the Algonquin Hotel?

The Round Table? She most certainly would.

Had she seen Beatrice Lillie and Gertrude Lawrence in *Charlot's Revue?*

At an Actors' Fund Matinee.

Had she read what he'd written about it?

She surely had.

In the Sunday paper as well?

Oh my, yes.

Did she know anything about tonight's opening? Noel Coward's *Hay Fever?*

A great success in London.

Dear Noel.

By then the cab was approaching Maxine Elliott's Theatre. According to show business rumors, the playhouse named for the great star had been erected with money advanced by the financier J. P. Morgan, although there was never any proof. There seemed to be no doubt in anyone's mind, surely not in Mr. Woollcott's, that Miss Elliott and Mr. Morgan's friendship was of a most intimate nature.

The cab stopped in front of the theater. Mr. Woollcott helped Miss Hayes out, paid the driver, and then they were engulfed by a small sea of first-nighters. An opening on a Sunday evening made it possible for every Broadway star to attend. A Noel Coward opening made it imperative.

Using his vast stomach as a buffer, Woollcott forged a path through the crowd. Miss Hayes and her escort entered the theater and bowed their way down to Woollcott's regular opening-night seats—sixth row on the center aisle. At least Woollcott bowed his way down. Miss Hayes followed obediently in his wake.

Robert Benchley, another drama critic, had taken his seat directly behind Woollcott's. George Jean Nathan, a third drama critic, sat behind Benchley.

A genial "Hello, Bob" for Benchley, a frosty stare at Nathan. A few whispered words across the aisle, a glance at the program; the house lights went down, the curtain went up, and the play began.

"It was a comedy," Helen Hayes remembered, "so I laughed to

help the actors, but Woollcott sat there stony-faced during the entire play."

Just before the final curtain descended, he nudged her. Seizing her coat, she dashed up the aisle after him and out onto the sidewalk. They walked west on Thirty-ninth Street to Broadway and then north into Times Square.

No garish neon lights poured onto the worn cobblestones. No recorded music blared through the air. Steel rails were embedded between the stones, and trolley cars with cheerful bells made their way up and down the great avenues. Incandescent bulbs lit up the theater marquees and an unknown copywriter had coined the phrase "The Great White Way." Ladies of the evening were not allowed in Times Square in 1925. Nor were empty taxis unless they remained in line at hack stands. The air was fresh, the streets safe, and the entire area looked clean, appealing, and romantic.

On Forty-fourth Street, they turned east and walked under the elevated railway that ran above Sixth Avenue until they arrived at the Algonquin Hotel. Once there Woollcott saw to it that Miss Hayes was seated at the best table. He then excused himself to go to the second floor, where he and another drama critic, Heywood Broun, kept a room in which they wrote their reviews. Tacked onto the door read the saucy message: "CAUTION! MINDS AT WORK."

Downstairs in the warm, comfortable dining room with the dark woodwork and the pink walls, Helen Hayes waited apprehensively. She had no clue as to what Woollcott thought of the evening's play. Its leading lady, Laura Hope Crews, had been a successful actress for many years. Quite naturally Miss Hayes identified with her. She was aghast to see Woollcott returning to the table after only thirty minutes.

"He came back brushing off the sleeves of his jacket," Helen Hayes recalled, "as if he were brushing off some foreign thing that had landed on him."

Woollcott smiled, pleased with the effect he had created.

"I'm just wiping off the blood," he told Miss Hayes. To her

astonishment he sat down and consumed an enormous meal. Dozens of his friends stopped by, and in between eating he cheerfully informed them how he had punished poor Laura Hope Crews for overacting and his very good friend, dear Noel, for under-writing.

In the cab on the way back to Miss Hayes's apartment, Mr. Woollcott turned once again to light conversation.

Did Miss Hayes believe that Noel Coward told the truth about taking only three days to write *Hay Fever?*

Three days did seem a very short time.

Mr. Woollcott was of the opinion such gibberish required but two days.

Really?

Mr. Woollcott thought they should have the cab turn about and take them to Noel's studio at the Hotel des Artistes. They were both invited to the party.

She'd love to go but it *was* quite late.

He understood completely. He'd confront dear Noel by himself.

"Right here, driver," he called to the cabbie when they reached Miss Hayes's building. "And hold your meter. I'm going on."

She thanked him for the evening.

He was grateful to her. They must go to the theater more often.

That would be nice.

Good night, my dear.

Good night, Mr. Woollcott.

With a surprisingly light step for so heavy a man, Aleck jumped onto the running board of the taxi, entered it, and closed the door.

"The Hotel des Artistes," he instructed the driver. "That's on Sixty-seventh Street and—"

"Don't tell me, don't tell me," the cabbie answered.

The Hotel des Artistes still stands on Central Park West and Sixty-seventh Street in New York, a citadel of luxurious living and the capital of Art Deco.

The apartment leased by Noel Coward was a sublet from Mae

Murray, a veteran of the *Ziegfeld Follies* and now, in the mid-Twenties, a star in the silent pictures produced by Hollywood. The reigning fashion at the time was to demote movie queens to consorts of European nobility. Pola Negri, a West Coast star, had married a Polish count. Gloria Swanson had gone her one better and become the wife of a French marquis. In 1925 Mae Murray selected the Russian prince David Mdivani to be her husband.

Noel Coward, fresh from triumphs in London, had come to Manhattan to star in his play *The Vortex* and to co-direct his other play *Hay Fever*. Needing a place to stay, he leased Miss Murray's apartment.

It was large, expensive, and far above the street. The living room was two stories high. The east wall, made up of several clear panes of glass, provided a magnificent view of Central Park day or night. The north wall contained a stained-glass window that portrayed a ship under full sail fighting against a storm at sea.

Statuettes of slim young nude women with small, tight breasts and overlong legs filled the rooms. The draperies were of red plush and most of the furniture was of wrought iron. In the center of the huge living room stood a high Renaissance chair with a red velvet cushion. Concealed under the chair a Victrola poured forth the flat, monaural tones of last year's hit song "Tea for Two." Over the doorway to the dining room hung tin grape leaves painted green. Many of the anxious guests looked the same color, which they attempted to change by consuming large quantities of Haig & Haig Pinch that had been delivered by one of the theatrical community's favorite bootleggers.

When Woollcott entered the studio, the feeble conversation of the opening-night party sagged to a whisper. The entire cast of *Hay Fever* and their guests watched him.

Handing his hat to a man at the door, Woollcott thrust his walking stick at another man, slipped out of his cape, and resolutely marched down the long flight of stairs to the wrought-iron gates that led into the studio.

Vinton Freedley, a Philadelphia Main Liner turned successful Broadway producer, watched Aleck push open the gates and walk directly toward Noel Coward.

"Aleck?" his host greeted him apprehensively.

"Magnificent," Woollcott pronounced.

"The play?"

"No, the apartment." His eyes drank in the high windows and his head nodded appreciatively at the twinkling lights lining the drives in Central Park.

"But what about *Hay Fever?*" Coward asked anxiously.

"My dear boy," Woollcott replied, "you should have taken two or three more days to tinker with that play."

"You didn't like it at all?"

"I wrote perfectly dreadful things about all of you terribly talented people," Aleck answered with a wave of his hand in the direction of the cast.

"And concerning you," he said blandly to the young English author and director, "as far as your playwrighting goes, I believe I wrote that Noel Coward as an industry is in its infancy. But . . ." and everyone waited, ". . . as a director, if I recall correctly, I ended my piece by praying the next time a play of yours goes into rehearsal, you be locked in a cellar."

While the women moaned and the men cleared their throats, Noel Coward uttered a single word.

"Calamity."

"Nonsense," Woollcott answered as he put his arm around the saddened playwright. "That's what they said about me, at my very beginning. 'A calamity!' And look at me tonight—bursting with good fellowship!"

2 Snow Boy

ALEXANDER WOOLLCOTT HAD OFTEN HEARD AC-
counts of the circumstances surrounding the day of his birth. Early
on the morning of January 19, 1887, a light but constant snow
began to fall over Red Bank, New Jersey. By breakfast the snow
drifts became so deep that sleds had to be used.

Getting to school posed no problem to the four Woollcott children. They and their many cousins lived on a commune called the
Phalanx, and it was within the confines of the house itself that they
received their education.

While the children climbed the stairs to the schoolroom, Frances
Bucklin Woollcott sent word to fetch the local physician, for she
could feel the intervals between her labor pains grow shorter. Having a doctor present was just a matter of form. The women at the
commune could have served as midwives. Frances Woollcott faced
the pangs of childbirth with the same equanimity she showed during
the daily travail of her life. She bore the pain without complaint.

Dr. Kimball arrived in a horse-drawn cutter by midmorning. He
entered the neat, eighty-five-room wooden house that smelled of
stored apples, cinnamon, ginger, cloves, dried berries, and above
all the odor of logs burning in numerous fireplaces. A short time
later Frances Woollcott gave birth to a son.

What few sounds came from the commune were muffled by the

29

still-falling snow. Alexander Woollcott, a man who would make so much noise in so many great cities, came into this quiet, rural world inauspiciously.

While nature enforced a silence outside, sounds could be heard in the house. A few doors away from the delivery room, the new mother's aunt Anne wept.

"A calamity," she kept repeating. "A calamity and a scandal."

Her sister, Frances' aunt Julia, bitterly complained of the arrival of the new child.

"They can't afford the first four," Aunt Julia muttered. "Why now this one?"

Both women remained inconsolable and kept to their rooms the entire day.

The father, Walter Woollcott, was an English-born rascal who could be seen only occasionally at the Phalanx. He had eyes for easy money, easy women, and especially an easy life for himself. The problems encountered by his wife and children were to be handled by his father-in-law, John S. Bucklin.

A New England man, John Bucklin had been one of the founders of an experiment in communal living inspired by ideas imported from France under the name Fourierism. This commune flourished longer and more successfully than its better-known counterpart, Brook Farm. Into it were drawn Presbyterians, Unitarians, Jews, Quakers, Shakers, and agnostics. Among them was Horace Greeley, whose advice to young men to go west took him no farther than Red Bank, New Jersey, where the Phalanx was located. Others involved in the experiment included Albert Brisbane, father of the journalist Arthur Brisbane, and Charles A. Dana, publisher of *The New York Sun.*

At the beginning all men, women, and children worked and shared equally. While the members successfully canned the vegetables they raised, little else at the Phalanx went well. It was rich only in gossip. Outsiders suspected that "free love" was being practiced. Socialism, communism, unorthodox methods of raising children and crops, every topic of malicious talk was part of the Phalanx

legend. When the founders erected the large house they considered
it luxurious. It was, however, more penurious. Although the house
boasted a ballroom, cows and goats foraged as close as the veranda.
Disciples dropped away almost as fast as the peaches in the orchard.

During one of the Phalanx's many reorganizations, John Bucklin
and his family took over the operation of the cannery. The ram-
shackle house became their home, their stronghold, their refuge.

While his son-in-law Walter Woollcott amused his daughters and
nieces and drank a hot toddy toast to the newborn boy, John Bucklin
and two of his hired men took time off from hauling potatoes to
drink to the boy's health in hard cider.

Earlier when Aleck's brothers, sister, and cousins learned from
eleven-year-old Julie Woollcott that a new baby had been delivered
to her mother, they stopped their study of Dickens' novel *Bleak
House*. Selecting a line from Dickens that read, "A young gentleman
has arrived whose name is Mr. Guppy," one of them scribbled it
onto a note and it was surreptitiously passed back and forth.

The children smiled and giggled until lunchtime. But they never
forgot the nickname they gave him that morning. His family called
him Mr. Guppy for years. As a child Aleck knew no other name.
When he started to talk, he tried referring to himself as Mr. Guppy
but could only manage "Guffy."

In the bed in which she had given birth, Mrs. Woollcott rested
and meditated, her newborn child safely tucked beside her. She
decided she would name her son after the husband of her best
friend. Eva Gallaudet had married Alexander Humphreys, a utilities
tycoon with connections as close as New York, Newark, and Philadelphia and as far away as Omaha, Nebraska, and Kansas City,
Missouri. Alexander Humphreys was a crackerjack businessman, a
clear-seeing, prominent community leader. It pleased Aleck's
mother to think that she would choose the name of a man her little
son could follow and perhaps emulate. She smiled contentedly as
she drifted off to nap.

The forty-year-old Frances may not have been as happy had she
known a medical fact. The closer the female is to menopause, the

greater the chance of a congenital defect in her infant. Modern medical science acknowledges that Alexander Woollcott was born with an abnormal condition which did not become apparent until the approach of puberty. Frances *never* seemed aware of it.

As Walter Woollcott made it his business to be away so much, Frances took it upon herself to look after their children. When he did put in an appearance at the Phalanx, Walter was sarcastic and even brutal in his speech to those he did not like. Aleck's outwardly cruel personality can be traced at least in part to his father.

Weary of raising five children without even the financial aid of her husband, Frances persuaded Eva Humphreys to find employment for Walter. Alexander Humphreys could deny his wife and therefore his wife's friend nothing.

When Aleck was two years old, his father took a job with the Kansas City Light and Coke Company that had been arranged by Alexander Humphreys. Leaving Frances and the children at the Phalanx, Walter Woollcott arrived in Kansas City, where he boarded at the home of the most beautiful widow in town. While there he joined the Kansas City Club and established a reputation as a part-time whist player and a sometime charmer. Most people thought he was a bachelor until, after six months of flirtations, he rented a house and sent for Frances and the five children.

Frances was overjoyed. She now had a home of her own, her children were with her, and Walter had just been promoted to the post of secretary of the K.C. Light and Coke Company.

Her youngest child was the pampered darling of his older sister and all of the teen-age girls in the neighborhood. They rouged and powdered Aleck's cheeks and photographed him over and over again wearing dresses. Julie's next-door friend Lucy Christie remembered that before Aleck was old enough to enter school he seemed content to play with laces and ribbons, often posing in front of a long mirror. Today, such behavior might cause trauma in some families, but in the 1890's little was thought of it.

What the Woollcotts realized *did* influence Aleck enormously and lastingly was the presence of a neighbor who lived across the street. His name was Roswell Field and he was the brother of the poet Eugene Field. Although being brother to a poet seemed grand, it was not nearly so important to Woollcott as the fact that Roswell Field was a drama critic. When Aleck was six years old, Field took him to a performance of Eddie Foy in *Sinbad the Sailor.*

From that moment Woollcott was trapped by the glitter and magic and imagery of the theater.

When Aleck became a first-grade student at the Franklin Elementary School, even his youthful and inexperienced teacher, Miss Sophie Rosenberger, recognized his precocity. He remained so fond of her that he kept up a loving correspondence with her his entire life.

His father, Walter Woollcott, who had a variety of English accents, sincerely enjoyed reciting Shakespeare to anyone who would listen. As a little boy Aleck became enamored with the works of the world's greatest playwright. But none of Walter Woollcott's socially accepted traits fooled the new management that had bought the K.C. Light and Coke Company. He had been kind to those beneath him and arrogant to those above him. He had absented himself from Kansas City for lengthy periods of time. The result was predictable. After six years, the longest he had ever held any job, he was fired, and the family trekked back to the Phalanx in New Jersey.

Aleck, who never saw much of his father, had by the age of eight acquired a distinct animosity toward him.

"The son of a bitch left us dangling from the brink of insecurity over the pit of poverty," he complained to the historian Margaret Leech Pulitzer. "What on God's good earth was there for me to love about my father? Or even admire?"

Having returned his wife and children to New Jersey, Walter Woollcott disappeared again. Young Aleck did not miss him. Although the boy retained only the haziest memories of the Phalanx, he was happy to be back.

"At the Phalanx it was plain living and high thinking," Polly Murphy, one of Woollcott's nieces, remembered. They rode to town in an old farm wagon. More often they walked. They planted, weeded, plucked, and canned tomatoes at the Bucklin cannery. They swam in Hop Brook and Trout Brook in clear fresh water. The old Indian burial grounds on the Phalanx land were respected and undisturbed. Behind them stood a hillock they called Sugarloaf.

Since the Phalanx could no longer support its own teacher, Aleck and his favorite brother, Billy, walked the two miles each day to the local grammar school. Culture, however, continued to be greatly valued at the Phalanx. Dickens was read at about the same pace that the Pilgrims studied the Good Book. Fourier having been a Frenchman, it appeared necessary that everyone at the commune learn French. In later years Woollcott boasted of his fluency in that tongue. No less an authority than Janet Flanner, who, as Genêt, was the Paris correspondent for *The New Yorker* and an old friend of Woollcott's, said of his ability to speak French, "It was lousy. Good chatter French, yes. He could sling a conversation with a waiter, but he couldn't read Marcel Proust and get anything out of it."

His friend George Backer, the author and editor, confirmed Janet Flanner's opinion of Woollcott's expertise. Backer said, "Of course he could speak better than Harold Ross. Ross's idea of French was '*Je suis, je suis* going to Bordeaux.'"

No matter what Janet Flanner and George Backer eventually thought, Aleck, then ten, and his sister and brothers were dabbling in French and settling down to the good rural life in Red Bank. Suddenly Walter Woollcott reappeared after two years of dodging about the country. Even more surprising, he had a paying job again.

This time it was the good fortune of the United Gas Improvement Company of Philadelphia to secure the services of Walter Woollcott.

The job had come his way as the result of considerable pressure exerted by Alexander Humphreys.

It had been the elder Woollcott's plan to leave his wife and brood at the Phalanx and move to Philadelphia to work and lead the life of a single man. Frances had other ideas. Believing that her youngest child had outgrown the district schoolhouse in Red Bank, she insisted that Aleck be permitted to continue his education in Philadelphia.

That posed certain problems for her husband. It would be impossible for Walter to carry on his charming escapades while sharing his quarters with his youngest son. Frances was adamant about Aleck's education. Knowing only too well that the husband of his wife's best friend got him the job, Walter struck a bargain with Frances.

Both Woollcotts, father and son, would move to Philadelphia. Walter would live in one place, and Aleck would become a boarder in another.

Frances journeyed to Philadelphia briefly to enroll her son in class and while there found a kindly, well-to-do family with a boy exactly her son's age, George Smyser Agnew, Jr. The Agnew family gladly took Aleck in. For the first time in his life Woollcott got a glimpse into how the wealthy lived.

This idyll lasted only a few months. Although Aleck and young Smyser Agnew were to become friends for life, Mrs. Agnew handed the eleven-year-old boy to a pair of elderly spinster ladies who made a genteel living by opening their home to well-bred, paying guests. Frances made sure her husband underwrote their son's room and board.

"I went to the Germantown Combined Grammar School where I neither distinguished myself nor disgraced my kin," Woollcott once told the famous humor columnist Franklin P. Adams.

In 1899 his father finally believed he was on the way to becoming a wealthy man. Together with a speculator named Gibbs, Walter Woollcott invested heavily and successfully in the stock market.

Feeling prosperous, he brought his wife and daughter, Julia, from the Phalanx to Philadelphia and set up housekeeping. Aleck left the spinster ladies and moved in with his temporarily affluent parents.

At the beginning of the year, before calendàrs changed from 1800's to 1900's, Aleck started a diary. On his twelfth birthday, January 19, 1899, the diarist listed his loot. *"The Golden Age* from Julia and candy from Polly. I had diarea [sic] and was absent from school all day." A typewriter, a bicycle, and a gold watch followed.

Further excerpts from the Woollcott diary reveal that the writer enjoyed eating and making such sweets as peppermints and fudge and that he was a great drinker of soda and lemonade. He was also unathletic, preferring books to sports and the library to the gym. He was a constant "purchaser" of flowers: carnations occasionally, more frequently violets. He wrote at length of "the great blizzard of '99," devoting six consecutive entries in the diary to that memorable Philadelphia storm.

Three more additions bear special attention: (1) "Wednesday, March 1. Mr. Murray came to visit us tonight. He is a very interesting talker"—this from the boy who upon becoming an adult turned into one of the most brilliant conversationalists in America. (2) "Friday, March 3. Bananas for supper!" He who at thirty would have eight-course dinners and savor four desserts. (3) "Saturday, March 4. This afternoon Mamma and I went to see Nat Goodwin and Maxine Elliot [sic] in *Nathan Hale.* She cried and I cried and everybody cried." Here is the Alexander Woollcott who did not change. He was always easily moved by emotional scenes.

As a future drama critic young Aleck chronicled the plays attended by his father, mother, sister, and himself. At another date he noted that he "went to see Dan Dailey in the *Belle of New York.* Lovely." Fifteen years later, "Lovely . . . N.Y. *Times"* would look good in any theatrical advertisement.

The diary of 1899 shows that the twelve-year-old boy went to Sunday school regularly, attended frequent baptisms at the First Baptist Church on Price Street, and appeared at funerals held in the Catholic church as often as twice a day. Apparently young Aleck found the rituals of the Roman Church dramatic and moving. In addition, he was a member in good standing of the Christian Endeavor, a nondenominational society composed of young people who belonged to an evangelical church. Moreover, he made extensive notes in his diary of the "sessions" he attended, but since the Phalanx did not believe in organized religion Alexander Woollcott was not baptized. When he grew older, few of the group with whom he associated believed in God. Aleck joined the nonbelievers. At twelve, though, he impressed and rather amazed his family with his keen religious interest.

On Saturday, July 1, 1899, he left Philadelphia, writing in his diary, "I went back to the Phalanx with Aunt Anne."

It was fortunate that Aleck had returned to the family stronghold, for by the end of the summer the bubble blown by his father had burst. To return to so inferior a post as employee of the United Gas Improvement Company was unthinkable. Walter Woollcott resigned and "took to his bed for two years," as niece Polly Murphy related.

In the autumn Aleck again became a boarder in Germantown. Within two years he was ready to enter the Germantown High School. Among his classmates were Harry Scherman, who some years later founded the Book-of-the-Month Club, and Ed Wynn, the future Broadway and Hollywood comedian.

By now he was pudgy, lacking in poise, myopic, and only too aware that he was different from all other boys of his acquantance. He was unable to understand or express to anyone the sorrow, disappointment, and bitterness he felt at this time in his life. In the years to come he was able to say, "I forsook God when I realized that He had forsaken me."

As an adolescent Woollcott began to realize *how* he differed from others. His sexual urges were not at all similar to his classmates'. In fact, those urges appeared mute and twisted. Precisely why this was so neither the boy nor medical science was then prepared to answer.

Later in his life Aleck unburdened himself to a few friends.

Some of them have described his dilemma, and doctors today can readily comprehend and explain it.

Woollcott was born with a hormonal imbalance * that resulted in an inadequate testicular system. Dr. Mortimer Shapiro, the eminent neuropsychiatrist, said:

> Woollcott had the fat, stuffy, amasculine appearance which one usually associates with testosterone deficiency. Testosterone is a hormone secreted by a part of the testicle that provides the secondary male characteristics such as beard and distribution of fat. The absence of it tends to give a softness to the skin and a plumpness around the hip area generally associated with female appearance.

Grafted to this constitutional defect was a psychopathological process in which he identified with a loving mother and pushed away any male identification because of a rejecting father. Given those two basic flaws, he probably had little active sex life, even though, as some prominent physicians describe it, "He was left with clusters of desire." These clusters may have ranged from heterosexual to bisexual to homosexual, but the taboos of his time were so strong they frightened off his freedom of sexual expression. An exception may be found in the inscription on the back of a photograph of a teen-aged Aleck, garbed in women's clothing, complete from dress to shoes to gloves to hat but without his ever-present spectacles:

> Under the influence of some intuitive yearning and Rose Field—at the instigation of Ivy Ashton Root—and By The Grace of God—THE PHALANX DUSE OF 1905.

Dr. David Abrahamsen, a foremost psychoanalyst, said, "He is an outstanding example of what to do with an abnormal inclination. I hardly know anyone who has succeeded in sublimating

---

* Dr. Shepard Aronson, an endocrinologist, is inclined to believe that Woollcott was born with a chromosome defect which resulted in a hormonal imbalance at puberty.

his thwarted sexual feelings in such a way as Woollcott did. He had to fight daily in order to overcome it and in order to sustain the loss of never feeling completely potent."

High school was a part-time horror. Aleck, who had known all of his life what it was to be an outsider, now found himself increasingly excluded from the class as boys from his own school and girls from a nearby school became more interested in one another.

To compensate—and all of Aleck's days were a series of compensations—he turned away from people and immersed himself in books. He always had been an ardent reader. Now came the opportunity to become a critic. It arrived in the person of a not-too-distant cousin, Miss Helen Sears. Miss Sears ran the book page of the Philadelphia *Telegraph* and her arrangement with Aleck was simple: he could keep the books he reviewed. A few years earlier he had filled up his little wagon with a dozen volumes a week at the library, but these works had to be returned. This time his cousin gave him the chance to keep *and* to review them as well.

"I devoured everything from Aristophanes to Zola. That period did not improve my eyesight, but it did wonders for my insight," he once said.

In his senior year Aleck invited Harry Scherman to his room. It was small and shabby, but piles of books rose from the floor like broken columns in a Grecian field. The floor, the bed, the table were littered with newspaper clippings and photographs. Grabbing one of the pictures, Aleck held it in front of Scherman. When he looked at it, Harry saw a composite photograph of some forty or fifty Broadway celebrities.

"That's what I'm going to be," Aleck announced.

"An actor?" his friend asked.

"A dramatic critic."

Woollcott always remembered the skeptical look that crept across Harry Scherman's face.

As Aleck approached graduation from high school, Frances Bucklin Woollcott, whose father was dead and whose husband was nowhere to be found, courageously reached a decision unprecedented in her family. Never before had a Bucklin or a Woollcott attended college, but her last-born, she determined, should do so.

Ivy Ashton, a Broadway playwright, had often visited the Phalanx. In 1905, when Aleck was eighteen and had just graduated from high school, the playwright and her husband arrived again. Ivy was married to Edwin B. Root, whose grandfather had been "Cube" Root and whose father had been "Square" Root. These gentlemen had held chairs in mathematics at Hamilton College, a small institution of higher learning located in the Oriskany Valley of New York State. Edwin's uncle, Elihu Root, had gone on to become Secretary of State, but the Roots' heritage remained in Hamilton.

Through their influence they were able to arrange a four-year scholarship for Aleck. But young Woollcott still faced the problem of finding money to buy texts, food, and clothes. That's where the utilities magnate Alexander Humphreys once again came to the rescue. He offered the boy named in his honor three thousand dollars. He could repay it if he wished or eventually give that sum to another deserving and needy young man.

"With old Humphreys' cash and a suit of Ned Root's I joined my peers that fall at Hamilton College," Woollcott said. "They weren't exactly my peers," he added, "because no one in the class was as downright poor as I. Nonetheless, I *was* Woollcott of Hamilton, '09!"

3 Class of '09

ACADEMICALLY, COLLEGE WAS A BREEZE. SO-cially, it was a torment. Hamilton plucked the protected Woollcott from the security of the Phalanx and the genteel life of boarding with two maiden ladies in quiet Philadelphia and threw him into the roisterous, sex-starved, sex-talking, sex-wondering world of an all-male college.

In this milieu Aleck fared badly. He looked, talked, dressed, and thought unlike the others. The price he paid was not banishment, but certainly a form of isolation and, as a result, rejection.

Upon his arrival at Hamilton, Woollcott stayed on the top of the college hill as a guest of the Root family. During the rushing period he was backed by the Roots, but the more prestigious Greek-letter fraternities, Alpha Delta Chi and Sigma Phi, both of whose houses stood on the crest of the hill, refused to yield to pressure and would not accept Aleck as a pledge. Not only his appearance—quite dissimilar to the other fifty-four members of the freshman class—but his intellectual and literary self-assurance filled the older boys with distrust and even more with envy.

"They could not understand a freshman who had pondered, read, and thought so much," said Lloyd Paul Stryker, a senior when Aleck entered his first year and who was to become a famous lawyer.

If the Alpha Delts and the Sigma Phis could afford to be choosy, Theta Delta Chi, then a fraternity of considerably less importance then it is now, began to regard Woollcott as a possible pledge.

Its members did so reluctantly. A considerable number of Theta Delts threatened to blackball Woollcott if he was asked to join.

"I wonder," one of them queried, "if he has to sit down to pee."

Merwyn Nellis, a hulking athlete, and at that time rated as the finest center the Hamilton football team ever had, served as president of the fraternity. He scrutinized Aleck, who possessed a high-pitched voice, a slightly effeminate manner, an unusual personality, and an eccentric appearance.

"He looks so far from the norm that the first impression on a lot of boys is that he's a freak," Nellis told Royal Wilbur France, a Theta Delta alumnus who had returned to help with the rushing.

Aleck had come to Hamilton with letters from prominent Theta Delt alumni. France decided there might be more to Woollcott than his outer appearance. Royal France recalled the young Woollcott he knew then:

I undertook to find out more about Aleck and invited him to take a walk with me. If he knew he was under critical observation, he gave no indication of self-consciousness. We walked down to the Oriskany Creek, turned west into the fields toward Kirkland, circled the hill, came up on top, and sat there for a couple of hours looking out over the valley and talking about literature, art, and life. I forgot my errand in my charm and delight in the boy himself. I was a little older—a little more mature—but he was my superior in the breadth and scope and understanding of his reading and equal to anyone I have known in the quickness and freshness of his attack on life and his sensibility to the beauty about and below us. The fields were colorful with the shades of the grasses, the goldenrod and purple asters, the trees were beginning to turn; it was a day of blue sky ridden by white clouds of many fanciful forms and the hours passed and dusk began to fall before I realized it.

I went back to the house, took Nellis aside, and told him that Aleck Woollcott was a real person, one whom the world would someday recognize, and that if I had any influence with him I wanted him to help me in getting Aleck pledged.

The football player and the recent graduate invited the dissenters into a room and convinced them that a vote for Woollcott was not a vote for depravity. The Theta Delts pledged him but without much enthusiasm.

All of Hamilton did not take to Aleck as quickly as Royal France or as obediently as the voting members of the Theta Delt house. Time and again Aleck was thrown into the campus fountain. Bigger boys, stronger boys ganged up on him and pitched him into the cold waters regardless of the hour or the temperature.

"And what, my young friend," a visiting alumnus asked Woollcott upon seeing him emerge from the water, "is our Alma Mater training you to become when you go out into the world?"

"A fish, you damn fool!" Aleck answered.

It should be noted that Woollcott the correspondent had a way of glossing over the true situation.

"I continue to love it here with all my heart and everything is just ideal," he told Smyser Agnew in the black November of his sophomore year, when he was as close to ending his life as he would ever be.

Through those first two years the bullies waited and pounced upon him.

"He never shirked a fight and never won one," recalled Alex Osborn, Woollcott's classmate. Osborn, whose name appears at the end of that magical quatrain of advertising agents Batten, Barton, Durstine, and Osborn, constantly encouraged Woollcott.

"Aleck, you're going to be another Dr. Johnson," Osborn told him. "You're going to be a greater Dr. Johnson. Don't let them get you down."

Osborn became the far-seeing exception, because the kindest word Hamilton pinned to Woollcott was "sissy." "Putrid" was another nickname they used for him, and when they shortened it to "Putt," Aleck was almost grateful that they were aware of his presence. How could they *not* notice him? Until he went to Hamilton, Aleck always had his own room; he chose his own company. Now, in the tight, close quarters of collegiate living, much of what he had always hidden so successfully became visible.

When the freshmen and sophomores listened to the upperclassmen boast of the whorehouses in the nearby towns or faraway cities such as Buffalo, Boston, New York, or even, for the well-traveled, Paris and Berlin, Aleck sat silently.

It was only when he came across Baron Richard von Krafft-Ebing's *Psychopathia Sexualis* that Woollcott read ceaselessly, over and over, in a frenzied wish to find out under which category *he* belonged.

The baron's book was of no help.

"I've been flowing through Krafft-Ebbing [sic] but the tide simply isn't in," he wrote to his friend in Philadelphia. "Actually, I am more wild about Wilde." He referred to Oscar Wilde, the Irish-born English writer of plays, poetry, and prose after whom Aleck might have copied his eccentric dress and somewhat aesthetic manner.

Further reading, however, convinced Aleck that Havelock Ellis held more for him than the baron. Ellis emphasized biology at a time when the clinical methods of the Freudians were attracting the most attention. His six volumes on the psychology of sex began to appear just at the time when Woollcott needed them.

The more he read, the more Aleck realized that his condition placed him forever in the category of those unhappy individuals whose lives are different.

By his sophomore year Aleck returned to Hamilton with a revolver. How much was melodramatic invention and how close he edged to suicide were never put to the test. Although he spoke darkly of turning the gun on himself, by the beginning of his junior year his relationships with his fellow students took a decided turn for the better.

The Charlatans, Hamilton College's first dramatic club, was founded by Alexander Woollcott. Receiving permission from college authorities to proceed with this project meant much to Woollcott. Receiving the cooperation of his fellow students meant more. Suddenly, the Charlatans and Aleck were accepted. Success, the very first Aleck had ever tasted, proved heady.

The price the founder of the dramatic club extracted from its membership was that he be allowed to play all of the feminine leads in its plays. From there he took the short step toward appearing at parties in women's clothes. The powder and rouge applied to his cheeks by his sister and her friends in Kansas City smelled strangely familiar to him. It was like putting on an old coat that had fitted well.

What fun he had passing himself off as a girl! He even had calling cards printed that read "Alexandra Woollcott." He reveled in all of it.

His schoolmates, content that he never made a pass at any of them, allowed this eccentric the privilege of dressing as he pleased.

By his junior year, even though he achieved acceptance at Hamilton, he still fretted about his image in the eye of his Philadelphia correspondent.

"You needn't sniff at my occupation for the summer," he wrote Smyser. "Almost all the waiters at Chautauqua are college men and we get board and room for our pains. All we need to do is come in at meal times, serve our table, and clean it away. . . . My other job, as janitor, requires a half hour's sweeping every day and I have to take tickets for the occasional lectures and concerts given in that hall—so you see I have most of my time to myself."

His brothers in Theta Delta Chi who had wondered if they had done the right thing in pledging Woollcott and later initiating him into their fraternity now found that his drawbacks were being outweighed by his more positive virtues. For one, there was the matter of grades. Aleck's almost straight-A academic standing raised the house average considerably. Next came the Charlatans, and finally the editorship of the Hamilton literary magazine was bestowed upon Woollcott.

Socially, it became impossible for Aleck to continue as a neuter. To wear women's clothing on occasion was equally dangerous, pleasing though it may have been. As a result Aleck began a life-long series of fabled and fake romances.

"What woman does not wish to be told she is desirous?" Aleck asked. "Where is she who will not accept a few posies, a box of candy, and a few carefully chosen compliments? I have yet to meet her."

And so it began. First people gossiped about Aleck's rumored love for a Root girl, and then about his love for a young woman whose father served as a minister in nearby Utica. His fraternity brothers talked of Aleck and the young lady whom he invited up from New York City for the Hamilton hops and who taught him to dance. But that's all it was: talk.

During his third year he started to project a gift for humor that people in later days associated with the name Woollcott. When his classmate Hawley Truax asked him how he managed to exist financially in Philadelphia, Aleck had a ready reply.

"I maintained myself by running errands for Benjamin Franklin," Woollcott answered loftily.

In the fall of his senior year Woollcott sought out the possibilities of gainful employment following his graduation from Hamilton. "Primarily, I wanted to become a teacher and actually got as far as to apply for the principalship of the high school at Hudson, New York," Woollcott wrote.

"The Hudson school board was gracious and encouraging, but during the tea table conference in what passed for a mansion in Hudson one of its more taciturn members took me aside.

"In a whisper he explained that, whereas the ordinances of the town were modern enough to frown on corporal punishment, it was an open secret that the principal must be prepared to thrash the occasional hoodlum among the students. Tranquil months might drift by without its ever being necessary actually to join combat. But that would only be because the principal was able subtly to convince the entire student body that he could, were he so inclined, take the toughest brute in the senior class and beat the living daylights out of him.

"This colloquy was held in a bay window which looked out on the elm-lined street of the old riverside town not far from Albany. At the moment three students were on their way home from football practice, their alarming bulk increased by the doggy high-necked sweaters of yesteryear.

" 'There,' said my counselor on the school board, 'could you scare the wits out of one of those?'

"So I decided to become a reporter."

The first job he attempted to obtain was on a Philadelphia newspaper. Instead of going to the managing editor, Woollcott, who always had a fondness for little old ladies, took tea with the wife of the editor-in-chief. She refused to write a letter of recommendation on the basis that it would be too much of a bother, but she did promise to telephone the managing editor as soon as he left.

Aleck made his good-byes but dawdled at the front door long enough to hear his hostess make the call.

"Mr. Dwyer, I don't know whether the boy will be able to write," she said into the phone, "but he should make a good reporter because"—and then she raised her voice and made her point—"he is the damnedest, nosiest person I have ever met!"

Woollcott let himself out and returned to college, chastened but ready to petition Samuel Hopkins Adams, an earlier Hamilton man, for a letter to a New York periodical. He received two. The first was a note that Aleck delivered during spring vacation to Carr V. Van

Anda, managing editor of *The New York Times.* He received no response. The second was a recommendation that Aleck held ready to take to Van Anda immediately after receiving his degree.

Graduation festivities called for much celebration for almost everyone except Woollcott. The carefully guarded Humphreys money had run out. He could not afford to invite a young lady to the various social events. Instead, he remained in the alcoves watching the waltzers and two-steppers. He sallied forth occasionally to make conversation with the wallflowers. His restlessness for the affair to be over was soon rewarded. The visiting young women were escorted back to their rooms, and although most of the Hamilton graduates were weary from the all-night party celebrating commencement, Aleck remained awake.

He excitedly packed and repacked, eager to be aboard the train that would take him to New York and his future.

4 Letter of Recommendation

*F*ORGOING HIS MORNING MEAL, A HIGHLY UNUSUAL
omission for him, Alexander Woollcott met two of his friends and
classmates, Hawley Truax and Philip Welch, at the depot of the
New York Central Lines in Clinton quite early in the day. The cows
on the neighboring farms had been milked but the dew in the fields
had not yet been burned off by the sun. These three young men
had been graduated the previous day from Hamilton College.
Woollcott and Welch were on their way to New York City to seek
employment as journalists. Truax was merely going home, but he
would end up as a valued member of *The New Yorker* magazine.

"Riding the New York Central in the summer is like taking an
extended tour of hell," Woollcott complained to Truax. "Everything
is there: the heat, the cinders, the wailing of infants not yet baptized, and the devils who march up and down the aisles selling
inedible sandwiches at outrageous prices."

Although his complaints were real, his mood did not match them.
Tucked inside a pocket of his jacket was the letter from Samuel
Hopkins Adams to Carr V. Van Anda supposedly recommending
Woollcott for the post of reporter on the staff of *The New York
Times.* Adams had made a name for himself as one of the early
American muckrakers. Woollcott, who always respected fame that

49

came from success, rejoiced at being the subject of the letter from Adams.

Adams wrote in his book *A. Woollcott,* "My support was on the cautious side. I guaranteed nothing, but gave my opinion for what it was worth, that the young man had possibilities, and that it might be worthwhile, to give him a trial." It did not read like a glowing letter of recommendation urging Carr V. Van Anda to hire Aleck Woollcott on the spot. But Woollcott didn't know the contents of the sealed envelope, so with the hope and foolishness of youth he confidently headed for New York.

In 1909 the *Times,* under the editorship of Carr V. Van Anda, was a long way from being the newspaper of record it is today. "At that time it was not one of the top circulating papers," Iphigene Ochs Sulzberger, daughter of publisher Adolph Ochs, recalled in her eightieth year. Van Anda had been plucked by her father from another New York daily, the *Sun,* and entrusted with the task of making the paper into one of the most respected and powerful journals in the nation. Van Anda, a highly educated, extremely intelligent man, had the ability to see into the immediate future and discern a great news story from a fair one, a good reporter from a plodding journalist.

Although the thick-bespectacled Woollcott was not yet a reporter, Hamilton College considered him to be one of its better writers. Twice he had won the college literary prize. Apparently he was endowed with *some* talent as well as the intelligence it took to be elected to the Phi Beta Kappa honorary fraternity in his junior year.

Throughout his entire life intense enthusiasm made up part of Woollcott's behavior and the letter he carried from Adams served to heighten it. He was not in the least disappointed that the recommendation was not addressed to one of what were then the great newspapers of New York City, the *World,* the *Post,* the *Sun,* the *Tribune,* the *American,* the *Herald,* or the *Journal.*

Woollcott had grown up accustomed to hand-me-down clothes, waiting on tables, very little spending money, and scholarships. Now those days of genteel poverty would soon be finished. The smoky train didn't move quickly enough down the Hudson Valley. New York City awaited him and he eagerly awaited its acceptance.

Late that afternoon Carr V. Van Anda scanned the Adams letter offered to him by Alexander Woollcott. He then quickly placed it face down on his desk.

"I'm sorry, Mr. Woollcott," he said. "I have nothing for you."

The letter proved strong enough to get him past the office boy but weak enough to keep him off the payroll.

The family of his classmate Hawley Truax lived in Manhattan. They were financially comfortable and socially acceptable, and they rented an apartment on Fifty-seventh Street. Hawley had no worries. Aleck's other classmate Phil Welch had been promised a position on *The New York Sun*. Heaven was already within his reach.

Truax and Woollcott stood on Forty-second Street in front of the Times Tower. The late afternoon sun hung over the Hudson River to the west.

"Where are you going, Aleck?" Truax asked his bitterly disappointed friend.

"To Twelfth Street and despair," came the reply.

For the twenty-two-year-old Woollcott despair was not in the apartment that he shared with his older sister, Julie, and Phil Welch. He rather enjoyed living with the two of them. Despair turned out to be found in the Chemical National Bank.

Alexander Humphreys, after whom Alexander Humphreys Woollcott had been named, for years had been instrumental in getting jobs for Woollcott's father. Now he used his influence to see that Aleck received employment first as a messenger, then, during lunch hour, as a teller in the Chemical National Bank.

During those early days in New York, Woollcott conformed as he never had before and never would again. Fear of being forced to return to the tomato patches of the Phalanx made him unusually polite and pleasing. He wore the high rounded starched collars that pinched the necks of countless American office employees in the early decades of the twentieth century. At Hamilton, Aleck had sported a red fez on his head and a variety of costumes of his own design. Now he donned a dark business suit: trousers, jacket, and vest complete with watch and fob.

"I looked like I was either in a perpetual state of mourning or was a constant candidate for the state legislature," he reminisced to producer-director Herman Shumlin.

In contrast to his later years, Woollcott kept his voice subdued in tone and his vocabulary guarded. In the future Aleck's public personality would employ shock and his private character would be a mixture of marshmallow and prussic acid. But for now he behaved very much like Charles Dickens' creation in *A Christmas Carol*, Bob Cratchit. Being an ardent devotee of Dickens from the age of ten years until his death, Woollcott successfully managed to play the role of a humble clerk.

As a teller at the Chemical National, Woollcott loathed the duties of accepting deposit slips, stamping passbooks, counting currency and silver in exchange for checks, drafts, and letters of credit.

"I wasn't exactly revolted by the sight of money," he told the literary critic Clifton Fadiman many years later. "It was the fact that I was paying it out instead of receiving it."

Spurred by his own outrage as well as a frenzy to get into the world of the written word, Woollcott showed up each Saturday afternoon in the city room of *The New York Times,* asked for Mr. Van Anda, and inquired if there might be a place for him. The answer was always negative.

Then there came a Saturday afternoon when he did not appear at the *Times.*

Half a century before Christ, Herodotus wrote about mumps. *Epidemic parotitis*, the Greek historian called it.

"In the ordinary case there may be a little discomfort," Dr. Herbert Porter, a practicing pediatrician, explained, "little aches and pains, headache, perhaps, but primarily children complain of a painful swelling below the ear and around the side of the neck. The disease runs roughly a week and there is no medication for it save for an aspirin if there is a bit of fever or headache. With male adults, it can be a different matter."

On July 15, 1909, Aleck, then twenty-two, awoke to find a swelling behind his ears. He suspected the diagnosis at once.

"That suggested mumps. It took me about two minutes to fly into my clothes and start for the Phalanx . . . I was pretty sick and got worse. By Saturday I couldn't move and had to be lifted from the bed—and then that beastly complication set in. . . ."

Although the local doctor knew nothing about hormonal imbalance and other such matters as Woollcott had been experiencing since puberty, he thought he understood the consequences of adult males' contracting the mumps. After morphine and time had eased the intense pain Aleck suffered, the attending physician had a long talk with the patient. The mumps, he told Aleck, when they were caught by grown men, could leave serious permanent scars.

Orchitis was the Latin term, and it was a grim business. He explained that one or both testicles could be affected. If only one testicle was injured, it made little difference, but if both gonad glands were attacked, chances were extremely high that future sexual relations might prove impossible.

After examining the patient the doctor felt his medical opinion had been correct. The worst had happened.

Aleck waited until the doctor had left. The mumps hadn't changed him. If every act had a reaction, if a little good comes out of every disaster, then surely, Aleck knew, he had been provided with an acceptable explanation for his weak sex drive.

"That beastly complication," he would tell those who dared to ask. And then everyone would understand. Lying in bed Woollcott arrived at a decision. He would play the role of "semi-eunuch" who, by reason of the mumps, had been afflicted in early manhood and never had to explain more.

The story that has been spread about him—that he had mumps and thereafter became sexually impotent—is no more than a myth. Today most doctors agree if a man has mumps after puberty, even if both testes are affected, he can still consummate the sex act.

Aleck quite deliberately caused confusion among his enemies and even his friends about his sexual abilities.

"Woollcott made a game of it," Janet Flanner recollected. "He told me he'd been lying under the sun and had a heat stroke and was thereafter unable to indulge in sex."

On the other hand, George Backer reminisced: "Aleck and I were on a four-day gastronomic tour of France. We found ourselves in one of those minor French cities in the south of France. We had a marvelous meal, and at Woollcott's insistence we went to a little red-light district, and literally, that's what it was—a house with a red light. We had a glass of wine and there was the most awful, dreary prostitute I ever saw. She had gold teeth and she must have been over fifty. I laughed because Aleck never was an Apollo-like figure, but even he could have done better. Woollcott took her upstairs and after ten minutes came down and said, 'Well, that's my orgasm for the year!'

"I reminded him of it on another trip," Backer continued, "but he grinned and said, 'She was a hardworking woman who needed a few minutes of rest.'"

For the remainder of his life people would guess, gossip, or claim that at best Aleck's bitchiness came from the time he had the mumps. At worst an acquaintance would say, "Aleck Woollcott was a fag but nobody ever caught him."

On his first day out of bed at the Phalanx, he timidly and cheerlessly approached the old discolored mirror in his bedroom. He forced himself to gaze at his reflection. He saw in himself a solemnity that was akin to hopelessness.

"What did I have on my side?" he said later to Dr. Frode Jensen, his protégé and friend. "I was hole-in-the-pocket poor. I had a father who was known to pawn brokers all over the east and mid-west. I had received an education that trained me only to be a well-spoken weekend guest.

"I wobbled over to the window and watched the children play-ing in the summer grass. None of my young cousins had ever been the least bit impressed with me. To them, I was flat as a shadow. Right there I decided that when they grew up the name Alexander Woollcott would matter. I swore that by the time those tots were men and women, when I entered a room everyone would take notice.

"That much I knew," Woollcott concluded, many years after his bout with the mumps, "and that much I accomplished."

5 Once a Critic . . .

FOLLOWING HIS ILLNESS ALECK RETURNED TO Manhattan. His position as messenger-clerk at the Chemical Bank was still open to him. But something within him sent him to *The New York Times* again.

"I looked positively atrocious," Aleck recounted with relish to the attorney Morris Ernst. "The circles under my eyes were vast and so saucer-like that even my eyeglasses failed to conceal their enormity. Perhaps it was out of a misplaced sense of pity, perhaps it was because I had been calling upon him so regularly, and he knew that one of the mainstays of a good reporter was that he return constantly to his source. In any case, Carr Van Anda, quite intelligently and most happily for me, engaged me as a member of the staff of the *Times*."

For eight years, since 1904, when the Board of Aldermen of New York City changed the name of the southern portion of Long Acre Square to Times Square, the Times Tower stood magnificently over its domain. It was the second tallest building in town—the Park Row Building in which the *Times* formerly had been housed was the tallest.

Behind the Times Tower stood the Rossmore Hotel. Across Seventh Avenue and a few feet toward the west on Forty-second

Street appeared the New Amsterdam Theatre, where Florenz Zieg-feld produced his *Follies*. Directly across Forty-second Street were the Hammerstein's Victoria Theatre, the Republic Theatre, and the New Lyric Theatre. Southeast of the Times Building opera stars and theater luminaries stayed at the Knickerbocker Hotel. One block north on Broadway was the Hotel Cadillac, where publisher Adolph Ochs often lodged during the construction of his Tower.

A few doors away on the same side of the street stood the famous restaurant Rector's, named for its proprietor, George Rector. It was he who said, "I found Broadway a quiet little lane of ham and eggs in 1899 and left it a full-blown avenue of lobsters, champagne, and morning-afters."

Across Broadway, running from Forty-fourth Street to Forty-fifth Street, was the New Astor Hotel, its public rooms aglitter under the twinkling of cut crystals hanging from scores of chandeliers.

"It's great up here in the *Times*," Woollcott wrote excitedly to his Philadelphia friend Smyser, shortly after he went to work on the paper. "We are in the Tower of the Times Building and can see all over the city on all four sides. It's great at night and will be fine as an observation ground during the coming weeks.

"I can't tell you how much I enjoy my newspaper work." And then he predicted, totally inaccurately, "It will never bring me any money but I love it and that's enough." (He also told relatives and friends, "I get $15 a week and I consider myself vastly overpaid.") He continued by writing:

My first assignment was an obituary of a woman who'd expired that afternoon. A woman of no importance but she'd given up the ghost in a fashionable neighborhood and, since all newspapers are snobs, this made her passing worth at least a paragraph. With anxious care as to street number, date of birth, spelling of name, etc., I wrote that paragraph and turned it in to the night city editor, Frederick T.

Birchall, who's since become famous as a foreign correspondent. In those days Boss Birchall had a red beard and a roving eye and the curious habit of addressing everyone from the police commissioner to the office boy as either Sweetheart or Dearie. I stood by while he inspected my first effort. Neatly typewritten, it began with the sad news that Mary Van Rensselaer Whoozis had just died of heart failure. When he got that far, the boss gave a low moan and began plucking hairs from his auburn beard. Next he seized his pencil, struck out the word "failure" and in its place wrote the word "disease." Then, turning as if to rend me limb from limb, he noticed for the first time that I was a newcomer, and straightway took the trouble to give me my first lesson in journalism. "Not heart *failure*, Dearie," he said, "we all die of that."

In ten seconds he'd taught me more than I'd learned in all my courses in composition at school or college.

The city room of a newspaper may be, if the student is willing, as good or even better a place to learn than most academies and universities. As it was in Woollcott's day and is now, the city room of *The New York Times* could be found on the third floor of what was then called the Times Annex, at 229 West 43rd Street. Shortly after Aleck joined the paper, the city room had been moved into those quarters from the Times Tower. Desks, typewriters, telephones, wire-service machines, pencils, and ream after ream of cheap yellow copy paper made up the properties on this set. Reporters, rewrite men, and editors formed the cast.

A spacious room, it was manned twenty-four hours a day. The *Times* was a morning paper, and the staff started drifting away as successive editions of the paper appeared. From midnight to 8 A.M. the city room contained only a few people. By midafternoon the work load increased until it reached the frenzy of its first deadline early in the evening.

Although it has undergone numerous changes, expanding east-
ward into what was the Paramount Theatre Building, westward
over a demolished apartment building known as Westover Court,
and northward over what was once the Forty-fourth Street Theatre,
the essential quality of the city room now remains as it was then.
It is a place of rushing and hurrying, of deadlines, of the excitement of getting out the news as quickly and as accurately as
possible. Fluorescent lighting has replaced incandescent bulbs, but
the staccato of the typewriters and the jangling of the telephones
today are essentially similar to what the city room was like in
Woollcott's time.

From the routine of covering New York's criminal courts Woollcott worked his way through the various staff assignments of a
large metropolitan newspaper.

That his carriage appeared more distinguished and his speech
more elegant than that of most reporters was apparent almost at
once. Aleck's behavior reminded his employers of an earlier anecdote involving their newspaper. The press had occasion to call at
the home of a society matron, Mrs. Paran Stevens. The butler threw
open the door to her drawing room.

"Five reporters, madam," he announced, "and a gentleman from
The New York Times."

A year later, in Coatesville, Pennsylvania, a black man shot and
killed a police officer. Infuriated townsfolk stormed the hospital
where the prisoner was being held, dragged him out to a slow
fire, and roasted him to death. Aleck, along with other New York
reporters, took the first train to Coatesville.

While most of the press milled about, Aleck marched directly
into the mayor's office.

"I represent *The New York Times,*" he informed the mayor
grandly, "which must insist that you take immediate measures to
fetch the perpetrators of this wholly unnecessary outrage to book
or justice or whatever your quaint custom may be here in Coatesville."

The local official looked at his young visitor, not knowing what to say.

"My personal feelings and opinions aside," Aleck admonished, "it becomes again necessary for me to warn you that *The New York Times* will not overlook reticence on your part."

The mayor shook his head as Aleck strode from the room.

The story Woollcott filed was as colorful as his approach to the mayor.

The day his piece appeared, a telephone rang in the *Times* city room.

"Can you tell me who wrote that Coatesville lynching story?" a voice asked.

"A young man named Woollcott," the city editor answered. "Who's this?"

"Richard Harding Davis," came the reply. "They don't do newspaper writing any better than that."

Aleck had been an ardent follower of Davis, a great reporter. After that he became a complete devotee.

On Sunday, April 14, 1912, at 11:40 P.M., the British steamship *Titanic*, traveling at full speed on her maiden voyage from Southampton to New York, struck an iceberg in the Atlantic. Two and a half hours later she sank. Of the more than two thousand persons aboard, only 705 were saved.

Woollcott, sent to Halifax by Van Anda, stared at the scores of bodies that had been fished out of the water-glass calm sea by rescue vessels. The sight of those corpses stacked like cordwood on the wharf at Halifax moved him deeply. The silence of the bodies seemed to shout at his nerves and notebook.

"There were moments," he told his brother Billy, "when I wished I was back at the bank."

When he returned to New York, he was considered one of the best reporters on the *Times*.

On July 19, 1912, Herman Rosenthal, gambling-house keeper, was shot and killed on a brightly lighted street outside a restaurant in the theatrical district. That seven policemen were close by and not one of them attempted to apprehend his murderers or obtain evidence of any sort caused a public outcry and newspaper charges of police corruption.

It was precisely the kind of story that intrigued Woollcott. Lizzie Borden, who took an ax and gave her father forty whacks and then gave her mother forty-one, was almost a heroine to Aleck.

"Writing about those cases," Dr. Yela Lowenfeld, a psychoanalyst specializing in problems of young people, said, "seemed for Woollcott a safe way of getting rid of his own impulses. Such sadistic and murderous feelings are a kind of catharsis."

Other papers assigned three to six reporters to the Rosenthal case. Woollcott covered it alone for the *Times*.

On July 29, ten days after Rosenthal's murder, a police lieutenant, Charles Becker, was arrested and indicted. Although Becker's annual salary had been $2,250, District Attorney Whitman disclosed that during the previous eight months, Becker had deposited $65,000 in cash in his own personal bank account.

Convicted on October 24 of instigating Rosenthal's murder, Becker was sentenced to death by electrocution.

Apparently, the pressure of overwork and Aleck's acute obsession with the subjects he covered deeply affected him. At the climax of the Rosenthal-Becker case, Woollcott suffered a nervous breakdown.

"It was a minor nervous breakdown," Aleck explained. "I say *minor* because the *Times* only allowed me six weeks to recover. If they had given me twelve weeks I may have referred to my debilitation as major."

When he went back, he was through as a reporter. He asked for and was given a job on the rewrite desk, where he became so proficient that in a short time he was called the biggest space-grabber on the *Times*.

He was still a loner, still very much the misfit. His abilities in crap shooting and poker grew rapidly but not with the speed of his writing. He actually enrolled in the Graduate School of Columbia University with the intention of obtaining a master's degree or even a doctorate, but after a semester he forsook the classroom for the newsroom.

It was in the city room of the *Times* one night that a telephone call came for Woollcott. He listened briefly and then replaced the receiver on its hook.

"Deal me out," he said. "I'll be back in less than an hour."

It took him that long to ride the subway to the Brooklyn morgue, identify the remains of his father, Walter Woollcott, who had collapsed and died on the street, order his father's body to be cremated, and ride back to the *Times* city room.

Inwardly, Woollcott did not realize that his father's death had any effect on him. Curiously, however, a short time later he began to repeat the same dream.

"All my life I have had a recurring dream," he told Herman Shumlin. "I dream I am on a train rolling north along the river. Next to me is a large, burly sort of man, a detective. I am manacled to this man and I know I am on my way to Sing Sing, *and I am the happiest man that ever lived.*"

The psychiatrists and psychoanalysts interviewed agree that it is most unprofessional to discuss a dream without the dreamer present, but they also agree that it is a fascinating series of images that Woollcott related. They volunteered to give some of the interpretations that could be made of them.

One analyst said, "If you ask ten doctors you'll get ten interpretations." He was wrong by six.

A strict Freudian said, "Woollcott's dream may have revealed his great desire to be with his father and it may have also revealed that unconsciously he had great love for his father."

Another Freudian pointed out that death held no fears for Woollcott because the greatest fear of all for a man had already happened to him: the fear of castration.

Only one of the many doctors consulted said, "A typical homosexual dream."

The consensus of the majority, however, was that Woollcott suffered from guilt and shame and his dream showed him with a father figure who was taking him to be punished—a punishment he felt he deserved because of his difference from other men and his hostility resulting from that difference.

The truth is probably a combination of all theories. Any man crippled in Woollcott's way would suffer from guilt, even while realizing he was not responsible for his condition. He might seek punishment for the unacceptable sexual desire he felt and he might seek the father he never had.

Woollcott himself put no store in Freudian doctrine.

"I don't believe in psychoanalysis," Aleck told his colleague on the *Times,* Murdock Pemberton. "I think it dangerous to probe the human brain. The unconscious should remain just that: unconscious."

An older Woollcott was to look back twenty-two years and give his portrait of himself as a *Times* newspaperman.

His name is Woollcott. Alexander Humphreys Woollcott. Later he'll throw that middle name overboard as too darned heavy to carry. He is twenty-five and the young among you would be surprised to learn how many things he doesn't know. We might describe him in terms of them.

Let's see. He's suffering from an inferiority complex but he's never heard of one. He's never heard of daylight-saving. Nor rayon. Nor Soviets. Nor jazz. Nor insulin. Nor G-men. Nor broccoli. He's never seen a one-piece bathing suit nor read a gossip column. He's never heard of a fox-trot. Nor a step-in. Nor inhibition. He's never tasted a tomato juice cocktail. He's never heard a radio nor seen a talking picture nor listened to the whir of an electric ice-box. He's never seen an animated cartoon nor a cement road nor a Neon light. No, nor a trailer, either. Nor a filling station. Nor a wrist watch.

You see, he does live in a world quite different from the one to which you and I must soon return. His very ideas are different. Take two as a sample. What does he think a job is? He thinks a job something any man can get who's willing to work. And a war? Why, war is a practice still carried on only by remote, comic opera countries in Central America and the Balkans. How much he has to learn!

As he grew more secure in his job at the *Times,* Aleck's personality opened up—particularly in terms of his favorite subject, theater. Once he said to the gang in the city room: "Mr. Clark played the king all evening as though under the impression that someone else was about to play the ace." Aleck gave credit for that line to Eugene Field when that gentleman was drama critic on the Denver *Tribune.*

Encouraged by the reporters' laughter, Aleck used another of Gene Field's lines:

"So-and-so played Hamlet last night at the Tabor Grand. He played it till one o'clock." Well, that was more amusing than murder or mayhem.

Frequently, he credited an earlier critic:

"To say of a bad play that some of it is pretty good is a little too much like saying of an unpleasant egg that at least part of it was fresh."

Nineteen-ten. Nineteen-eleven. Nineteen-twelve. Nineteen-thirteen. The years raced by. Woollcott's sister, Julie, married a printer named Charles Taber. Aleck stopped in often to offer gifts of food and necessary surprise packages of clothing. Much financial aid was needed by his mother, who remained at the Phalanx. Aleck gave it.

At the *Times* he continued to drop jewels of theatrical wisdom. He was devoted to Coleridge's comment on Kean's Hamlet: "Seeing it was like reading Shakespeare by flashes of lightning." It was a good line and Aleck liked it.

He also delighted in a line of Sir Arthur Tree, the British actor-manager-director. "Ladies," Sir Arthur said at rehearsal once, "ladies, just a little more virginity, if you don't mind."

The city room roared and Aleck enjoyed hearing the laughter. It was a friendly sound, amiable, likable—all the things Aleck wished people to think him. Laughter, however, is also a noise, and noise caught the attention of Carr Van Anda. Rather than lecture Woollcott on the duty of the journalist to act as a serious member of society, Van Anda waited. One day he might very well repay Woollcott in kind.

It is impossible to determine whether Aleck deliberately planted an aura of theatricality about himself or whether it was an unconscious wish to get those free seats Roswell Field had been given back in Kansas City. When he was seventeen, Aleck had decided to become a dramatic critic. It wasn't until he was twenty-seven that luck and a lady stepped in.

Miss Jane Cowl, as she preferred herself to be billed, was a star of the first magnitude in her day in the American theater. She had been born in Boston three years before Mrs. Woollcott gave birth to Aleck in New Jersey. As an actress she had beauty, intelligence, and talent. No one could or did ask for anything more. Three years after Woollcott joined the *Times*, her name appeared above the title of the play *Within the Law*, guaranteeing her billing as a star.

Two years after that, Miss Cowl and Adolph Klauber, dramatic critic for *The New York Times*, decided to marry. Klauber would give up his work as a newspaperman and become her husband and producer. His marriage to Miss Cowl did not last forever, and eventually he would return to the *Times*. However, the prescient Van Anda could not forecast such events and he had to decide how to fill the vacancy left by Adolph Klauber's sudden departure.

There had been many good drama critics in the United States: the poet and short-story writer Edgar Allan Poe had written dramatic critiques; Nathaniel Hawthorne, the novelist, had done the same; so had Walt Whitman, poet and conscience of the North during the Civil War. The list was long and distinguished. All of those men suffered from a common malaise: it was the somewhat unpleasant job of the drama critic on American newspapers to solicit advertising from the theatrical managers or producers.

More often than not, the amount of space purchased was determined by the quality of the review written by the drama critic.

When Carr Van Anda offered the post to Woollcott, Aleck was stunned, overwhelmed, grateful—and yet he had a single request: might policy be altered so that the drama critic of *The New York Times* did not have to solicit advertisements from the management of the plays he reviewed?

Clearly this raised a question Van Anda could not answer. It was sent to the publisher.

Adolph S. Ochs was born March 12, 1858, and began earning his living at the age of eleven. He carried newspapers for the Knoxville (Tennessee) *Chronicle* at twenty-three cents per day. At the age of nineteen, he and two other men, F. S. Paul and J. E. MacGowan, started a newspaper in Chattanooga, Tennessee. It was called the *Dispatch* and it folded within six months. According to his biographer, Gerald W. Johnson, Ochs "was left literally without the price of a ticket to Knoxville."

Eventually, Adolph Ochs did return to Knoxville, where he became a printer. A few years later he became publisher of the *Chattanooga Times.* His capital at the age of twenty was $12.50! His purchase of *The New York Times* in 1896 grew out of a disastrous real estate investment. Ochs could have erased the debt by declaring bankruptcy but his personal integrity was such that he put up the *Chattanooga Times* as collateral and bought *The New York Times* for $75,000. In 1896 the *Times* was "a wreck of a great newspaper."

Adolph Ochs was short in height but a giant when it came to publishing a newspaper. When the question was put to him, Must his drama critic solicit ads? the answer was a single word: no.

In declaring that simple, one-syllable word, Ochs struck a blow for the freedom of drama criticism throughout America.

" 'Standing, one winter evening of 1914,' wrote Samuel Hopkins Adams, "at the Knickerbocker Bar, where the jolly and luminous Maxfield Parrish mural of Old King Cole lent a special savor to one's cocktail, I was accosted by a rotund young man who said with an air of reproach verging upon accusation:
" 'You don't remember me. I'm Woollcott.'
" 'I do,' I said. 'How are you?'
" 'You told Mr. Van Anda that I would make a good reporter.'
" 'Are you a good reporter?'
" 'I was,' he said with empressement.
" 'Have you left the *Times?*'
" 'No. I've just been made dramatic critic.'
"He was bubbling with enthusiasm," Adams recalled.

"I took the job," Aleck told the boys in the city room, "because I thought Jane Cowl went with it."

That was Aleck on the surface. Underneath he could scarcely contain his zeal. His boyhood fantasy had become reality. With great pride he wrote his mother of his advancement. She answered with a dash of cold water.

"I should think it would be very narrowing," Frances Bucklin Woollcott said in a letter to her son.

Alexander Humphreys Woollcott spent the rest of his life proving how broadening the post of a drama critic could be.

Moreover, in contrast to the harsh realities he had spent so much time observing, the world of make-believe opened gentler vistas.

He remained in New York writing reviews until June. Then it was thought by Van Anda that Aleck needed an education in the European theater. The *Times* packed him off to London, Paris, and Berlin.

"Prior to my departure," Aleck wrote, "I received an anonymous note in the mails from a person whom I took to be a nonadmirer. He reminded me of John Fuller's quotation, 'If an ass goes traveling he'll not come home a horse.' The letter writer must have received one of my neighs already. He should practice his braying while I am gone."

Woollcott fell in love with London at once and forever. Those four weeks in the British capital as the drama critic for *The New York Times* gave him a sense of confidence and pleasure such as he had never before known. He was shedding the many protective layers that he had accumulated over the years and began to feel free and, what's more, important. He was, he realized, Alexander Woollcott of *The New York Times*. At last the sense of belonging began to set in. It excited him and pleased him. Being somebody was infinitely better than being nobody. The longer he contemplated his new station in life, the more exquisitely good he felt about it.

In Paris, Aleck met his New York colleague Burns Mantle, an older and more sedate drama critic. The older man lectured him. No reviewer should associate with actors. They were fascinating people, but if a critic became involved with their personal likes and dislikes, he could no longer be objective, and as a result he would lose prestige for himself and his newspaper.

Woollcott listened politely. How could he tell Burns Mantle that he already had an appointment the following day with Mme. Sarah Bernhardt?

As Europe was preparing to slaughter its men in World War I, Woollcott sailed for home. Mme. Bernhardt and Mrs. Patrick Campbell were indelibly marked as actresses of heroic stature, while Laurette Taylor and Ada Rehan were etched in his mind as their American counterparts.

His reviews during that 1914–1915 season read quite badly today. They were saccharine, partisan, and filled with such trite
phrases as "these old eyes" and "this thoroughly wretched reviewer."

Woollcott's critiques were always honest, though they were, as
Burns Mantle had cautioned him, prejudiced in favor of those he
liked. In addition to Ada Rehan and Laurette Taylor, the Barrymore family—Lionel, John, and eventually Ethel—became his pets.
He lavished praise with a heavy, sugary hand. What he wrote,
however, began to attract the attention not only of readers of the
Times but of others who were interested in the theater.

Conceivably, he might have been content with his slowly increasing prestige, had not the Shubert brothers declared war
upon Woollcott. The conflict in Europe claimed enough attention,
but open hostilities in the New York theater were immediate and
dramatic.

They took Woollcott from obscurity to prominence, and they
helped give the *Times* the circulation necessary to become one
of the nation's top-ranking newspapers.

David Szemanski was a peddler from Poland. A pogrom drove
him from his native land to New York City. A year later, in 1882,
he sent for his wife and six children, Levi, Sam, Jacob, Fanny,
Sarah, and Dora. The family then moved to Syracuse, where David
had relatives. The name Szemanski was changed several times
until it became Shubert. Levi went to work in a haberdashery,
Sam got a job in a local theater, and little Jacob sold newspapers.

Within five years Sam became treasurer of the theater, and
when *The Texas Steer* folded there he took over the production.
He booked the show throughout the Mohawk Valley with such
great success that he eventually toured it across America.

By then Sam S. (for alliteration) was a financially solid teen-
ager. The question to be faced: Should Sam join his older brother
Levi in the haberdashery shop, or continue to promote *The Texas*

Steer? As Levi was spending all of his spare time at the theater, Sam decided he would remain in show business. Levi (it was shortly shortened to Lee) watched the store and waited. Jacob (eventually he would be called J. J., the second *J* having as much meaning as the second *S* in Sam S. Shubert) was different from his two older brothers.

They were dark-haired, dark-skinned, dark-eyed, brooding, short, thin men. Jacob had pink skin and blue eyes, was five inches taller and built like a hog butcher. He also enjoyed fighting, a necessary attribute to his vocation. His favorite place for selling newspapers was outside a hotel frequented by horseplayers. If they were lucky, the tips were big; if not, it was merely a penny for a paper. Many boys tried to take that location by force but none succeeded, because when Jake fought it was to win.

By 1915 Sam was dead. Lee and J. J. were in New York City and well on their way to taking over the American theater.

That they hated each other didn't matter as much as the fact that they despised everyone else: Klaw and Erlanger, kings of the legitimate theater; Keith and Albee, rulers of the world of vaudeville. All Lee and J. J. loved was the theater, money, their mother and sisters in that order.

On March 17, 1915, St. Patrick's Day (as good a night for a fight as any), the Messrs. Shubert opened a small French farce, *Taking Chances.* "In light of what happened," wrote Jerry Stagg in his biography of *The Brothers Shubert,* it was "a prophetic title."

Suspecting what the reviews might be, the Shuberts took ads in all fifteen New York dailies to appear on the morning after *Taking Chances* opened.

TO THE PUBLIC

Do not believe everything you see in the notices today. And though some of the critics, lacking in humor, may try to make you believe that somewhere there is something a

little bit off the line in *Taking Chances,* the management
is not taking any chances in extending its assurances to you
that this impression is decidedly wrong. You will like *Taking Chances* just as the rest of the audience did last night,
when the play scored one of the most sensational comedy
hits ever known in the American theatre.

The Management

There was one good review, six noncommittal ones, and
eight pans. The one good review ran in a newspaper owned out-
right by the Shuberts. The remaining fourteen reviews, six so-and-
so and eight pans, included a blast from *The New York Times.*

Under ordinary circumstances, critics receive their opening-
night tickets either at their homes or their offices. It was, therefore, something of a mild surprise to Woollcott to walk into the
Times city room to be told that the managing editor held a pair
of seats for that night's opening of Charles Dillingham's play at
the Maxine Elliott Theatre. A note accompanied the tickets. As
the Maxine Elliott was a Shubert-owned house, would Mr. Van
Anda be kind enough to have anyone on the *Times* staff, with the
single exception of Alexander Woollcott, review the play?

"I don't take orders from the Shuberts," Woollcott remembered
Van Anda saying. "If you're our critic, review Dillingham's play."
And he tossed the tickets and their note to Aleck.

Woollcott never got inside the Maxine Elliott Theatre that night.
J. J. Shubert, flanked by two house managers, physically barred
the entrance.

By the time Woollcott plodded back to the newspaper, Van
Anda had already left. Frederick T. Birchall, the night city editor,
did not have the authority to act. Privately Woollcott wondered
to his sister, Julie, and a few friends if his time as drama critic
had run out.

What were the Shuberts up to? Van Anda asked the next morn-

ing. Were all the critics barred who disliked *Taking Chances?*
Again Carr Van Anda went to see Adolph Ochs. The issue was
plain, freedom of the press! The cause would become a newsman's
jihad, a holy war.

Ochs, still short on cash but long on genius, filed for an injunction in the courts to bar the Shuberts from keeping his critic out
of their theaters. On the day the injunction was served, Ochs informed the Shuberts that no advertisements for any Shubert theater would be accepted in the pages of *The New York Times,*
effective as of that date! The battle had been joined.

What started out as a local dispute spread in prairie-fire fashion
across the country. It was indeed a journalistic holy war. Woollcott
and the *Times* became banner headlines and the foremost editorial
writers in the nation began attacking the Shuberts.

The first round went to the *Times,* but the Shuberts appealed
at once. By now Aleck, who had talked his way into a column on
the Sunday drama page—"Second Thoughts on First Nights," he
called it—suddenly found that the publisher would accept four
columns.

It wasn't that Ochs was entranced by Woollcott.

"My father never liked him. He wasn't his type," Iphigene Ochs
Sulzberger, the remarkably candid lady of distinction, recalled.
"He thought he was a good critic but personally he didn't appeal
to him. Except my father firmly believed in freedom of the press
and he thought when he gave a man a job to do, it was his job to
do it the best he could and he would never bow to pressure from
advertisers of any kind."

So there it was. The issues were clear. And when the Court
of Appeals ruled in favor of the Shuberts and against the *Times,*
every editorial gun in the country went off.

By the end of hostilities Woollcott had been barred twenty-two
times from Shubert productions and not a single line of Shubert
advertising ran in Adolph Ochs's newspaper. Meanwhile, the
Times received a healthy boost in circulation. Aleck got a raise

in his weekly pay envelope and his first by-line. Only the Shuberts were being hurt.

Love of the dollar overcame the brothers' hatred of Woollcott. Although they were winning in the courts, they were losing at the box office. And if the Shuberts read anything at all, it was their own weekly box office statements. After almost a year peace overtures began.

It is doubtful that Ochs, a Southerner, believed in unconditional surrender. He didn't want Lee and J. J.'s theaters. He simply wished his reporters and critics to write as they pleased. Any tampering with their copy would be done by the editors of the *Times*. When the Shuberts agreed that Woollcott would be allowed inside their houses on opening nights, Ochs began to accept Shubert advertising again.

"For Lee, it's Appomattox all over again," Aleck remarked upon hearing of the cessation of belligerency on Forty-fourth Street. "Come to think of it, General Jake's lawyers can beat their swords into candy canes. He can sell them in the lobbies."

There was no doubt in anyone's mind as to who won and who lost. When the Shuberts, knowing of Aleck's newly found fondness for Cuban cigars, sent him an enormous box of the finest Havanas, Woollcott quipped, "The whole thing went up in a puff of smoke."

6 Safe for Democracy

WOOLLCOTT'S WAR WITH THE SHUBERTS WAS scarcely over when the war in Europe looked uglier for the Allies. German long-range artillery pounded Paris; the Mexican folk hero Pancho Villa invaded Texas; the Kaiser's U-boats indiscriminately sank Allied or neutral ships on the high seas.

The culmination of it all came in the spring of 1917.

On April 2, President Wilson appeared before a Joint Session of Congress and asked for a declaration of war.

On April 4, the Senate voted 82–6 in favor of such a resolution.

On April 6, the House followed the Senate, and Wilson signed a proclamation declaring that "a state of war exists between the United States and the Imperial German Government."

It was a war for which they really wrote songs. The French had one called "La Madelon," while the British chipped in with "Tipperary." Not to be outdone, the Americans came through with George M. Cohan's "Over There" and Irving Berlin's "Oh, How I Hate to Get Up in the Morning."

The Conscription Act established the draft. War Loans raised money to finance the conflict. Al Jolson, Elsie Janis, W. C. Fields, Ed Wynn, and other theatrical stars stood on street corners during the lunch hour and sang and joked so that ticket buyers on Broadway and stock buyers in Wall Street would contribute.

Victory Gardens were started by any city dweller who had a

patch of soil that could grow potatoes, tomatoes, or beans. Hamburgers became Victory Steaks. Tens of thousands of citizens whose families originated in Germany or Austria anglicized their names.

Everywhere James Montgomery Flagg's classic poster of a stern Uncle Sam pointing his index finger directly at the viewer read, "I Want *You* For U. S. Army!"

Because his manhood had long been suspected by his family, his friends, and himself, because he loved England and was entranced by France, because Americans in those innocent days thought of warfare more as a sport than a massacre, Alexander Woollcott, who was always seduced by the dramatic—and what appeared more dramatic than war?—was among the first to volunteer.

A single look at his pear-shaped torso with its flabby muscles and bulging belly made it instantly clear that he was not material for the infantry. Or the cavalry. Or the artillery.

Still, there *had* to be a place for someone with as much desire to serve his country as Woollcott. And to serve meant not some stateside desk job, but overseas in France.

The same determination that landed him a position on the *Times* got him a khaki uniform. Volunteers from New York's Postgraduate Hospital formed a medical unit. The officers were mostly the doctors and nurses. Woollcott was permitted to enlist as a medical orderly.

He was quite a sight. After two months of training on Governor's Island in New York harbor, Private Woollcott waddled up the gangplank with his backpack, barracks bag, gas mask, canteen, mess kit, and a new life preserver. At the first boat drill a popeyed officer called out, "For God's sake! Who's the pregnant mermaid?"

The officers and men of U. S. Base Hospital #8 embarked from Hoboken aboard the *Saratoga*, a fruit ship that had been taken off the Central American run and diverted to the use of her country. The *Saratoga*, carrying an apprehensive Woollcott, sailed for France and went as far as Staten Island, when it was rammed and sunk by the liner *Panama* just in from Colón.

Fortunately no one was injured, and two days later the medical unit shipped out again. On the journey across the Atlantic, Aleck, who had been brushing up on his French, offered to instruct the officers in the intricacies of irregular verbs. As a result Private Woollcott was moved from the steamy bowels of the ship to the cool and comfortable forecastle.

After disembarking in St. Nazaire, the commanding officer of Base Hospital #8 ordered his troops to march thirty-five kilometers to the village of Savenay. Thirty-five kilometers meant twenty-one miles, and with full equipment and a hot August sun beating down upon them, the men hardly thought of it as a stroll around Times Square. On the day of the landing, Aleck, already wise in the ways of soldiering, conveniently tripped on the deck of the troopship, tore a ligament in his ankle, and rode in a transport to the base.

Eventually, to make the world safe for democracy, Aleck did hike and worked a good deal of suet off his rotund body. He was, after all, thirty years old, while the bulk of the enlisted men in Base Hospital #8 had been Princeton boys who, as he claimed, had enlisted in May to escape the June exams.

Newspaper correspondents from New York located Woollcott and came to visit him. Heywood Broun and Ruth Hale arrived to find him hiding in a shed, refusing to participate in close order formation under the command of a captain.

"I will not be drilled by a dentist!" Woollcott railed, and then grinned at his own joke.

His mother died while he was in Savenay, and Aleck was inconsolably depressed. Promotion to sergeant did little to boost his morale. It was only when a telegram arrived inquiring if he could be assigned to *Stars and Stripes* that he perked up. As the colonel was away at the time, Aleck and the adjutant collaborated on a telegram: SERGEANT WOOLLCOTT HAS DONE MAGNIFICENT WORK HERE BUT CAN BE SPARED.

Immediately after Aleck arrived in Paris, checked into the Hôtel

Continental, and walked out onto his balcony for a view of the city, the heavens burst into a hysteria of aerial warfare. Searchlights sweeping the sky illuminated the dogfights. Fires from falling bombs added more color. Sirens wailed.

Heywood Broun, who joined Aleck during the bombardment, inquired if he was afraid.

"After you've carried a bedpan in a syphilitic ward you're not afraid of anything!" Woollcott snapped.

He added that the entire display looked like the Hippodrome director's idea of warfare.

The reticence of the French impressed him greatly. That Paris could be bombed so heavily every night without a word of it seeping out seemed a tribute to Gallic stoicism. Not until the next morning did he learn that this bombing had been the worst air raid Parisians had ever undergone.

Somewhere, somehow, someone got the idea of having an enlisted man's newspaper, which was called *Stars and Stripes*. At the beginning the paper was under the command of officers, but quite early in its history the lower ranks voted to keep officers out of the day-to-day publication of the newspaper. A private and a sergeant sent the officers out on assignments. A reporter, beaten to a news story by another publication, wound up in the guardhouse. *Stars and Stripes* was that kind of paper.

The officers included Lieutenant Adolph S. Ochs, nephew of the publisher, Lieutenant Grantland Rice, Captain Franklin P. Adams, Captain Stephen Early, and Captain Guy Viskniskki. Following the war, Grantland Rice became one of America's foremost sportswriters. Adolph Shelby Ochs became general manager of the *Chattanooga Times*. Stephen Early became Franklin Roosevelt's press secretary. Franklin P. Adams was and continued to be America's finest humor columnist. He and Aleck stayed close companions for the rest of their lives.

The staff was composed of men who had worked on newspapers

in the States. The most important were a former ship's reporter from the San Francisco *Call,* Private Harold Ross, and, of course, Sergeant Alexander Woollcott.

The enlisted men elected Ross as one of the editors. He was twenty-four years old, tall, gawky, and brilliant. Half a dozen years later Ross founded *The New Yorker* magazine. He continued as its editor until his death in 1951.

The second most important staff member was its frontline correspondent, Sergeant Woollcott. Although Ross and Aleck were destined to spend much of their lives together, Ross always looked slightly askance at Woollcott because of those sergeant's stripes. John T. Winterich, one of the founders of *Stars and Stripes,* said, "Woollcott probably got into the Army as a result of a clerical error." Woollcott had wanted to see the front ever since Wilson's declaration of war. Ross gave him the chance.

There were two million American troops in France by the end of the conflict, and General John J. Pershing commanded them. Probably more doughboys saw Woollcott than Pershing. What the Shuberts had started, the war finished: Aleck became famous. Wally Wallgren's cartoons of Sergeant Woollcott fearlessly mincing his way across the tops of trenches, totally oblivious to incoming small-arms fire and artillery rounds, ran regularly in *Stars and Stripes.* Wallgren's cartoons of Woollcott often showed the intrepid correspondent carrying a single rose in one hand, an image to which Aleck strenuously objected. Woollcott quickly learned the price for being sketched without the offending flower. Whenever he returned to Paris he had to keep Wallgren completely saturated in cognac. If he failed to do so, the audacious Woollcott appeared in *Stars and Stripes* bearing the solitary rose.

The doughboys chortled at this version of Aleck but their whistles and hoots did not stem from derision, for they saw Woollcott personally covering every major battle from the first commitment of the United States Marines in the battle of Belleau Wood to the last shots fired before the Armistice on November 11, 1918.

Traveling with a pass signed by the highest military authority in Paris, Woollcott went everywhere, saw everything, and wrote it all up. He slept in the back seats of automobiles, and failing that, near any convenient haystack, from which he pulled down enough hay to make a soft bed.

Aleck's frontline dispatches were cold, careful reporting of a brutal war. His behind-the-lines features ranged from a sentimental story about a dog and her attachment to a Marine to a hard-boiled cook who pulled a .45 on an M.P. when he was stopped from delivering hot food to the boys in the trenches.

Aleck was the first to write about an immaculately dressed brigadier general who stood on the sandbags atop the trenches in full view of the German gunners and coolly surveyed their position through a pair of field glasses. His name was Douglas MacArthur.

Aleck was also the first to mention the chaplain of New York's Sixty-ninth Regiment. His name was Father Duffy, and the northern pie wedge of Times Square where his statue stands today has been renamed Duffy Square.

Woollcott did not resemble any other American soldier in France. He bulged in the wrong places, his puttees dragged. Somewhere he found a German officer's sheepskin coat and liberated it. In front of the coat he wore a frying pan, and behind it he wore a shawl around his shoulders.

During a brief stay in Paris, Aleck dined with the sweetheart of the American Expeditionary Force, Elsie Janis, and her mother. It was a lavish dinner and Sergeant Woollcott was footing the bill. Midway through the meal Mrs. Janis mentioned the draft back in the States and how men of all standing were being conscripted into the armed forces.

"That means *you*'ll have to go into the Army, doesn't it, Aleck?" Mrs. Janis asked innocently.

Even the glories of French cooking were ruined for Woollcott, at least for that evening.

At a time when patriotism appears to be wavering, it is necessary to report that Woollcott's devotion to his country, its flag, its ideals, and, above all, to the men who fought and died in the mud of a foreign field was absolute.

Stars and Stripes served to keep American troops informed and entertained. It also proved an excellent channel for opinions of the General Staff to reach the enlisted men without going through the chain of command. The day after the Armistice in November, 1918, every American division in France decided that it should be shipped home immediately. Grumbling grew loud when transports were not available.

C. Le Roy Baldridge, another cartoonist on *Stars and Stripes*, put an end to the complaints with what is still one of the most moving drawings of that or any other war.

"It was simply a chill corner of a battlefield," Woollcott wrote in the *Saturday Evening Post* in 1928, "bare as the face of the moon. The drawing showed two stretchers covered with a muddy blanket. It was a sight too many of us had seen not to have known from the very contour and folds of those blankets that there were dead men underneath—dead men waiting for the burial squad to saunter past and stick them somewhere underground. But it was the title of his cartoon that transformed it into as telling a tale as ever I saw—effective in its little movement of time as sometimes a hand may be when it is lifted to still a tumult. The drawing was called 'THE FIRST TO GO HOME.' "

In 1919, Aleck traveled to Germany with the Army of Occupation. With his mother dead, the Phalanx was empty of Woollcotts. He felt no need to rush home.

Alone in Germany, he once again became unsure of himself and uncertain of the future. He hung around the Rhineland until he heard that the younger men on the staff of *The New York Times* were referring to him as "God's Big Brother." Delighted that people at home still remembered him, Woollcott sought and received an immediate honorable discharge. He returned to New York in June, 1919, with a large portion of the staff of *Stars and Stripes.*

The America he found was already racing toward the Volstead Act, paved roads, bobbed hair, short skirts, flappers, Warren G. Harding, and "normalcy."

"I scarcely had time to get on the merry-go-round," he told playwright Russel Crouse, "but when I did, first thing I grabbed was the brass ring."

7 ... Always a Critic

WOOLLCOTT ARRIVED IN TIME TO ATTEND GRAD-
uation exercises at Hamilton College. From there he took the train
back to New York, turned up at the *Times*, and asked if his old
job was still open. Once he learned that it was, he was instantly
relieved and made the rounds of the city room.

It was there that he first met a tall, dark-haired young man who
had been appointed drama editor while Aleck was away. Aleck
endeared himself at once. Having need of some minor legal advice,
Woollcott asked the reporters who gathered around him for an
attorney. One of them suggested a name.

"I need a lawyer, not a liar!" Woollcott declared.

The skinny, bespectacled assistant, George S. Kaufman, realized
from Aleck's first words that Woollcott was a man to whom he
could listen and learn.

Banter between these two men would continue throughout their
lifelong friendship. When asked to describe Aleck in a single word,
Kaufman replied, "Improbable."

When Aleck returned to Manhattan he had taken a single room
in the City Club. But loneliness forced him back to the arrangement of Hawley Truax and his mother on West Fifty-seventh
Street, where he had lived before the war began. Woollcott hated
living alone. The Phalanx made him crave communal living. He

had been enveloped there by his mother, his sister, his brothers, his cousins, his aunts, his uncles, and their many friends. Throughout his life Woollcott sought substitute relatives.

The Army provided enough companionship during the war. By returning to the Truax apartment, he knew he would be mothered by Mrs. Truax and befriended by Hawley, one of his closest college companions.

After moving in with the Truaxes he called on Al Getman, another Hamilton graduate, who by then had become a successful physician. Aleck borrowed a few thousand dollars from Getman. The reason for the loan was twofold: he had grown weary of Army khaki, and all that French and German cooking he scooped up during his postwar days had added many pounds to the Woollcott frame.

He began by buying an entirely new set of formal evening clothes. When Woollcott went to the theater next season, he would go in style!

Woollcott went back on salary at the *Times* on September 4, 1919. The beginning of the theatrical season signaled Woollcott's new policy. It may have been the war and its accompanying horrors, or the realization on Woollcott's part that the cream-puff reviews he wrote in the past were no longer appropriate drama criticism.

Whatever the reason, Woollcott, regularly writing under his own by-line for the first time, etched many of his reviews of plays and players in acid.

"The suffering of the audience was beyond words," a Woollcott notice read.

"The leading man should have been gently but firmly shot at sunrise," he wrote in a second review.

"Mrs. Patrick Campbell," he commented another time about one of his favorites, "is an aged British battleship sinking rapidly and firing every available gun on her rescuers."

"In his time, Woollcott was a *good* drama critic. Operating when there were 13 daily newspapers, he was the equal of any reviewer and superior to most," A. H. Weiler, a *New York Times* reporter and movie critic, observed. "He was, however, a man of feverish affections and feverish hates."

Viewing the performance of an actor, Woollcott proclaimed, "He snatched the play to his bosom, rushed to the Eltinge Theatre, and acted it all over the stage."

Hurt and alarm greeted Aleck's astringent comments. A performer who received unfavorable notice actually threw a punch at Woollcott.

Sigmund Romberg, the European composer notorious for stealing European musical themes for his songs, received two admonishments from Woollcott.

"The audience whistled the tunes going into the theatre" was Woollcott's first warning.

"The score is by Sigmund Romberg, who knows a good tune when he hears one" was the second.

His first sentence reviewing a new play proved even more devastating.

"*Number 7* opened last night at the Times Square Theatre," he asserted. "It was misnamed by five."

"Count Dracula walks the boards at last," Aleck mentioned in his review of that classic horror play. "Ye who have fits prepare to throw them now."

Not everyone thought his reviews were perceptive, or strong enough, or wise. His fellow critic George Jean Nathan, who at that time believed that only plays written in Germany, Austria, or Bosnia-Herzegovina had merit, attacked Aleck in a magazine called *The Smart Set*.

"The Seidlitz Powder in Times Square," Nathan entitled his tirade. He deprecated everything about Woollcott, from his "small up-state college" to his reviews that "read like a college boy writing and beseeching a lock of hair." Nathan complained that Woollcott was "forever crawling on his hands and knees to see something or somebody," and concluded by accusing him of a "lump-in-the-throat type of reviewing."

In his autobiography, *Present Indicative,* Noel Coward sharply disagreed with Nathan:

"Alexander Woollcott, in a rage, has all the tenderness and restraint of a newly caged cobra, and, when striking, much the same admirable precision. . . . He has in criticism brought me to the dust and raised me to high pedestals, usually giving a sly, rococo twist to the pedestals."

Despite his tough new attitude, Woollcott's zeal in promoting quality in the theater was undiminished.

"We opened on the same night eight other plays opened. I had no name, of course," Katharine Cornell reflected. "The next day we got our notices to close on Saturday night. The reason we didn't was Aleck Woollcott. He went to a Wednesday matinee and came backstage. We'd never met, but he came into my dressing room and said, 'This cannot close, this play. I will see that it does not close.' He went out and called Heywood Broun and said, 'Pull everything out for Sunday. Make your whole page *A Bill of Divorcement.*' And Broun pulled out his Sunday page and we went on for two years, all because of Woollcott."

That first season after the war, he praised Alfred Lunt in Booth Tarkington's play *Clarence.* Next year he wrote equally glowing words for Lynn Fontanne in Kaufman and Connelly's first hit, *Dulcy.* When Lunt and Fontanne appeared together for the first time, Aleck wrote prophetically:

"They have youth and great gifts and the unmistakable attitude of ascent, and those who saw them last night bowing hand in hand for the first time, may well have been witnessing a moment in theatrical history. It is among the possibilities that we were seeing the first chapter in a partnership destined to be as distinguished as that of Henry Irving and Ellen Terry."

Aleck had been touting a young dancer who, with his sister,

Adele, had been playing the vaudeville circuits prior to World War I. Shortly after Aleck returned to his post as drama critic on the *Times* in 1919, Fred Astaire opened in a Broadway musical, *Apple Blossoms*.

"There is a kid hoofer at the Globe that you ought to look over," he told friends and producers. Although Mr. Astaire recalled meeting Aleck only once, Woollcott spoke and wrote warmly and encouragingly of him.

Will Rogers, the Oklahoma cowboy, was another talented performer who had not become a close friend of Aleck's, but Woollcott had sat through his lariat-spinning act in several of the *Ziegfeld Follies*. The cowboy act didn't appeal to him but the ad libs did. Sensing there was more than "shucks" and "gee" and one-liners, Aleck introduced himself to Rogers and suggested that he turn to journalism. The extent of Will Rogers' writing consisted of his name on the bottom of a contract, but Woollcott remained firm. He dragged the reluctant cowhand to his old buddy from *Stars and Stripes*, Harold Ross, who at the time was editing *Judge*, a humor magazine. Ross listened to Rogers' monologue and decided to publish everything he wrote. From there Will Rogers went to *Life* and fame as one of America's foremost humorists.

As a critic Woollcott encouraged the young, not only with words but with money. He paid for his own seats in many productions of the Washington Square Players and other Off Broadway ventures. As a good baseball umpire, he called 'em as he saw 'em. When genius arrived, he recognized it.

"The most interesting playwright of the new generation in America," he pronounced, "is Eugene G. O'Neill. Short and long, experimental, a little undisciplined and exuberant, vigorous always and always somber, his plays have, by their own force, pushed their way up from the tentative little playhouses tucked away in Greenwich Village and have summoned imperiously the wider audiences of the pay-as-you-enter theatre. Not one of them but had its blemishes that would catch the eye of any dramatic critic over the age of two. But they have stature, every one of them, and imagination and a little greatness."

Some say that George S. Kaufman and Charles MacArthur became playwrights because of Aleck's encouragement, though he took no credit for their success. A stronger case can be made for his influence on Paul Robeson. The former All-American football player and Phi Beta Kappa from Rutgers had become an actor. Woollcott met him, liked him, and after hearing him sing a few folk songs at a party, urged him to try singing professionally. Robeson hesitated. Woollcott, backed by his fellow critic Heywood Broun, insisted and Robeson became one of the eminent bassos of the day.

Although most of his colleagues were quick to point out Woollcott's friendship with the leading men and women of the professional theater, he also encouraged amateurs. He immediately recognized the importance of the Washington Square Players, who were, at their beginning, composed half of amateurs and half of professionals. And when, within a few short years, they became the single most important Broadway producers utilizing the name The Theatre Guild, Aleck gave credit where due.

Aleck's opening-night seats were always directly in front of his fellow critic Robert Benchley. The two men grew to admire each other. On occasion Woollcott would encounter Benchley's whimsical humor during the course of an evening's play.

In 1922, at the opening night of *He Who Gets Slapped,* a Russian drama of disillusionment set in a circus, three white horses were brought out onstage. The center horse appeared to be grinning broadly, its large teeth flashing under the glare of lights.

Benchley leaned forward, tapped Woollcott on the shoulder, and whispered loud enough for Aleck and his feminine companion to hear.

"See that middle horse? That's Violet Kemble-Cooper."

As Benchley's son Nathaniel tells it in his biography, Woollcott gave a barely perceptible start, then turned halfway around and looked at the woman beside him.

"Miss Kemble-Cooper, may I present Mr. Benchley?" he said to the actress's younger sister.

Benchley had the most winning smile on Broadway. He turned it on like a bright bulb and said, "But it's such a beautiful horse!"

At the 1928 opening of a melodrama called *The Squall,* starring Dorothy Stickney, Blanche Yurka, and Romney Brent, the actors were obliged to spend the better part of the evening speaking pidgin English.

At one point in the play, the door flew open and a half-clad gypsy girl entered. She crawled across the floor and kissed the hem of the woman of the house.

"Me Nubi," the gypsy announced. "Nubi good girl. Nubi stay here."

Woollcott sensed a rustling immediately behind him as Benchley arose. Then, quite clearly, he heard Benchley speak.

"Me Bobby. Me bad. Me go."

In Woollcott's review next day, he took note of Mr. Benchley's early departure from the theater.

When Arthur Schwartz and Howard Dietz wrote the first *Little Show,* Aleck referred to one of the production's featured players, Clifton Webb, as "the general futility man." Dietz fired back by calling the drama critic "Louisa M. Woollcott."

The next time he met the lyricist, Aleck asked darkly, "Dietz, are you trying to cross me?"

His friend glanced at the mountain of flesh that loomed up from Woollcott's stomach. "Not without an alpenstock."

The name Dietz had given Aleck, however, stuck, and Woollcott had to spend years denying in print that he had grown up on *Little Women* and *Little Men.*

It was at this time that Aleck developed one of his great gifts, that of the raconteur. One of his better stories, which he repeated many times, dealt with professionals versus amateurs. "By definition, an amateur is one who does a thing for the love of it, but naturally enough and pardonably, the people of the theatre are wont to speak of an amateur as one who does everything incompetently. . . . All in all, the attitude of the professional players toward amateurs is best summed up in a raffish story they delight in telling on all occasions. It begins with a touching picture of an old broken-down tragedian sharing a park bench with a bedraggled and unappetizing street walker. 'Ah, madame!' says the tragedian, *'Quelle ironie!* The two oldest professions in the world ruined by amateurs!' "

As he was so firmly established, all of Woollcott's friends expected him to remain a permanent fixture at the *Times.* His little "2 by 4" office along the western wall of the city room had become a meeting place for reporters, actors, playwrights, and other drama critics. It is unthinkable today that such folk would gather together while the *Times* drama critic typed out his review of a play, but Woollcott's personality drew them together, and after work he would join them in a night on the town.

Conceivably, this convivial life could have continued as long as Van Anda and Mr. Ochs approved of their drama critic, and for all purposes New York proclaimed Aleck the most popularly read and believed play reviewer in town. The *Times* brass was content.

"Woollcott, obese and prolix, was the most celebrated [critic]," Brooks Atkinson, his eventual successor on the *Times,* said. "His mercurial enthusiasms and his rhapsodic literary style suborned more readers than any other critic of his time . . . his pinwheels of prose lighted the sky over Broadway."

Those sparks of light erupted from the *Times* for only three more seasons, and then Woollcott chose to change his base of operation as well as his entire fashion of living. Within those three years he changed not only his job but his living quarters. Although he clung tenaciously to his old friends, he also made a host of new ones.

First the job. Frank A. Munsey was a grocery store king who had a fondness for buying newspapers and hiring and firing editors and reporters in much the same way that he bought and sold fruit and vegetables. Kaufman had been fired by Munsey in Washington, D.C., when Munsey spotted Kaufman seated behind a typewriter.

"What is that Jew doing in my city room?" Munsey demanded. Ten minutes later Kaufman was on the street and out of a job. And now, in 1922, Aleck announced he was leaving the *Times*.

"You're actually going to work for that son of a bitch?" Kaufman asked.

"I'm going to work for that son of a bitch for two thousand dollars a month," Woollcott replied.

"That," Kaufman answered, "is what I call an incentive."

Two thousand dollars a month! No drama critic in America ever had received that kind of money. But Woollcott had made such a name for himself and had so great a following that penny-pinching Frank Munsey was willing to offer him that large sum.

"It was Anna Case, the opera singer, who nominated Woollcott for the Munsey job," Harold Ross asserted. "Mr. M. was courting her at the time in a mammoth way. I think Anna did more than nominate; I think she insisted. Aleck is one of the few drama critics who ever got his job so his employer could get a piece of nookie."

Woollcott explained the offer to the managing editor who gave him his start on the *Times*. To his surprise Van Anda actually urged him to accept. After all, it was a fortune compared to what he had been getting from the *Times*, which paid Woollcott at most one hundred dollars a week.

"Only three incidents ever brought tears to my eyes," Aleck told everybody, "when I was graduated from Hamilton, when I said good-bye to my buddies on the *Stars and Stripes*, and when I got my last check from the *Times*."

A touching statement but not true. Aleck cried at every available opportunity: class reunions, the death of a friend's cat, or almost any sad story.

His last check from the *Times* came on September 14, 1922. Woollcott cleared out his desk, got all his personal effects of thirteen years together, and then, like a naughty boy, sat down at his

typewriter. The last thing he wrote as a member of the staff of
The New York Times was a letter to the publisher's nephew,
Adolph Shelby Ochs.

"I have just resigned from this newspaper," Aleck typed on the
Times letterhead. "Now I won't have to kiss your ass any longer."

Years later, a still dazed Ochs said, "Amazing thing to write
because, you know, he *never* kissed my ass."

The next month Woollcott went to work as the drama critic on
Munsey's New York *Herald.*

James Gordon Bennett had started the *Herald* on May 6, 1835.
He was a tough old newspaperman whose son surpassed his father.
In his day Bennett the younger sent a reporter named Stanley into
Africa to find Dr. Livingstone. The younger Bennett also financed
expeditions into the Arctic and laid the transatlantic cables that
broke the monopoly of Jay Gould. He founded the Paris *Herald*
and established the James Gordon Bennett trophies in yacht, auto,
and airplane racing. On his death in 1918, the *Herald* went to
Munsey.

After October, 1922, no doubt existed as to the identity of the
most important critic in America. When Woollcott walked down
the aisle and took his seat at an opening night, almost everyone
on the orchestra floor turned or nudged or nodded. Too late,
George Jean Nathan!

Woollcott was immense in his cloak, immaculate in his white tie
and tails, and imperious in his hold on the attention of his readers.

"Lord! This man hath the power to make whatever he writes of
seem so interesting that when he writes of a play it seemeth to me
that not to have seen it is a dereliction of duty," wrote Franklin P.
Adams, as the modern diarist imitating Samuel Pepys. He considered that Woollcott had reached the acme of drama criticism.
It is possible, however, that Adams was prejudiced. An examination
of his daily columns shows that Woollcott's most frequent guest on
opening nights was F.P.A.

❉   ❉   ❉

Now for the change in his lodgings. Actually, it began in France during the war years, when Woollcott introduced Harold Ross to Jane Grant, a former society reporter for the *Times*. Miss Grant arrived in the French capital as a member of an entertainment unit. Ross took to her quickly, pursuing Miss Grant through the countless poker games that eventually gave rise to the Thanatopsis Club. With the war over, all of them returned to New York.

Ross was not wild about Manhattan, having tried twice to find employment as a reporter and failing both times. What kept him in New York was Jane Grant, and what kept Ross and Jane Grant together was her proposal of marriage and his acceptance of it.

With the possible exception of the bride and groom no one was happier about the forthcoming wedding than Woollcott.

"Leave it to me," he told Jane Grant and Harold Ross. "I'll take care of everything!"

And he did. When the judge they selected to perform the ceremony became unavailable, Woollcott arranged for the wedding to be held in the Church of the Transfiguration, its more conventional name to folks in the theater being The Little Church Around the Corner. Woollcott called a hotel in Philadelphia to arrange for the honeymoon. Woollcott secured seats in the parlor car on the Pennsylvania Railroad, went to the License Bureau in Ross's place, and even whisked Jane Grant into Tiffany's for a wedding ring. Since Ross was busy job hunting, Woollcott did the selecting. The clerk at Tiffany's understandably thought Woollcott was the groom. After the shoppers chose the ring, the clerk expressed approval and offered good wishes to Jane and Aleck.

"You've made a good choice, sir." The clerk smirked at Aleck. "And what is to be inscribed in it?"

"Nothing," Woollcott told him. "She might want to use it again."

The astonished clerk did what was known in vaudeville as a double take and then went to have the ring wrapped.

A few years later, Ross and his wife decided to buy a house. As Hawley Truax was then in the real estate business, they decided to accept his advice. Today the section in Manhattan where the Rosses found a place is called the Clinton area, but in those days it had the name Hell's Kitchen.

Two houses at 412–414 West 47th Street were made into one. Ross and his wife discovered that they had too much room for one couple. Jane and Ross turned to their friend Aleck, who solved the problem for them by moving tenants into the two apartments on the third floor. Kate Oglebay, a wealthy young woman from Cleveland, rented one suite of rooms. Bill Powell, not the movie actor but a public relations man, took the other. Hawley Truax and Woollcott moved into separate apartments on the second floor while Ross and his wife were allotted rooms of their own on the first floor.

In addition, the first floor contained the kitchen and the dining room, which served as a community room when it wasn't being used for eating.

Like Ruth Hale, Jane Grant refused to take her husband's name during the years of their marriage. An entire group of women at that time decided to keep their maiden names. All of them belonged to an organization called the Lucy Stone League, and George Kaufman observed, "A Lucy Stone gathers no boss."

Ross, particularly after drinking whiskey, told anyone who would listen, "I never had one damn meal at home at which the discussion wasn't of women's rights and the ruthlessness of men in trampling women. Grant and Ruth Hale had maiden-name phobias, and that was all they talked about, or damn near all."

An absence of locks on the interior doors turned out to be one of the less desirable features of the house. Arriving home late after an opening, Woollcott would march into the Ross-Grant bedroom.

"Come on, Ross," he would call as he entered the pitch-black room, not caring whether Jane and Harold were in bed, asleep, or what. "Three games. That's all I have time for!" And Ross would get out of bed and start for the cribbage board.

Worse were the nights when Woollcott didn't feel like playing cribbage. He would stomp into the Ross-Grant bedroom, turn on a light, pull up a chair, sit beside their bed, and tell Jane and Harold the plot of that night's play, who attended the opening, what they wore, and what he, Woollcott, thought of it all.

And then there were the nights when he would invade not only their bedroom but their bathroom as well. Jane Grant was a modern, liberal-thinking woman. Ross was a prude. But both took umbrage when Woollcott walked into their bathroom, stripped, turned on the water taps, and, with the door wide open, spoke animatedly to them on any subject he chose to discuss from their own tub.

"It is difficult to imagine a person more gregarious than Aleck," Jane Grant wrote. "Solitude to him was agony. In the years that followed we were generously treated to his need for companionship."

The gang at 412 continued its riotous pace for some years, during which time Ross founded *The New Yorker*.

8 Not for the Old Lady in Dubuque

*H*AROLD WALLACE ROSS WAS BORN ON NOVEMBER 6, 1892, in Aspen, Colorado. His father was a carpenter from Northern Ireland and his mother was a schoolteacher from Kansas City. After completing two years of high school, Ross dropped out. Although his formal education was finished, he never stopped learning or reading, particularly *Webster's Second New International Dictionary*.

A job as an errand boy on the Denver *Post* began his love affair with the newspaper business. Over the next few years he worked on the Salt Lake City *Telegram and Tribune*, the Sacramento *Union*, the Pasadena *Herald*, the Needles (California) *Bee*, the New Orleans *Item*, the Brooklyn *Eagle*, the Atlanta *Journal*, the Hudson (New Jersey) *Observer*, and the San Francisco *Call*. Evidently he was content to be a tramp reporter until the outbreak of World War I, when Uncle Sam pointed his finger at Harold Ross. Ross volunteered, joining the Eighteenth Engineers (Railway) Regiment.

The regiment's motto, "First to France, First to Fight," proved half true. Harold and the others arrived in France early enough, but then the dawdling began. When Ross learned that a newspaper for enlisted men was being started, he applied at once. When he heard nothing more, he went AWOL and walked and hitchhiked to Paris from an officer-training school in Langres. Upon being accepted for the staff of *Stars and Stripes*, Ross met an overblown sergeant from the Medical Corps who puffed in from Savenay with full field equipment, including a typewriter. Ross interviewed him.

"Where'd you work?" Private Ross asked Sergeant Woollcott in an effort to determine his qualifications.

"*New York Times*—dramatic critic," Sergeant Woollcott answered with the air of a man familiar with true quality in journalism. An eastern dramatic critic on an Army newspaper!

To the sergeant's surprise, the private threw back his head and laughed derisively.

Woollcott, who even then could sting like a hornet, waited just long enough, and while Ross was gasping for breath, replied, "You know, you remind me a great deal of my grandfather's coachman."

Ross stopped laughing and their friendship began.

In later years Ross would snicker, "My God, his grandfather's coachman. One of the farmhands at the Phalanx may have driven their surrey to Red Bank on Saturdays, but that's the nearest he ever got to a coachman." But Ross could never think of a fitting reply to Aleck's line. The moment their lifelong friendship began, so did their mutual animosity.

The tall, rawboned Ross had a head of brown hair that simply refused to stay down most of the time no matter how much water or stickum he applied. Catching him at a weak moment, Aleck observed, "Ross looks like a dishonest Abe Lincoln." The description clung to him.

Following the war, Ross got a job on an ill-fated magazine called *The Home Sector*. It lasted six months and folded during a printers' strike. Ross went to work on the *American Legion Weekly*. Following that, he wrote briefly for what then passed for a humor magazine, *Judge*.

In 1925, Ross conceived an idea for a new magazine. He tried it out on Woollcott.

"This is going to be a very special magazine, Aleck," Ross told him. "Can I count on you?"

"For a great deal of encouragement," Woollcott replied.

Ross explained the idea to his wife, Jane Grant. She in turn asked her editor at the *Times*, Carr Van Anda, what such a project would cost to launch.

"In the neighborhood of a million dollars" was the answer.

Ross believed he could get the magazine under way with an investment of fifty thousand. By pooling their savings, mortgaging their home, and tapping their friends, Ross and Grant were able to raise half that amount. The remaining $25,000 was put up by Raoul Fleischmann, an heir to the yeast and baking fortunes bearing his name.

The press agent John Peter Toohey came up with a title that Ross liked, bought, and paid for in stock. It was to be called *The New Yorker*.

The prospectus for the new publication, written by Ross himself, has become a classic in the opinion of other editors and publishers and is worth quoting:

ANNOUNCING A NEW WEEKLY MAGAZINE

The New Yorker will be a reflection in word and picture of metropolitan life. It will be human. Its general tenor will be one of gaiety, wit and satire, but it will be more than a jester. It will not be what is commonly called radical or highbrow. It will be what is commonly called sophisticated, in that it will assume a reasonable degree of enlightenment on the part of its reader. It will hate bunk.

As compared to the newspaper, The New Yorker will be interpretative rather than stenographic. It will print facts that it will have to go behind the scenes to get, but it will not deal in scandal nor in sensation for the sake of sensation. Its integrity will be above suspicion. It hopes to be so entertaining and informative as to be a necessity for the person who knows his way about or wants to. The New Yorker will devote several pages a week to the covering of contemporary events and people of interest. This will be done by writers capable of appreciating the elements of a situation and, in setting them down, of indicating their importance and significance. The New Yorker will present the truth and the whole truth without favor, but will not be iconoclastic.

Amusements and the arts will be thoroughly covered by departments which will present, in addition to criticism, the personality, the anecdote, the color and the chat of the various subdivisions of this sphere. The New Yorker's conscientious guide will list each week all current amusement offerings, worth-while theatres, motion pictures, musical events, art exhibitions, sports, and miscellaneous entertainment—providing an ever-ready answer to the prevalent query, "What shall we do this evening?" . . .

Judgment will be passed upon new books of consequence, and The New Yorker will carry a list of the season's books which it considers worth reading. . . .

The New Yorker expects to be distinguished for its illustrations, which will include caricatures, sketches, cartoons and humorous and satirical drawings in keeping with its purpose.

The New Yorker will be the magazine which is not edited for the old lady in Dubuque. It will not be concerned with what she is thinking about. This is not meant in disrespect, but The New Yorker is a magazine avowedly published for a metropolitan audience and thereby will escape an influence which hampers most national publications. It expects a considerable national circulation, but this will come from persons who have a metropolitan interest.

The New Yorker will appear early in February.

The price will be: Five dollars a year

                    Fifteen cents a copy

The first issue of *The New Yorker* appeared on February 21, 1925. Those who put it out were not altogether pleased with it.

The lights at 412 West 47th Street had been burning late for weeks, and they would continue to do so for many months to come.

With the exception of Kate Oglebay, the remaining tenants were caught up in the new magazine. Ross proved to be one of the great magazine editors of America. Boldly but wisely he collected a staff of editors, writers, and cartoonists comparable to none. E. B. White, who later wrote *Stuart Little* and coauthored *The Elements of Style,* was an early *New Yorker* author and editor. For many years he wrote the "Notes and Comment" page of "The Talk of the Town" and lived to settle in Maine and watch others try to write and cut copy equal to his. Ross gave White's wife, Katharine, the delicate and difficult task of editing Woollcott. James Thurber, Wolcott Gibbs, William Shawn, and a host of other brilliant blue-pencil people followed as editors. Artists included Rea Irvin, who drew the first cover of the Regency dandy looking through his monocle at the butterfly, Helen Hokinson, Peter Arno, Mary Petty, John Held, Jr., William Steig, and Charles Addams. Early prose writers and poets were Don Marquis, Ogden Nash, Dorothy Parker, A. J. Liebling, Sally Benson, John Collier, John O'Hara, Nancy Hale, Arthur Kober, Frank Sullivan, Ring Lardner, Corey Ford, Clarence Day, and scores of others known and talented enough but too numerous to list in these pages.

The incandescence of Ross made *The New Yorker.* Indeed, what Ross did for American letters in general was to tighten, simplify, straighten, and document them to a higher degree than they had ever been. He was as impassioned about clarity as Woollcott was about ebullience.

While the new publication took offices in a building owned by Raoul Fleischmann, many hours were spent working in their home. Ross roamed his quarters, muttered aloud, and wrote "Locate," "Who he?," "When happen?" in the margins of the copy submitted by his writers, at the same time that Woollcott entertained guests in a voice equal to the flourish of a trumpet.

Perhaps for Aleck the beginning of the end at West 47th Street occurred one evening when he returned unexpectedly and found other members of the household seated at a dinner party with several guests.

Realizing that only he had been excluded, Woollcott scorned the hastily drawn chair and the heaping plate of food that they quickly offered to him.

"Rather than touch any of that slop," Woollcott sneered, "I'd just as soon lie face down in a pail of Italian garbage!"

And with that he marched furiously upstairs to his own quarters.

The turmoil was too much for Ross. He decided that Woollcott had to go.

"Buy him out," he told Jane Grant.

To break the tie that bound him to their old fat friend was a delicate undertaking. Grant did not care for a confrontation with Woollcott. Ross, who rarely backed away from a fight, was not eager to initiate this scrap. His reluctance to fire anyone from *The New Yorker* was already known and noted.

Eventually, Grant threw down the taffeta gauntlet.

"How about your getting out of here?" she asked Woollcott. "I can't torture Ross any longer with this community living. You know we were doubtful from the beginning about the arrangement."

Aleck stood speechless and Jane felt sorry for him.

"We need this space," she told him gently.

A mistake—for Woollcott, with a mind quick as a cat's paw snaring a mouse, said, "I've got an idea. We'll commandeer Powell's apartment. I'll move in there and you and Ross can take this one."

In a trice Woollcott had checked them. Powell vacated his quarters, Woollcott went upstairs, but the conditions remained unbearable.

Eventually, Grant coaxed Aleck into moving into an apartment in the Hotel des Artistes, from where he announced to his friends that he would appreciate a china, linen, and silver shower.

F.P.A. sent Woollcott a moustache cup, a handkerchief, and a dime.

Many of those who write about *The New Yorker* side with Ross and are anti-Woollcott, claiming that Aleck removed his name from the magazine when he was a contributing editor, that he never allowed it to be used, that he didn't start writing until Ross's idea became a proven success. The truth is found in the pages of the magazine itself.

In the third issue on March 7, 1925, Woollcott wrote a profile of his old editor on *The New York Times,* Carr Vantell Van Anda. He followed that with another profile on June 20 of the same year. The subject was E. Haldeman-Julius, the last editor of the famous Socialist weekly *Appeal to Reason.* E. Haldeman-Julius was noted for his Little Blue Books, which were one of the first attempts at American paperback publishing.

His word portraits concerned themselves with people or institutions he favored: the Seeing Eye Dog training center, his friends Harpo Marx, Frank Lloyd Wright, George S. Kaufman, Marc Connelly, Alfred Lunt, Noel Coward, Charles MacArthur, Lloyd Paul Stryker, and his former office boy at *The New York Times,* Sam Zolotow.

He had a facile mind and quick fingers, and if his words were too sugary or too tart, if he became too adoring or too insulting, Katharine White sat in her editor's chair prepared to snip or, if need be, hack away at his copy. When she wasn't available, her colleague, Wolcott Gibbs, performed the editorial surgery.

The following example is a story that Mrs. White allowed to get by but which she and Ross considered to be beneath the caliber of the magazine:

> Then let me recount the misadventure in Vermont recently experienced by one Eppert R. McKay, who is a blameless resident of Springfield, Mass., where his father was a distinguished clergyman. The younger McKay is Division Toll Supervisor of New England Tel. & Tel., but his avocation is genealogy and it was on a quest for some dusty Vermont archives which took him to Vergennes not

long ago. As he drove into the tranquil and lovely old town, he swung near enough to the curb to ask a passing citizen where the courthouse was. The native, who was, it seems, a trifle deaf, answered apologetically, "We ain't got none. You gotta pick 'em up off the street."

But Woollcott would complain bitterly when he had been edited. So vociferous were his protests that a standing joke in the *New Yorker* offices was that anytime a telephone rang, someone would say, "There's Woollcott, calling up to resign again."

Old stories, fables, even a line worth remembering seemed to stay with Woollcott forever. From such a story came the title for his book and later for his column in *The New Yorker*.

And there sat in the circle at the Players Club one who spoke always with the accent of authority, giving the impression that his own story and the story of the theatre were two inseparable strands of the same woof. Indeed, he sometimes referred casually to the five seasons passed at the dear old Drury Lane. But one day someone asked him point blank what his role there had been. He had to explain then that his talent had always been devoted to off stage noises. Finally, he showed a Drury Lane program, yellow and creased and wine stained. There his name was at the end of the cast and opposite it was the role assigned him— Shouts and Murmurs.

Woollcott's weekly columns called "Shouts and Murmurs" consisted of a pastiche of past and present theatrical anecdotes, ghost stories, grisly murders, gossip about famous friends, and ladies of the evening. As he did when he started as a critic for the *Times*, Woollcott frequently tried to slip *double entendres* into his copy. Ross, as proper as a Boy Scout, hated him for this.

"All the time Aleck wrote for us he was a trial," Ross said, "something of a nuisance and an embarrassment. There was usually a jangle every week because he'd want to put in some off-color thing, a dirty word, or a for-men-only story. At that period he was for utter frankness of expression between the sexes and everybody else, free living, no marriages, recognition of the nobility of bastards, and so on. We had to fight to keep him printable, and he was harder to deal with than a Gila monster, which he sometimes resembled."

Ross agreed to the Woollcott column only if Katharine White would take full responsibilities. Mrs. White was of the opinion that Ross did not want to have anything whatsoever to do with the weekly contact with Aleck.

"I believe Ross made Woollcott promise not to call him on the matter of his page as a condition of taking him on," Mrs. White said. "The two men were intimate friends and constant antagonists —a very ambivalent relationship."

Staff behavior in the early days of *The New Yorker* was a good deal more collegiate than businesslike. Dorothy Parker, spotted by Ross in the middle of the afternoon in a speakeasy rather than the office, made a small but successful apology. "Someone else was using the pencil," she said.

Robert Benchley, an early contributor, arrived in Venice one day with his traveling companion, Jock Whitney. Benchley carried a suitcase filled with horse manure. Benchley had been told that no horse had ever been seen in Venice. In the small hours of the morning Benchley and Whitney placed their imported horse droppings at proper intervals in the Piazza San Marco.

Charlie MacArthur, Benchley's roommate, told the story proudly for years.

"The Venetians," he said, "considered that horseshit the only miracle of the twentieth century."

When Wolcott Gibbs took a turn at drama criticism, a wag in the office came up with "God, he's brilliant. He never likes anything."

The difference between Gibbs and Woollcott in their attitude toward the theater was clear. Gibbs liked nothing while Woollcott was the most excitable, explosive, and certainly the most devoted of the theatergoers. With one successful play he turned jubilant.

"This is written in gratitude for *The Corn Is Green*," he said in a letter to Herman Shumlin, producer-director of the drama. "That nourishing play, as it comes true at the National, renews one's faith in the eternal theatre. All the days of your life you will be glad you produced it and gave it your best.

"Words fail me—and it serves me right for having squandered them on lesser occasions."

Toward poor performances he grew bitter and vengeful.

"I do not know where this actor comes from, but wherever it is, he'd better go back there," Aleck once wrote in a review.

To his colleague and friend on *The New Yorker*, Frank Sullivan, Woollcott said, "If I were found dead with a dagger through my chest, the next morning three hundred actors would be arrested on suspicion of murder."

"Let's say it would be justifiable homicide," Sullivan added.

Sullivan was with him at the old Ritz Hotel's Men's Bar when Corey Ford, the humorist, entered. Ford had just begun working on *The New Yorker*. Without waiting for an invitation, Woollcott turned to him and announced, "Ford, I'm going to visit you in your new place in New Hampshire for three days next week."

Ford, ill at ease at the thought of having so demanding a guest, muttered, "That'll be nice."

"*I'll* be the judge of that!" Woollcott thundered as he held up his hand.

Quite possibly Woollcott's highest and lowest moments during his early and middle years on *The New Yorker* came at a single dinner party in London. The guest of honor was the Prince of Wales.

After the ladies had been excused and the gentlemen were about to start on their port and cigars, the Prince begged those present to retire as he wished a private conversation with Mr. Woollcott.

The gentlemen bowed out as requested, leaving his Royal Highness and a Woollcott whose imagination caught fire with probabilities: matters of state, perhaps, a speech to the Empire, or even an introduction by Woollcott to a volume of letters by Edward.

When the doors were closed, the Prince looked squarely at him and began with "Woollcott . . . ?"

"Sir," came the anticipatory reply. At that precise moment he might gladly have been willing to lay down his life for the Crown.

"You've something to do with that magazine from the States, *The New Yorker*, don't you?"

Woollcott's outthrust chest began to deflate and his spine sagged against the back of his chair.

"Yes, sir, I do."

"Then why the devil don't I get it more regularly? Do look into it, will you?"

And then they joined the ladies.

9 Master of the Hounds

AUTUMN, 1920. WHILE MOST AMERICANS SAT DOWN
to lunch at 11 A.M. or noon, in the city of New York the midday
meal for a certain group of men and women shifted to one o'clock.
The reasons were severalfold: some of the late diners had spent
the night carousing or playing cards or other games; many were
not expected to begin their duties at work until ten or eleven in
the morning; and the rest held positions that allowed them to
eat out when they chose, and the choice they made was lunch
at 1 P.M. at the Algonquin Hotel.

It was an odd group that met in the Algonquin dining room on
Forty-fourth Street between Fifth and Sixth avenues. Almost all
of them were rebels who had left their hometowns for New York.
For reasons that ranged from opportunity to be gainfully employed
to social and political dissatisfaction, they poured into Manhattan
and gave it an infusion of talent that it had not seen before. Mc-
Keesport and Chicago, Pittsburgh and the Fox River Valley of
Wisconsin, New Jersey and upstate New York all survived without
these people, but Manhattan blossomed with their presence and
they thrived in Gotham.

The emotional drum major of this band of talented folk was
Woollcott. At thirty-three years of age, Aleck emerged dynamic,
dramatic, energetic, and magnetic. Above all, he carried the stan-

dard for what New York considered the height of sophistication of that period. The group that gathered about him were all individualists, but they spent their luncheon hours with him because he aroused their appetites, stimulated their minds, and turned them into witcrackers.

Never before had America collected such a group of people at a daily table. It would thrive for a decade and then dissolve in 1930. Although many of the figures of literature, drama, and journalism were never included, so many were that the Algonquin Round Table has become a watermark of American culture. Whether it was a mark of high or low water is still being debated.

Many people become incensed at the mention of the Round Table. Even more become ecstatic. It would be impossible to write about Alexander Woollcott, however, without examining the phenomenon, for he was the master of that joking, bickering, jesting pack of men and women whose brightness still shines today.

Much has been committed to paper about the Algonquin Round Table—the witticisms, the puns, the sallies, the poker games. Just as no amount of practice is ever enough for a working concert pianist, no amount of research is ever enough for a biographer.

Take the line "Let's get out of these wet clothes and into a dry martini."

Ten years of checking made it certain that it was *not* Woollcott but Robert Benchley who spoke the jest. Committed to print, it read relatively well and received few complaints.

Two years later, an interview with Benchley's son Nathaniel turned up the mildly astounding news that his father had never spoken or written the words. A press agent, working on behalf of Robert Benchley, had come up with the line and, because he wished his weekly salary check to come through, passed it on to a columnist and gave credit to Benchley.

In spite of everything that has been written about the Round Table, its true beginnings did not come to light until a short time ago.

Murdock Pemberton was a reporter and the art critic for *The New Yorker*, and so silent and modest a man that the *Times* obituary on his wife a few years ago identified her as "the widow of the late Murdock Pemberton." Actually, Murdock Pemberton is alive and well, residing in midtown Manhattan. When Pemberton worked on the drama desk at the *Times*, he wanted a story on a George C. Tyler play. As the play had been reviewed and later discussed in the Sunday edition, there seemed only one way to get a fresh slant on it. Woollcott was back on the paper, and if Woollcott could write about the Tyler play . . .

Picking up the telephone, Pemberton called Tyler's press agent, John Peter Toohey, and urged Toohey to take Woollcott to lunch. Woollcott, who then lived at the City Club, was led ever so gently next door to the Algonquin. Aleck enjoyed the meal and wrote the story. Toohey alerted Pemberton, the *Times* ran it, and the rest may be described as a footnote in American humor.

Generally speaking, the Algonquin Round Table falls into nationalistic camps. Americans tend to like it. The British for the most part dislike it because it isn't their kind of humor. The French and the Germans have no understanding of it whatever, and the rest of the world gets along very well without it.

The men and women who made up the Round Table were continuously criticized for logrolling and back scratching.

However, when Frank Adams wrote a particularly brutal review of a book by Heywood Broun, Woollcott arrived at lunch well prepared.

"You can see Frank's scratches on Heywood's back yet," he observed with pleasure.

To his friend, former landlord, and current editor, Harold Ross, Woollcott sent a note. "I think your slogan 'Liberty or Death' is splendid and whichever one you choose will be all right with me!"

"Rancor was Woollcott's only form of exercise," Marc Connelly said with only a slight amount of exaggeration.

Logrollers? Back scratchers? "Their standards were high, their vocabulary fluent, fresh, astringent, tough," wrote Edna Ferber, the Iron Duchess of American fiction. "Theirs was a tonic influence, one on the other, and all on the world of American letters. The people they could not and would not stand were the bores, hypocrites, sentimentalists and the socially pretentious. They were ruthless toward charlatans, toward the pompous and mentally dishonest. Casual, incisive, they had a terrible integrity about their work and a boundless ambition."

Who were these ruthless, ambitious, yet sterling characters? For the most part they were newspaper people who began to use their typewriters for more than news stories.

Woollcott was a drama critic. So were Dorothy Parker and Heywood Broun. Robert E. Sherwood was an early movie critic. George Kaufman, Marc Connelly, Herman Mankiewicz, and Charles MacArthur were reporters. Most of these journalists were soon to be counted among the more successful playwrights in America.

F.P.A., Robert Benchley, and Ring Lardner were columnists. Harold Ross, Art Samuels, and Frank Crowninshield were editors. Edna Ferber was a short-story writer and novelist.

Tallulah Bankhead, Noel Coward, Alfred Lunt, Lynn Fontanne, Ruth Gordon, Margalo Gillmore, Harpo Marx, and Peggy Wood were card-carrying members of Actors Equity whose names appeared above the title of the play or picture in which they appeared.

Among the irregulars were Helen Hayes, Beatrice Kaufman, Herbert Bayard Swope, Deems Taylor, Donald Ogden Stewart, Margaret Leech Pulitzer, Jane Grant, and Neysa McMein.

Frank Case, the thin, soft-spoken man whose manners and taste were even more elegant than his properly cut clothes, had come from Buffalo and worked his way into the hotel business in New York. The Algonquin was originally designed to be an apartment building. As apartments were not selling well, the thought of opening a hotel arose. Its owner intended to call it the Puritan.

Case objected strenuously. A hotel named the Puritan!

"What's the matter with it?" the builder demanded. "Isn't it American, hasn't it splendid historical associations?"

Case agreed that it had. "But," he added, "it has come to have, too, an additional meaning which contradicts the spirit of inn-keeping. It is cold, forbidding, and grim. I don't like it."

"Well, *I* do."

Challenged to find a better name, Case delved into the books at the Public Library to learn that the first people in the neighborhood had been the Algonquin Indians. He immediately fell in love with the name and sold it to his boss.

Installed as the manager of the new Algonquin Hotel, Case brought much of his own personality into the residence and dining rooms on Forty-fourth Street. Case couldn't stand politicians. He had no use for athletes. He ignored businessmen. He turned up his nose at socialites. What Frank Case admired most in this world were men and women of talent.

"Gifted people not only should be tolerated," he said, "but they should be encouraged in their strange and temperamental antics."

He had more thoughts along those lines.

"People of unique ability are unique creatures, and it is only when they try to act like the rest of us that they are artificial and out of character."

In a short time writers, actors, producers, and editors were eating and living at the Algonquin. Case's instincts told him that the names of his talented young customers would someday line the pages of the future *Who's Who in America*. He instructed Georges, the headwaiter, to move their table to the center of the room. He assigned them their favorite waiter, Luigi, and before long he considered the big round table and its occupants as his "floor show." He was proven right.

People flocked into the Algonquin dining room to see these new celebrities and hear some of the *bons mots* traded at lunch each day.

In 1920, Edmund Duffy, artist on the Brooklyn *Eagle,* had drawn a caricature for his paper showing the diners at "Luigi's Board" in knight's armor. From then on, people dubbed them "The Algonquin Round Table Set." Lunch, five or even six days a week, became Case's most patronized meal.

Kaufman, returning from Philadelphia where he had witnessed the tryout of one of his plays, came to the Algonquin. Although his show received rave notices, George knew better than the Philadelphia critics.

"What *I* suggest," he told the group, "is that we leave the show in Philadelphia and bring the notices into New York."

The loudest laughter came from the group's leader, Alexander Woollcott. If he wasn't talking himself, and if the story didn't make him the butt, Aleck was a marvelous audience. Anything from gossip to intellectual parlor games could keep him giggling and guffawing. His smile was infectious, and his belly jiggled as he chortled. One of his own favorite lines was precipitated by the brilliant Dorothy Parker. Mrs. Parker had a trim figure, dark hair, darker eyes, and a wit that bit.

"A combination of Little Nell and Lady Macbeth," Aleck said in describing her.

At a Halloween party Mrs. Parker was asked to join the merrymakers who were "ducking for apples."

"Change one letter in that phrase," Dorothy remarked, "and you have my life story."

Because he was so jolly, so debonair, and his friend Kaufman's collaborator, Woollcott devoted no small amount of attention to Marc Connelly. Although he respected him immensely, Woollcott summed up Connelly almost as neatly as he had done Parker.

"He is an infuriating blend of poet, peacock, and procrastinator."

Returning from Europe, Connelly, met at the ship by the press, gave an interview. Next day the newspapers ran a story to the effect that "A sun-tanned Marc Connelly came back to New York with a new three-act play."

Speculation as to the probability of that allegation arose immediately at the Algonquin.

"Knowing Marc," a Round Table member said, "I'll bet he doesn't have a full three-act play."

"I doubt that he has two acts," replied a second.

Woollcott looked around the assembled group.

"I say he doesn't even have a suntan," he pronounced conclusively.

While Connelly's disinterest in work may have vexed Kaufman, Woollcott forgave him completely for a single line he uttered in the dining room of the Algonquin. Seated at the Round Table one afternoon, the puckish, uninhibited, and very bald Connelly felt a man run his hand from Connelly's forehead to the back of Connelly's head.

"That feels just like my wife's behind," the fellow said. Marc waited just a split second before he answered.

"So it does," came the reply.

A great deal has been written of the wit, rascality, and profanity of Alexander Woollcott. Much of that may be traced directly to the dialogue he picked up from the doughboys in France. Tramping through mud and freezing rain and eating cold meals gave the men who made up the American Expeditionary Force reason enough to curse. Barnyard language, steel-mill oaths, and choice phrases from the back rooms of saloons became the unofficial language of the American troops.

Woollcott absorbed and distilled it immediately into a smooth, 100 proof liquor of his own. The pleasure he found in shock value was undeniable. "You bet your sweet ass," he would say to a dinner partner. Eyebrows up and down the table would rise to the hairline. Other conversations would stop, and Woollcott to his delight would be holding center stage.

Today, when the ultimate in profanity is seen or heard everywhere with the possible exception of children's television programs, Woollcott's "Listen to me, you faun's behind" must appear pale. In its day, however, it was wicked, rash, daring, and ultra-sophisticated. Woollcott employed such comments for the same reason that drill sergeants blew their whistles: to gain attention immediately.

His wit, too, began to be shaped even further in France. Exposed to the banter among Franklin P. Adams, Harold Ross, and Heywood Broun, Woollcott quickly adjusted himself to the jibe, the jest, and to what was soon to be called "the wisecrack." Adoring the theater as he did, he picked up the timing that was necessary in delivering a line at lunch.

As for his rascality, he came by it naturally. As exalted as his enthusiasms could carry him, in a sudden fit of depression he could quite comfortably undercut anybody or any subject.

The insult is one of the easier forms of humor. It was used at the Round Table with great frequency, and in Woollcott's hand the insult joke became a flashing rapier. Few dared cross swords with him, and those who did generally came out second best. Hurt by nature before birth, Woollcott felt free to slash mercilessly.

"It is a tragedy that such a gifted man," Dr. David Abrahamsen said, "knowing so much of human nature, knew so little about himself. He found it necessary to challenge everyone because he felt a deep-seated need to be first."

To put someone else down seemed a means of putting himself on top, and since he did it with even more effectiveness than the others, Woollcott employed the insult with stunning results.

"That is what we psychoanalysts always see in every man who feels insecure in a psychological sense," Dr. Abrahamsen concluded.

"Hello, Frank, you greasy mass of Gentile self-pity," Woollcott greeted the short, slim, twinkling-eyed Frank Sullivan one afternoon.

Stung and puzzled, Sullivan replied, "Why did you say that?"

"I'm always using that on my Jewish friends," Woollcott answered. "So I thought I'd try it out on my Gentile friends."

Dorothy Schiff, presently editor-in-chief and publisher of the New York *Post*, remembered that, as a young woman whose married name was Hall, she met Woollcott at the Kaufmans.'

A dispute developed at the card game in progress. A few "damns" and "hells" were flying back and forth when Aleck put his cards face down on the table and raised his pudgy fingers in feigned horror at the profanity.

"What will Mrs. Hall think—if she thinks at all?" he asked.

Dorothy Schiff's manners were as perfect as her profile. She smiled politely and said nothing. A second incident came to her mind.

"He was visiting my home in Oyster Bay, spending a weekend. He and a few others were playing one of their endless card games. Lunch was served and the cardplayers got up. Aleck was a strong believer in punctuality. They left their cards on the table and went into the dining room. While we ate, a maid slipped into the room where the game had been. She emptied the ashtrays, cleared away the glasses, and neatly stacked all of the cards in a single pack.

"When he came back and saw his cards had been removed, Aleck blew up. He was outraged. He made a dreadful scene. I felt so guilty because it was my house and my maid, and Aleck had the ability of making me feel like a worm."

Heywood Broun and George Kaufman were extraordinary hypochondriacs—even for the Round Table. The difference between them was that Broun carried around vast stacks of his electrocardiograms. Coming in one day with a new batch, Broun spread them out upon the table.

"Heywood," Woollcott asked drily, "aren't you about ready to hold a one-man show of those things?"

When stopped by a man who had known him years before, Woollcott stared coolly at him.

"Hello, Aleck. You remember me, don't you?"

"I can't remember your name and please don't tell me!" Woollcott snapped as he walked away.

Defending his friend the author of *The Green Hat*, Aleck said, "Michael Arlen, for all his reputation, is not a bounder. He is every other inch a gentleman."

On Beatrice and George Kaufman's fifth wedding anniversary, they received the following telegram from Woollcott:

I HAVE BEEN LOOKING AROUND FOR AN APPROPRIATE WOODEN GIFT AND AM PLEASED HEREBY TO PRESENT YOU WITH ELSIE FERGUSON'S PERFORMANCE IN HER NEW PLAY.

Reviewing a volume of inferior poetry entitled *And I Shall Make Music*, Woollcott addressed himself directly to the woman who wrote it. "Not on *my* carpet, lady!"

Friends of Woollcott said he enjoyed playing a variety of games; that his favorites were whist, hearts, bridge, poker, cribbage, puns and anagrams, and croquet. Actually he preferred different games at various times in his life. At the start of the Algonquin period there can be no doubt that the game was poker.

Beginning in Paris during the *Stars and Stripes* days, this regularly scheduled game took hold in New York and shifted to various locations; Ruth Hale complained, and rightfully so, at the mess left after Heywood Broun, her husband, brought the Thanatopsis Club to their home. Frank Adams' wife had similar misgivings.

Imagine a game that began midway during Friday evening and ended in the neighborhood of nine o'clock Sunday morning. The debris on the table, the sideboards, and particularly the floor was astounding. Woollcott, Ross, Adams, and Broun continued under the impression that they were still playing cards in a restaurant in Montmartre. Anything that interfered with the game was moved to one side or thrown under the table.

All the members of the Thanatopsis Club belonged to the Round Table. The club naturally found a happy home in a suite on the second floor of the Algonquin Hotel. It was there that the weekly poker game became for a decade a permanent fixture of New York.

The variations in its name were many. The Young Men's Upper West Side Thanatopsis and Inside Straight Club is what Woollcott called it. Others referred to it as the Thanatopsis and Inside Straight Chowder and Marching Society. Although the combinations of names were endless, everyone knew it as the Saturday Night Poker Game.

Guests, from time to time, were permitted to sit in. Their eligibility depended largely upon the size of their fortunes and their lack of skill at poker. Not being the cardsharps they imagined themselves to be, the Thanatopsis regulars were taken as often as they did the taking.

One visitor of considerable wealth was brought in early Saturday evening by a member who secretly advised his fellow cardplayers that his guest was almost *too* easy.

Late Monday morning, a group of Thanatopsis players looked up the guest in Dun and Bradstreet. The sucker's fortune was listed as six million dollars. Immediately they sat down and composed a missive to that noted bureau of financial evaluation.

"Dear Sirs," it read. "He now has $6,000,410."

An occasional player at the Thanatopsis was the actor Herbert Ransom. When he held a good hand, his facial expressions were so evident that F.P.A. suggested a new club rule: "Anyone who looks at Ransom's face is cheating."

As long as the stakes remained comparatively low, members thought at least as much about the jokes they made as the cards they held. The grumbling began when Broun lost the money that he and Ruth had saved to make an initial payment on a house. The poker sessions reached a more serious level with the introduction of Herbert Bayard Swope, managing editor of the New York *World* and a multimillionaire.

From its earliest days in Paris when they played with francs and centimes, the betting had always been table stakes, that is, any amount the bettor chose to put up had to be matched by any of the other players if they wished to continue.

When Swope joined the club, betting rose drastically from a quarter to a dollar on the last card. The dynamic Swope thought nothing of backing his play with a thousand-dollar raise. Some even say he would wager ten thousand dollars on a single card to win a pot.

Successful as the Thanatopsis players had become, no one of them was in that financial league. After Broun's thirty-thousand-dollar loss one Saturday night, Woollcott dropped two or three thousand a few weeks later. For a boy who had grown up at the Phalanx, where there was *no* cash, the loss of two or three thousand dollars was not a matter to be shrugged off. Besides, there was something in Woollcott's makeup that made it very difficult for him to accept the loser's role.

In the fall of 1923, therefore, Woollcott, Broun, and Connelly, who was as constant a loser as one could find, handed in their resignations to the Thanatopsis. They intended never again to spend their hard-earned cash at the green-baize table on the second floor of the Algonquin.

But contrary to his written display of indignation—"[My] objection to poker is that it's a waste of time"—Aleck continued to play with the club whenever the mood moved him.

"I shall fold my tens like Arabs and silently steal away" was a line Kaufman said continuously and which Aleck quoted constantly and with increasing irritation.

Once an unexpected event took place before the game began. Members of the Thanatopsis Club had fallen into the habit of bringing delicatessen snacks into their second-floor headquarters. Understandably, the waiters who served the cardplayers all night began to complain about the lack of tips. One Saturday evening a large sign greeted the members as they gathered to play: "BASKET PARTIES WELCOME. FRANK CASE, PROPRIETOR."

The sarcasm offended their sensitive souls, and with an indignant sniff and an angry back of their collective hand, the Thanatopsis moved to the socially prominent Colony Restaurant, where the game became so big it divided itself into two tables, and the stakes became so high a lower-priced game took up sessions at the St. Moritz Hotel. They named the low-stake game the Hoyle Club. A branch even existed for a time in Los Angeles, alternately shifting from Chasen's Restaurant to the Hillcrest Country Club. Someone dubbed the Los Angeles group Thanatopsis West.

Gene Cavallero, owner of the Colony, was delighted to have the poker players and the press that followed in their wake. After two months, however, the Thanatopsis returned to its old stand at the Algonquin. Frank Case, proprietor, had been taught his lesson. But members of the club, when they were hungry, once again ordered food from the dining room.

Since the primary function of the Round Table was to eat lunch, it appears reasonable enough to examine the eating habits of Alexander Woollcott.

"Perhaps there is a speck of truth in this new Freudian foolishness," he told George Backer. "Perhaps food *is* a substitute for love. My capacity for the former makes me positively tingle at the possibilities of what might have occurred had I the aptitude for the latter. Had things been different, I might have been lean and lusty."

As for the appetites of the other members of the Round Table, they ranged from finicky food pickers such as George Kaufman to hearty eaters such as Heywood Broun.

"My theory about George Kaufman's eating habits in restaurants," Aleck told Thornton Wilder, "is that the boys in Jewish homes have devoted mothers who see to it that all nutrition is bound up with love. The mothers are martyrs to these special sons of theirs. Any dish in any restaurant therefore may be wonderfully prepared, marvelously served, but it doesn't have the element of love. It must taste like a glass of sand served off a shovel. There's a neurotic connection—the food and the mother."

Broun would eat anything put down in front of him, but no one could stand up to Aleck as a trencherman, and he who chose the Algonquin never had reason to fault its cuisine.

If it was breakfast for Aleck, he would begin with four eggs Benedict. He would wash down whatever accompanied this repast —rolls, muffins, and the like—with cup after cup of coffee. If it was lunch, double, triple, and frequently quadruple orders of dessert would be carefully considered and consumed.

If there was no rush to get to the opening of a play, Woollcott would dine more often than not at the Algonquin. If not there, then at the Kaufmans', where George's wife, Beatrice, became one of his great all-time favorites.

Beatrice's dinners were triumphs of Teutonic cookery. Everything possible was made with butter. Steaks, potatoes, rich desserts. Not all guests were entranced with Bea's table.

"It was heavy food, guaranteed to bring on indigestion," Jed Harris, the Broadway producer and dissenter, remarked. "It was as though you were condemned to eat at Luchow's every night of your life."

The playwright Ruth Goetz claimed otherwise.

"Beatrice's table was lavishly spread," Mrs. Goetz remembered. "The finest foods, the finest wines, all served exquisitely, were mixed with the best conversation in New York."

Bea, catering to her husband, also catered to Aleck and herself. While George remained a string bean, Bea spread almost as quickly and as broadly as Aleck.

George regularly nagged her to diet. He did not dare, however, to make such a suggestion to his boss. Eventually the carbohydrates conquered.

When the Round Table began, Aleck was a tubby fellow who at 195 was overweight by fifty pounds. By the end of the Round Table, ten years later, he had spread to a grotesque 255 pounds.

Sugar, cream, everything fattening appealed to Aleck. An outstanding example is the cocktail that Aleck and many other friends claimed was named after him. Others deny stoutly that the

Alexander was named after Woollcott. Aleck, they advised, merely appropriated the drink.

Instructors at bartending schools vary in their opinions as to the first Alexander. A menu from the once-famous Broadway restaurant Rector's, dated 1905, shows no mention of a cocktail named Alexander.

Whether or not he created the drink—one ounce heavy cream, one ounce crème de cacao, one ounce gin or brandy, add cracked ice and shake well—it is certain that he consumed it before dinner. Two, even three, if time allowed.

As caloric intake continued, Woollcott's two tentative double chins now became three distinct areas of fat. His face changed in shape from oval to round. His ever-thickening eyeglasses magnified his pupils so that they appeared to be immense. These, combined with a little beak-shaped nose, gave him the look of an owl. The first subject for every caricaturist in New York was Woollcott.

"I don't mind the pen-and-ink boys," he told the Round Tablers. "They've made me look so smart that Hamilton College wants to give me an honorary degree."

In the mid-Twenties his Alma Mater honored Woollcott by awarding him a doctorate. He accepted it in Clinton and hastened back to New York to announce to his luncheon colleagues his appreciation of his newly acquired title.

"Now whenever I'm at an opening night," he claimed, "and the manager comes out and asks, 'Is there a doctor in the house?' I'll be able to stand up and say, 'Here I am!' "

Miss Kate Sproehnle, F.P.A.'s young cousin from Chicago, came to New York for a short visit and sat next to Woollcott. A discussion of a theater benefit for the A.S.P.C.A. came up. The price of a single ticket was so high that the young woman exclaimed, "Goodness! It would be cheaper to buy a horse and just be kind to it."

Margaret Case Harriman, daughter of the proprietor of the Algonquin, reported in her book *The Vicious Circle* that an unwritten but strictly followed law at the Round Table allowed no one to use the words spoken during lunch without giving credit to their originator.

A few days later Douglas Fairbanks, the silent-movie star, was called upon to speak at a banquet. He used Miss Sproehnle's words and unintentionally failed to mention the young woman who first spoke them.

The next morning F.P.A.'s column in the *World* chastised him soundly. That noon Fairbanks showed up at the Algonquin hoping to make amends.

"I didn't know this Sproehnle kid was a relative of yours, Frank," Fairbanks apologized to Adams.

"Relative or no relative," F.P.A. advised him, "plagiarism is plagiarism whether her name is Kate Sproehnle or Lizzie Borden."

"Oh," Fairbanks retorted immediately, "if her name had been Lizzie Borden I'd have known *Woollcott* said it!"

Striding into the Algonquin one day came Heywood Broun, half a dozen galley proofs in his hand and a smile on his face. Broun was one of the editors of a book to be called *Nonsenseorship*, a series of belles-lettres against the evil practice of interfering with the rights of authors. He had just received the proofs of a Woollcott article that so delighted him that he brought it to lunch and showed it to the members of the Round Table. Woollcott's attack was as follows:

> They derive a curious comfort from the story of the reviewer for a Boston journal who once described a musician as remaining seated through a concert in the pensive attitude of Buddha contemplating his navel. It is a story within whose implications lies all that has ever been said, or ever will be said, about censorship. The copy-readers and make-up men, it seems, could see nothing especially infamous in their reviewer's little simile. . . . At all events, the offending word passed all the sentries and was printed, when, too late, it

caught the horrified eye of the proprietor. At the sight of so crassly physical a term in the chaste columns of his own paper, he rushed to the telephone at the club and called the managing editor. That word must come out. The paper was already on the presses. Even as they spoke these were whirling out copy after copy. Too late to reset? Yes, much too late. But was there not still some remedy which would keep at least part of the edition free from that dreadful word? Wasn't it still possible to rout out the type at that point, to chisel the word away and leave a blank? Yes, it was possible. So the presses were halted, the one word was scraped out, the presses whirled again and the review with a gape in the line went up and down Beacon Street, reading ". . . a musician as remaining seated through a concert in the pensive attitude of Buddha contemplating his   ."

Verbal thunderbolts were employed by three members of the Round Table, Woollcott, Parker, and Kaufman. While they were not always on the same side, Mrs. Parker used shock in her humor with great success.

When she was being walked through an elegant Manhattan apartment by a real estate broker, the diminutive Dorothy shook her head.

"No, no," she complained. "All I need is room enough to lay a hat and a few friends."

Of a book on science Mrs. Parker, the critic, complained, "It was written without fear and without research."

At his bridge club one afternoon, the incomparable Kaufman shuddered at the atrocious playing of a fellow member. When the hand was finished, the bungler sensed disapproval in Kaufman's silence.

"All right, George," he protested, "how would you have played it?"

Kaufman froze him with, "Under an assumed name."

Broun invited Lardner to a poker game at the Thanatopsis. "Can't make it tonight," Lardner explained. "It's my little son's night out and I've got to stay home with the nurse."

"The trouble with this country," Franklin P. Adams observed at the Algonquin, "is that there are too many politicians who believe, with a conviction based on experience, that you can fool all of the people all of the time."

"Ninety-two percent of the stuff told to you in confidence," F.P.A. whispered at lunch one day, "you wouldn't get anybody else to listen to."

Aleck frequently found himself on the receiving end of the barbs hurled at the Round Table. The beautiful Peggy Wood, actress and operetta star, arrived at the Algonquin in time to hear Woollcott pontificating upon a revival of *Macbeth*.

"We're talking casting, Peggy," Aleck began afresh. "I don't think you'd make a good Lady Macbeth. Do you?"

"No," Miss Wood replied sweetly, "but you would."

Myra Hampton, an actress who hadn't worked as much as she would have liked, found herself seated next to Jascha Heifetz at the Round Table one day. The noted violinist complained bitterly.

"Every time I go to a party people ask me to play."

Miss Hampton nodded sympathetically.

"How would *you* feel," Heifetz continued, "if every time *you* went to a party people asked you to get up and act?" Myra Hampton's eyes lit up.

"I'd *love* it!" she answered.

Robert Benchley came to lunch ready with an opinion concerning the previous night's entertainment.

"It was one of those plays in which all the actors unfortunately enunciated very clearly."

After a particularly wet session of the Round Table, Benchley found himself outside the Algonquin looking at a uniformed fellow he took to be the doorman.

"Would you get me a taxi, my good man?" Benchley asked politely after tapping him on his shoulder braid.

"See here," the man responded icily, "I happen to be a Rear Admiral in the United States Navy."

"Perfectly all right," Benchley said with a small hiccup. "Get me a battleship then."

George S. Kaufman, always in and out of the *Times* city room, hurried into the Algonquin with information that The Theatre Guild had a problem. The Guild had just started rehearsals of the American premiere of Shaw's *Saint Joan*. While the rehearsals were going well, the play lasted three and a half hours, far beyond the usual curtain time. Cabling Shaw that suburban theatergoers would miss their trains home, the Guild urged the author to cut the play. George Bernard Shaw's reply had just arrived in Lawrence Langner's office: "BEGIN AT EIGHT OR RUN LATER TRAINS."

Kaufman also reported to the Round Table about his collaborator on *June Moon*, Ring Lardner. The play was being tried out in Atlantic City, and the local critics wrote that it had a sensational second act but the first and third acts badly needed rewriting. Lardner, shuffling gloomily along the boardwalk, encountered a friend.

"What are you doing here?" his friend asked.

"I'm down here with an act," Ring answered.

Jests, laughter, fun—this was the theme of post-World War I America. "The pursuit of happiness" was not merely a phrase from the Declaration of Independence, it became the postwar way of living.

New York was smaller in the Twenties. Subways and trolleys

cost a nickel. Times Square was bright and exciting. Appreciation of art was everywhere. There were no prostitutes, no pimps, no winos in Woollcott's world. Drug addicts and panhandlers didn't exist between the Algonquin and Times Square. It was the time and the place for bright lights and fun. The Depression and the Crash were words waiting to be coined. Breadlines and the New Deal were impossible to imagine. Theater was still concerned with the carriage trade. "Talkies" was a word nobody had heard. Radio was in its infancy, television hadn't entered the laboratory.

For Woollcott and his cronies the Round Table was now. They were amazed to find a few years later that it was they who made up the lost generation.

10 Around the "World"

*I*T WAS A TIME OF INNOCENCE IN AMERICA. TODAY newspapers are filled with international, even interplanetary subjects. In the Twenties the best reporters spent their energies on more local topics, matters of greater human interest. Herbert Bayard Swope, who in 1919–1920 covered the Versailles Peace Conference in striped trousers and a cutaway coat, returned home and promptly reported the Dempsey-Carpentier prizefight, quoting no less an intellectual than George Bernard Shaw on the outcome of the match.

Heywood Broun, who devoted large quantities of his work to liberal politics, took time off to write a serious article on the death of the circus's bearded lady in a small Oklahoma town with a population of two hundred. Today her passing would probably not make the obit page of *Variety*. Then it was big news in the pages of Pulitzer's *World*.

Many people actually believed that Herbert Bayard Swope was the illegitimate son of Joseph Pulitzer. The life-sized photograph of Pulitzer that Swope kept on the wall behind his office desk chair bore a startling similarity to Swope himself. That Pulitzer first made good as a publisher in St. Louis and that Swope was born in that city served only to further the rumor.

In truth, Herbert Bayard Swope was born, quite legitimately, in

1881 to Ida S. and Isaac Swope. Beginning as a reporter on Joseph Pulitzer's St. Louis *Post-Dispatch,* he served his apprenticeship there and then joined Robert McCormick's *Chicago Tribune.* Pulitzer, however, lured him back as a reporter for his New York *World,* and in that capacity he covered the 1914–1918 war in Europe as a correspondent behind the German lines. His articles on the Central Powers were so effective that he received the Pulitzer Prize for reporting in 1917.

By 1920 he had assumed the position of executive editor of the *World.* His personality was as vivid as his red hair, his aggressiveness as positive as his jutting jaw. His energy, his ego, and his capacity for work were all as tall as the man himself—well over six feet.

As a reporter for the *World* during the prewar years he had beaten Woollcott and every other reporter assigned to the Rosenthal-Becker murder case. As the editor of the *World* in the postwar years he watched Woollcott the drama critic and waited.

Munsey's paper, the *Herald,* on which Woollcott worked, suddenly began to lose large sums of money. It was sold and then merged with the *Tribune* in 1924.

"I don't see what the *Herald* can contribute to the *Tribune* except a hyphen," Woollcott said.

Munsey, still knowing a good thing when he had it, moved Woollcott to his afternoon newspaper, the *Sun.*

While Woollcott was on the *Sun* he fathered, mothered, and seemingly delivered to the waiting world Adolph, Leonard, Julius, Milton, and Herbert Marx. The Marx Brothers were escapees from the two-a-day milieu of vaudeville.

Arriving at the Casino Theatre in New York, they were scheduled to open in a musical comedy with the vamp-until-ready title *I'll Say She Is.*

No first-string critic, drunk or sober, in or out of his right mind, planned to go to the opening. Woollcott expected to attend a drama that night. Much to his annoyance the management post-poned the performance. Every other critic took the evening off, but Woollcott, who loved the theater with so much passion, agreed with reluctance to attend *I'll Say She Is*.

Under the vague impression that he was about to see a group of acrobats, Woollcott went to the Casino Theatre.

When he came out he wrote, "Surely there should be dancing in the streets." There was much more, all typical Woollcott ginger-bread: ". . . splendacious . . . harlequinade . . . behooves . . . vouchsafed."

From that night forward Aleck, although he later acknowledged Minnie as their mother and Frenchy as their father, considered the Marx Brothers his own. He doted upon them, particularly Adolph, or, as he became better known, Harpo.

Despite the occasional discoveries he made, Aleck was not happy on the *Sun*. He took it into his head that the only critics that car-ried any weight in the theater were those who wrote for the morn-ing papers. It is not a play on words to write "carried any weight." Percy Hammond, Heywood Broun, and Alexander Woollcott all tipped the scales at well over two hundred pounds each, and they were accordingly known as "The Three Fat Fates of Broadway."

To find himself on an afternoon paper after all those years put Woollcott into a pout.

Swope pulled him out of it with a three-year contract at fifteen thousand dollars a year and a thirteen-week vacation during each of the three years. Aleck went to work for the *World* in August, 1925.

That year proved to be an exciting theatrical season. Fred and Adele Astaire were in *Lady Be Good*; *The Jazz Singer* had George Jessel; Ina Claire starred in *The Last of Mrs. Cheyney*; and Rodgers and Hart wrote *Garrick Gaieties*.

Nothing pleased Aleck more than when Irving Berlin, George

Kaufman, and Morrie Ryskind teamed up to produce a vehicle for the Marx Brothers called *Cocoanuts.* It turned out to be a smash hit, and Woollcott, content that so many of his friends found success in a single production, took his contractually agreed-upon leave from the *World* the next summer and sailed for a holiday in Europe.

The going-away party for Aleck was much too large for his cabin. That small stateroom could hardly contain the multitude of gifts brought by well-wishing companions: toy trains, teddy bears, and drawing slates competed with presents his chums felt he could not find in Europe. Robert Benchley arrived with a plate of wheat cakes while Marc Connelly and Alexander Clark, an actor, contributed a bowl of goldfish and a two-foot bust of Schiller weighing 120 pounds.

Two months later Aleck returned to New York, to be met by many of the same people who saw him off. They had arranged for him to go through customs without the usual delay and examination. He ordered his steamer trunks, his valises, his Gladstones, his portmanteaus, and his satchels to be delivered directly to 412 West 47th Street.

Then, bidding sweet and pungent farewells, he left by taxi for the Lyric Theatre on West Forty-second Street to see the Marx Brothers. Accompanied backstage by two of the musical's authors, Kaufman and Ryskind, Woollcott found his favorite zanies in their dressing rooms. He tried to get them to welcome him, but the Marx Brothers, who were really as wild offstage as they appeared to be onstage, gleefully greeted Aleck by stripping him down to his underwear.

Kaufman, incredibly shy, winced and walked away. Ryskind, younger and more daring, remained to watch the show. What would Woollcott do?

Woollcott had no chance to respond. Groucho was ready with a line.

"Tell us, Aleck," Ryskind remembered Groucho asking, "when you were in France, were you laid?"

Woollcott paused for a moment and then spoke with a marked wistfulness.

"Infinitesimally," he replied.

Then, with sublime confidence, Aleck casually began to dress himself.

Jeffrey Holmesdale, an attractive blond young man, served as Aleck's assistant on the *World*. He seemed a quiet, unassuming Englishman, and after a year or so of faithful service, he approached Woollcott and asked if he might be allowed to return home for a short visit, as his father was ill.

Aleck granted the request and thought no more about it, until a photograph accompanied by a news story with a London dateline came to his attention. The fourth Earl Amherst had died. His son, Viscount Holmesdale, succeeded to the title. The fifth earl, the news story read, had been pursuing a literary career in New York.

Picking up the picture, Aleck saw his assistant decked out in the coronet and ermine robes of a belted earl. A few days afterward, the bearer of one of the noblest titles in England returned to the *World* and without a word picked up where he had left off—as Woollcott's faithful assistant on the drama section.

After Aleck's first successful book had been published, he viewed his former assistant's loyalty with a certain amount of assumed irritability.

"With the exception of Mrs. Stanley Baldwin and two or three articled clarks living near Liverpool," he confided to Noel Coward, "the entire citizenry of the British Empire has written me with great enthusiasm about *While Rome Burns*, all explaining that they had borrowed their copy from Earl Amherst. This would seem to indicate that thanks to his Lordship's lavishness all sales of the book in England and the Dominions had been rendered unnecessary. I hope the little bleached son of a bitch fries in hell!"

Woollcott did almost everything in triplicate. At any given time, if one asked, he would name three "first ladies of the American theater." He discovered Katharine Cornell in *A Bill of Divorcement* in 1921. Lynn Fontanne was uncovered by Woollcott in *Dulcy* in 1922. Helen Hayes had to wait until *Coquette* in 1927.

It was not at all inconsistent for Woollcott to proclaim each as the ruling lady of the American theater in three successive columns. The only difference between the coronation of Miss Hayes and those of the Misses Cornell and Fontanne was that he had known Miss Hayes socially.

Although she claimed, "I was a creation of his," when Helen Hayes starred in her first great hit, *Coquette*, the critics wrote wildly complimentary notices—all except Woollcott.

"An unfortunate thing occurred at the Maxine Elliott Theatre last night" was the way he started his review.

Later, however, he returned and paid his proper respects. Helen Hayes forgave him and Woollcott repeated the marriage-broker role he had played in the Grant-Ross wedding.

On the afternoon of August 17, 1928, the forty-one-year-old Aleck arrived at the small apartment Miss Hayes shared with her mother, Brownie. Solemnly he walked to the phonograph and placed upon it a record of "Drink to Me Only with Thine Eyes." Miss Hayes, about to marry Charles MacArthur of the playwriting team of Hecht and MacArthur, was forced to listen to the record several times before the hour struck. Then Helen Hayes, her mother, her groom, and his best man, Aleck Woollcott, taxied to Forty-second Street to be married in the office of Judge Obelwager.

The judge, a man who never avoided the opportunity of getting his name in print, invited the entire New York press corps to the festivities. When the marriage ceremony ended, Mr. and Mrs. MacArthur and all the photographers and reporters descended in a large elevator. The silence was broken only once and that was when Woollcott spoke.

"Every girl," he said, "should be married to Charlie MacArthur at some period of her life."

Always-the-best-man-never-the-groom was a role that Aleck had been playing with increasing regularity. Peggy Wood married John V. A. Weaver, a Hamilton graduate, with the aid and assistance of A. H. Woollcott.

Irving Berlin, the composer, married Ellin MacKay, the socialite, with Aleck doing everything except performing the ceremony and cutting the cake.

When Bill Murray, the critic-turned-artists'-representative, married Natalia Danesi, Woollcott once again served as best man.

When asked why *he* never took the marital plunge, Aleck always referred to Frank Crowninshield's statement: "Married men make very poor husbands."

About the only one with whom he didn't walk down the aisle was Edna Ferber, and Miss Ferber had a ready line for that. "Being an old maid is like death by drowning, a really delightful sensation after you cease to struggle."

If he didn't find her a husband, Woollcott did the next best thing. Edna Ferber gave him credit for acting as the marriage broker between her novel *Show Boat* and Jerome Kern and Oscar Hammerstein's musicalization of it.

Another instance of his matchmaking came during lunch one day when he found himself across from the table at which Arthur Hopkins was eating.

"You wouldn't want to read a play, would you?" Woollcott asked the producer.

Hopkins paused.

"I forgot. You're a producer. You don't read plays."

Hopkins couldn't allow such a remark to go by without comment. He'd be glad to read any play Woollcott suggested.

"This is a war play," Woollcott continued. "Nobody wants to

read a play about the war. That's over. Done. Best be forgotten. Am I correct, Hopkins?"

Hopkins had no alternative but to say he'd be pleased to read a war play even if such works weren't popular at the time.

Four days later Hopkins announced that he had taken an option on a work by two young newspapermen on the *World*, Laurence Stallings and Maxwell Anderson. Their play, *What Price Glory?*, was one of the big successes of the next season.

Abie's Irish Rose was a comedy that almost every New York critic sliced into shreds—except for Alexander Woollcott, who to everyone's amazement conceded that it left much to be desired as a work of art but predicted that the public would keep it open. The cries of outrage from his colleagues were heard up and down Broadway, but after 2,327 consecutive performances, *Abie's Irish Rose* became the longest-running play in Woollcott's lifetime.

Benchley vehemently campaigned against the play. He even offered a prize for the best capsule review of it. Aleck was properly proud when Harpo Marx won the contest.

"No worse than a bad cold," Harpo said.

"What's the prize?" an Algonquinite asked.

"The prize," Harpo answered with a straight face, "turns out to be I don't ever have to see it again."

That Harpo Marx could write a terse dramatic criticism reminded Woollcott that another of his friends, Tallulah Bankhead, the throaty southern beauty, had once performed a similar feat. Aleck had taken her to a rather tedious revival of a Maeterlinck tragedy.

"There is less here than meets the eye," Tallulah murmured as they rose to leave.

No one appreciated her summation more than Aleck and no one more employed succinct and concise comments of the drama than Woollcott himself—that is, when he wasn't gushing.

"In retrospect it is not very easy to evaluate him as a drama critic," Wolcott Gibbs (no relative) wrote in his profile of Woollcott in *The New Yorker*.

> He had enthusiasm, an honest love for the theatre, and a gift for the neat and deadly phrase. On the other hand, he was sentimental, partisan, and maddeningly positive about everything even before he had been a critic long enough to know much about anything. His style, which could be lucid and witty, could also be muddled and frantic, and reading him in this mood often made subscribers feel as if his hot breath was actually on their necks. The short space of writing time allowed by a morning paper, of course, had a lot to do with that, for the Woollcott style, pouring too richly from his heart, needed a great deal of skimming and straining before it was fit for public consumption. He was aware of this himself and once, when an admiring lady asked him how he ever wrote so much in such a short time— most of his reviews were turned out in less than an hour—he answered her reasonably.
>
> "If I had twice as much time, my blossom," he said, "my pieces would probably be half as long."

A play in nine acts, *Strange Interlude* by Eugene O'Neill, had a somewhat shaky start. The Guild had offered it to Katharine Cornell, who courteously turned it down. Alice Brady also refused it. Pauline Lord would have none of it. Finally the Guild begged Lynn Fontanne to play the leading role. Miss Fontanne agreed to appear in it but she had many misgivings. Her husband, Alfred Lunt, claimed that if the play had two more acts he could have sued for desertion.

During rehearsals Lynn Fontanne slipped a copy of the script to Woollcott, who read it and promptly wrote an article about it in *Vanity Fair* that was tantamount to a poor review.

"Swope thought that a man who already had taken a public

stand about a dramatic offering was disqualified from reviewing it objectively," E. J. Kahn, Jr., wrote in his biography *The World of Swope*. "*Strange Interlude* was probably the most important new play of that season, but Swope nonetheless ordered Woollcott to step aside and let Dudley Nichols substitute for him. Then to demonstrate there was nothing personal in it, Swope gave Woollcott his own opening night tickets. The muzzled critic escorted Swope's wife to the performance."

It does not seem fair to call the premiere of *Strange Interlude* an opening night. The play began at five-fifteen in the afternoon, ran for two hours, took time off for dinner, and started up again at 8:30 P.M. The curtain came down shortly after eleven.

It was not only an endurance test for cast and audience alike; the opening also proved to be a great social occasion. Otto Kahn, the financier and patron of the arts, arrived at the afternoon session accompanied by the actress Elsie Ferguson. He wore formal afternoon clothes, striped worsted trousers, a charcoal swallow-tailed coat, and a gray cravat. After dinner he returned in resplendent evening attire, white tire and tails. This time he was accompanied by the German impresario Max Reinhardt.

Woollcott leaned toward Margaret Swope and whispered, "Kahn must have inadvertently hung Elsie Ferguson in his clothes closet."

To the surprise, dismay, delight, disappointment, disdain, and distress of everyone in the theater, depending upon who you were and how much he liked you, Alexander Woollcott suddenly made it known that he would stop his daily reviews of plays with the expiration of his contract with the New York *World* in May, 1928.

The decision came as a blow to the theatrical community. A year earlier Equity, the actors' union, had voted Aleck "the most discriminating" of all drama critics. Now he appeared to be forsaking them at the very height of his power.

One reason Broadway gave for his abdication was that Aleck had grown so fat he was unable to squeeze into the rather ordinary confines of a theater seat. Another reason concerned his continual feuding with the *World's* managing editor. Herbert Bayard Swope reveled in sending the red-hot and biting memos that he fired off to the heads of many departments on the *World.*

Woollcott protected the drama desk from these barbs. His assistants, Jeffrey Holmesdale and Alison Smith, never faced the wrath of Swope while Aleck was there to shield them, but his relationship with the flamboyant managing editor began to deteriorate. Personal friends though they were outside the office, Swope hectored Aleck by narrowing the time from the end of a new play to the deadline when Woollcott's copy was due downtown in the *World's* city room, at 63 Park Row.

At the end Swope decided that Woollcott's copy had to be delivered by midnight. As openings in those days began at 8:30 P.M. and were over at approximately 11:10 P.M., this gave Woollcott fifty minutes to race up the aisle, catch a cab, or walk as rapidly as he could to a room in the Astor Hotel. It was a block and a half closer to most theaters than the Algonquin, and Aleck was no longer as fleet of foot as he used to be. There a typewriter and a telegrapher awaited him. As rapidly as Aleck turned out a paragraph—and he was as fast a typist as any newspaper had in those days except for George S. Kaufman—the telegrapher would lift each paragraph out of the machine and send it to Park Row.

The pressure proved too much for a man who had lived under such stress for almost two decades. He made light of leaving his post. Years later he told Lynn Fontanne:

> My profession made me hard on watches. In my nights as a dramatic critic I used to prop mine beside the typewriter as I wrote and about once a month would knock it off onto the concrete floor. My bills for repairs at Tiffany's took about all my income. I decided I must get something cheaper and less fragile and picked out a nice plain one, in a Fifth Avenue shop, that seemed to be encased in gun metal.

Obviously it was better than a mere dollar Ingersoll watch but what if it cost $5 or $10? They told me the price was $1,500. So I went out onto the sidewalk, did some figuring on the back of an envelope and decided it would be cheaper to give up being a dramatic critic.

Management of the *World*, which had wanted to save the high cost of Aleck's weekly stipend, suddenly changed its corporate mind. Swope offered him charm and a thousand-dollar raise, all to no avail. Came May, Alexander Woollcott, after fourteen years as a drama critic—with time out for the war—after nineteen years on newspapers, quit while he was ahead and on top.

That he regretted his departure, from the parade down the center aisles at the opening nights to the deadlines to the smell of the freshly printed papers, may be seen in the many magazine pieces he wrote in the years that followed. That he brooded about it, that he turned melancholy into depression over the abdication of his power as a critic is, however, nonsense. Woollcott, always one to plan ahead carefully, left New York for a grand holiday in a villa on the French Riviera. A year and a few months before the Black Friday that left Wall Street so impoverished that it required thirty years before The Street recovered, Woollcott, Bea Kaufman, Alice Duer Miller, and Harpo Marx sailed on the S.S. *Roma* for a summer that few would forget.

11 On the Riviera

*L*ONG BEFORE ELSA MAXWELL SMOKED STOGIES, Woollcott smoked cigars. And long before Elsa Maxwell gave parties for a living, Woollcott gave them for the pleasure of his friends' company. Although there had been many parties in the past and although there would be still more parties in the future, the most glorious, the most glamorous of them all was a three-month binge Woollcott arranged in a villa on the Cap d'Antibes.

It was beautifully planned and exquisitely executed, and if there was an occasional bit of skinny-dipping, anything went during the summer of '28.

There was more than a touch of the tour guide in Aleck. Although he did not look the part, he was in reality one of the most organized of men. Specific people at specific hours at specific places for specific reasons—at this he excelled. He even booked hotel rooms for himself and his party of three during the week that it took to ready their villa for occupancy.

In 1928 the hot, dry mistral blew as relentlessly as it does today. Then, the Riviera had few homes and a small population. The summer sun baked everyone and everything. It burned down on the gay red-tiled roofs and the pastel walls of the houses. Only the lush foliage of the coast thrived. Lemon, palm, pine, and silver olive trees hid the Moorish balconies that looked out onto the

Mediterranean. The sea was warm, the sky appeared cold, and the sunlight fused both into a horizon beyond which lay Africa. That year the air itself was perfumed by burning eucalyptus from fires behind the rocky beaches.

Once installed in the Villa Ganelon, Woollcott donned a two-piece yellow bathing suit with broad black stripes. This outfit, along with a canvas sailor cap, proved to be his uniform for the better part of the summer.

"That bathing suit didn't make him look any slimmer," Mme. Ruth Dubonnet reflected. As the young widow of a remarkable portrait artist, she thought Aleck was "delightfully charming and bright because he made everyone around him sound and feel so charming and bright. The protruding tummy made no difference."

Another young widow who arrived on the Riviera and remained for the summer was Aleck's dear friend Ruth Gordon. Her husband Gregory Kelly had died the previous year, and Miss Gordon, one of Woollcott's chosen actresses, was received with great welcome and much warmth.

"Ruth Gordon was ever so gay as Nibs," Aleck had written in the *Times* in 1915, while reviewing what he considered to be the greatest production of *Peter Pan* starring Maude Adams. His throwaway line for Ruth Gordon wasn't much but he more than made up for it in the years that followed.

When asked to choose the proverbial woman with whom he'd be willing to spend the rest of his life on a desert island, Woollcott named Ruth Gordon. People close to them claimed that Aleck had launched her literary career by urging her to broaden her talents to include writing. He liked to tell people that he had fallen in love with her, and even wished to marry her.

"They were always saying that Aleck and I were engaged," Miss Gordon said. "Rubbish! If we'd announced our engagement who would have printed it?"

Aleck took to his typewriter and addressed another woman close to him.

"I am leading the life of a rosy, middle-aged dolphin," he wrote Edna Ferber, urging her to join his merry band on the Riviera. He was forty-one at the time and had five more careers to pursue.

The French in those days ignored the Riviera, preferring instead the beaches of Deauville. That summer the Americans and a few British had the coast from St. Tropez to Monaco to themselves. Ernest Hemingway was there. Zelda and Scott Fitzgerald were at Juan-les-Pins. Dwight Deere Wiman, whose money came from the Deere tractors and was plowed into Broadway musicals that made him even wealthier, summered on the Riviera with his wife and their children and their children's governesses. Harold Guinzburg, co-founder of the Viking Press, and his wife, Alice, spent the summer at Antibes. Other Americans included the noted actor Otis Skinner, his wife, Maud, and his daughter, Cornelia Otis Skinner, Peggy Hopkins Joyce, and Grace Moore.

Montagu Norman, governor of the Bank of England, and three writers—Somerset Maugham, H. G. Wells, and G. B. Shaw—made up the van of the British contingent.

Woollcott visited each of them and reciprocated their hospitalities one by one. Shaw caused the greatest stir. Having invited Mr. and Mrs. Shaw to lunch and having the Shaws accept the invitation, the entire Villa Ganelon—hosts and staff alike—were thrown into a panic. Shaw was a vegetarian. What to have for lunch?

Four days were given to the debate. On the fifth day lunch was ordered and prepared. For Woollcott it was the social coup of the season. For Harpo Marx it didn't mean quite as much. Actually, Harpo had heard the name Shaw discussed at the Round Table. He was an English writer, politician, something.

Bored with the breathless preparations being made by Woollcott, Mrs. Miller, Mrs. Kaufman, and the cook, Harpo took a dip in the blue Mediterranean and then stretched out for a bit of nude sunbathing. Shortly thereafter he fell asleep. But not for long.

" 'Halloo! Halloo! Is there nobody home?' " a man's voice called out.

"I wrapped the towel around myself and scrambled up the rocks to see who it was," Harpo wrote.

It was a tall, skinny, red-faced old geezer with a beard, decked out in a sporty cap and knicker suit. There was a lady with him.

"Where the devil's Woollcott?" the guy asked. Without waiting for an answer he said, "Who the devil are you?"

I told him I was Harpo Marx.

"Ah, yes, of course," he said, with an impish grin. He held out his hand. "I'm Bernard Shaw," he said. He caught me flat-footed. Instead of shaking hands he made a sudden lunge for my towel, snatched it away, and exposed me naked to the world. "And this," he said, "is Mrs. Shaw."

"From the moment I met him," Harpo concluded, "I had nothing to hide from George Bernard Shaw."

As deeply as Aleck loved Harpo, Harpo was always at work trying different means by which he might embarrass Woollcott. And Woollcott was not a man who embarrassed easily. There was a night on the Riviera, however, when Harpo outdid himself and Woollcott reaped his revenge.

One evening Aleck decided to treat Bea Kaufman, Alice Miller, Cornelia Otis Skinner, and Harpo to a sumptuous dinner at the Café de Paris, to be followed by roulette at the Grand Casino at Monte Carlo. The ladies wore long skirts, Aleck wore a dinner jacket, and Harpo dressed in the style in which he felt most comfortable: slacks, a blazer, and an open-neck polo shirt.

"How can I explain you to the French?" Aleck asked impatiently of Harpo. "They have no word for 'boob.'"

At the door to the casino, an attendant stopped Harpo. He regretted, but the rules of the establishment were certain beyond a doubt. No gentlemen were permitted to enter without neckties.

"Serves you right, Marx," Aleck told him grandly. "Find some other divertissement to occupy your idle time." And with that he swept the ladies gallantly through the double doors that opened before them.

Harpo was not only intelligent but inventive as well. Going around the corner, he took off his two black socks, put one of them in his pocket, and knotted the other one as a bow tie around his neck. He returned to the entrance of the casino, where the doorman, noting the black tie, apologized completely.

"You perceive how it is, m'sieur, rules of the house, *n'est-ce-pas?*"

Harpo nodded tolerantly.

"If you will, m'sieur, your friends will be waiting for you," the doorman said as he bowed Harpo in.

Miss Skinner recalled that when Woollcott looked up from the roulette table and saw Harpo his eyes did not flicker for even a second. He merely placed his bet and turned toward the croupier. Harpo began betting extravagantly and losing just as easily. When he finally ran out of money—something he obviously had been trying to do for the better part of an hour—Harpo reached inside his blazer, withdrew his passport, tore out his passport photograph, and placed it on the table, smiling broadly, as if a picture of Harpo Marx were legal tender in Monte Carlo.

That finally proved too much for Woollcott. Leaving his place. at the table, he walked around to where Harpo stood and without a word took the thumb and forefinger of his left hand and pulled at one end of the tie around Harpo's neck. A single tug and the bow tie became a sock in Woollcott's fingers. With his other hand he beckoned an assistant manager.

"I understood," Woollcott told the assistant manager, "that gentlemen were not allowed in the house without cravats."

Shepherding his three ladies before him, Woollcott left, his chins and nose pointing toward the baroque ceiling.

Four liveried attendants closed in on Harpo, and for him the evening was over.

Noel Coward came by to reinforce the British. Charlie Mac-Arthur descended to amuse the Americans. King Alfonso of Spain

arrived as a relief to the people of Madrid. The holiday was drawing to a close and there was time for only a pair of parties.

One of the very few times in his life when Aleck was tight
occurred at the first affair. When the Fitzgeralds, Zelda and Scott,
were around, everyone drank doubles. Hear it from the beautiful
blonde who began in Irving Berlin's *Music Box Revue* and ended
up as an opera star, Grace Moore.

> Our little season on the Riviera that year was officially
> closed with the farewell dinner we gave for Aleck Woollcott
> and my beau from Paris, Chato. Zelda Fitzgerald threw her
> black panties at Aleck and Chato. Aleck, dear prim soul,
> was too shocked to make more than a pretense of reaching
> and Chato naturally caught the prize. . . . We all dashed
> down the rock after Chato and soon everybody was in the
> water still fully clothed.
>
> The effect of salt water on the alcoholic content of Vin
> Rosé simply produces the familiar blur. We all edged out
> to the parked raft before it got to us. But suddenly, we
> noticed Aleck emerge completely naked out of the shadow
> of an overcast moon. Apparently, he had lost all his clothes
> in the Mediterranean plunge, and now blissfully unaware
> of his native state, was climbing a ladder to the shore. He
> walked over to where he had left his straw hat, solemnly
> put it on his head, lit a cigarette from the case that had
> been left there and walked with great dignity up the path
> and to the hotel. We watched him with a kind of fascinated
> and dulled horror, loath to remind him of his lack of
> clothes because we knew, knowing puritanical Aleck, how
> strong his reaction would be. We didn't see him again that
> season. He had already departed for Paris by the time we
> could get the end of the story from the room clerk. Aleck,
> we were told, had fortunately come into an empty lobby.
> Unaware of the picture he made with hat and sans clothes,
> he came up to the desk, and with habitual pomposity, said

to the clerk in perfect, although not overfluent French, "Donnez moi le clef." Then, clef in hand, he vanished straw hat and all. . . .

The last night at the Villa Ganelon saw a gala that lasted through the dawn. "Everyone" was there, including the French sewing-machine heiress Daisy Fellowes. Glancing about the room at those who were still on their feet, Daisy realized what extraordinary company she was in. Daisy, who had two yachts in the harbor and a villa in Antibes, said, "You are so gifted. You write, you dance, you sing. But I do *nossing*."

Woollcott looked at her attractive face and sensuous body. "Puss, I've heard differently," the dear prim soul told her.

Next day they were in Paris, the day after that they boarded the *Ile de France* for home. Aleck's holiday was over but not the games of chance, for his gambling in New York in the autumn of 1928 would be more serious, less frivolous than at Monte Carlo.

A free lance in the time of the medieval knights meant a soldier whose services were purchasable, a person who acted on his own responsibility. This was what Aleck came back to New York to face, being an uncommitted knight with a pen for a lance.

At the Lambs Club, once a noted actors' hangout, they celebrated. "The First Grave Digger," as Aleck had been called, "won't be on the aisle this season."

12 Words for Sale

*U*PON HIS RETURN TO NEW YORK, WOOLLCOTT found himself in an entirely new position. When he had been a child his mother or Julie or his brother Billy told him what to do. At high school and college he had to obey the rules and orders of his teachers. On the *Times,* the city editor, the managing editor, and, when needed, the publisher could make certain decisions for him. In the Army there had been an endless chain of officers over him.

In the autumn of 1928, Woollcott had no masters, no superiors. For some men that kind of limitless freedom brings on fear. They need guidelines to point them in the right direction, handles to grasp should they slip. Woollcott had no need for such supports. From the time he had been a small boy writing served as his outlet and a release for his anxieties.

Once home he cleared his desk, removed the oilcloth cover from his typewriter, and submitted articles to magazines. After viewing a play a night for so many years and turning out a Sunday piece as well, he found magazine writing to be relatively easy. What made it even more pleasant was his ability to sell everything he wrote. And after he got into it, he quite often sold the same story to two or three different periodicals. Needless to say, several editors were wild with rage each month, but Woollcott had enough muscle—thanks to "Shouts and Murmurs" in *The New Yorker*—and enough personal charm to soothe them.

Through a mistake on the part of a secretary, two magazines received permission to reprint the same story Woollcott had already run in *The New Yorker*. The author called that magazine's editor and bellowed the information into the telephone.

"How do you know?" Ross asked reasonably.

"I just got two checks in the same mail."

"What are you going to do?"

"Go right down to the bank and deposit them," Woollcott said as he hung up the phone.

In the early days of *The New Yorker*, Ross paid Woollcott four hundred dollars for a single printed page, more than any other writer. This practice Woollcott took to be standard. When he wrote, he expected and received top money. The magazines which published his work ranged from *The American Mercury* to *McCall's* to *Vanity Fair* to *Cosmopolitan* to *Collier's* to *Pictorial Review*.

Aleck had three primary categories in which he wrote: theater, books, and assorted fragments from murders to memories of World War I.

The income from those magazine articles and the savings from twenty years of weekly salary checks slowly grew to $100,000, a sum Woollcott never dreamed he could amass. But he was like many Americans who put their trust in the stock market during the euphoric 1920's. Only Aleck got his tips from the adviser of Presidents of the United States and Prime Ministers of Great Britain. Under Bernard Baruch's watchful eye Aleck took his $100,000 and invested shrewdly. Before very long his money doubled. He calculated this fortune would be enough for his old age, but Black Friday came first.

This was followed by Black Monday, Black Tuesday; in fact, every day of the week in the fall of 1929 proved a disaster. The stock marked plunged as fast as brokers leapt from their office windows.

Woollcott, along with everyone else, was wiped out.

"I don't know that it was overnight," he quipped. "It may have happened in the morning or the afternoon. All I know is that every penny I had in the world has gone where every other penny has gone."

Considering that $200,000 was as much money as he could ever conceive of having, he took the news of his financial downfall extremely well. Woollcott was like everyone else. When the news arrived that he had been financially destroyed, all the torments of a childhood filled with poverty came back to haunt him. However, after the initial shock of being poor once more, Aleck quickly realized he was on his way toward becoming solvent again. Unlike most people's, his mailbox kept receiving checks for magazine articles. The Crash even served as the springboard for one of his better-remembered remarks.

"A stockbroker," he said, "is someone who runs your fortune into a shoestring."

The era that saw Hoovervilles and breadlines and veterans being chased from the Capitol steps by the U. S. Cavalry came into being with a painful thump. Small businessmen went bankrupt, Big Business banked its fires and laid off its workers, Al Smith lost his race for the Presidency, and Herbert Hoover, the man who beat him, hopefully predicted that "Prosperity is just around the corner." It never arrived.

Luck at that period seemed to be only on Woollcott's side. While almost everyone else was having a hard time of it, Mr. Hoover's prediction came true for Aleck. When others tightened their belts, Aleck bought a new and bigger one.

An acquaintance trying to make small talk on a large subject asked Aleck, "What do you think of the Depression?"

"I can see nothing in its favor," Woollcott answered, "except that Frank Case has lowered the price of his desserts."

That was Woollcott the imperturbable. Throughout the Depression, though, Aleck shared generously what he had with his less fortunate friends. Down deep he knew that very often he was wrong, even cruel toward those around him. He sought to atone for such despotic behavior by charitable contributions. Feelings of guilt that he carried with him from childhood, and a sense of conscience at having money at a time when others did not, drove him to support many less lucky than he. His tips to waiters grew larger, out-of-work newspaper colleagues were invited to elaborate dinners, and former buddies from his war days had checks pressed into their hands.

Heywood Broun's telling comment on the times became one of Aleck's favorites.

"I've known people who stop and buy an apple on the corner and then walk away as if they'd solved the unemployment problem."

Woollcott not only generously gave financial assistance, he also used his position to aid the underdog. In 1929, Robert Blake, a convicted murderer awaiting execution in the Huntsville, Texas, prison, sent an article from Death Row to H. L. Mencken. Mencken ran it in *The American Mercury* magazine three months after the author had been electrocuted.

Upon reading the article, the playwright John Wexley wrote a drama castigating capital punishment. It was the first of the many prison plays and movies to explode violently in the Thirties and Forties.

Herman Shumlin produced the play early in 1930. On opening night Shumlin fidgeted and nervously walked in and out of the theater, as authors, directors, and producers still do on such occasions. Only when the third-act curtain had fallen did the producer return to the theater's lobby.

"Someone came running up to me and said, 'Alexander Woollcott is backstage looking for you.'" Shumlin remembered clearly. "I told him to say I was gone, I couldn't think of going backstage.

"In a few minutes, Woollcott strode toward me. He was wearing his typical opening-night outfit. It was a dark-blue cape and a large black felt hat. His voice was trembling with feeling."

"This is one of the most extraordinary experiences of my life," Woollcott told Shumlin. "I can't begin to tell you how important this play is to me. I'm not a critic anymore so I can't write a review of it in the newspaper, but if there is anything I can do for you, just tell me."

Shumlin thought for a moment and then suggested that perhaps Woollcott might be willing to compose a short letter that could be used as an advertisement.

"Two days later, I received it in the mail. It was a very passionate letter which concerned itself with execution by the State and what a wicked thing it was. The next day I ran it as an ad in every newspaper in New York."

It is difficult to imagine a working drama critic or any retired drama critic being so intensely interested in a play that he would take the time to do what Woollcott did for *The Last Mile*.

Aleck, however, was not finished with his good works. Early in May, 1930, his detailed article on *The Last Mile* appeared in *Collier's* magazine. He gave its entire history, from Robert Blake in Huntsville prison to the young actor who made such a hit on Broadway playing the lead, Spencer Tracy.

By spring of 1930 Woollcott was on his way to Europe again. On April 26, he wrote Beatrice Kaufman from London.

My Blossom:

Noel [Coward] is the only gamester I ever knew with my own whole-heartedness. We played backgammon or Russian Bank all the way over. I had never before crossed the Atlantic without once laying eyes on the darned thing. The other passengers were mysteriously angered by this single-ness of purpose. They would stop by and say: "Don't you two ever tire of that game?" or "Still at it?" or, in the case of the German passengers, they would merely say "Immer!" to each other in passing. . . .

I did not have much luck. Paid for my passage but not much over. . . .

Cavalcade last night. Noel's party in the royal box. A convenient arrangement, with a salon behind it for coffee and liqueurs and an adjacent room for the relief of the royal kidney.

Adele Astaire and Lord Cavendish in the next box and the Duke of Bedford in his. The audience gala, with much cheering at Noel's entrance, a speech afterwards from the stage. The show very moving. Also a good play. No one had ever told me it was that.

I am lunching today with Jeffrey Amherst, dining tonight with the incomparable Rebecca [West], lunching tomorrow with Mrs. Belloc Lowndes. Tomorrow afternoon, Lilly [Bonner] arrives by plane from France. Program from then on a blank, but probably a week-end at Noel's, which is near Dover and might be taken in en route to Paris. . . .

I must make clear a curious illusion of which I am conscious. If I write a note to either you or George Backer, I feel as if I were writing it to both of you . . .

Joyce [Barbour] and Dickie [Bird] are immensely bucked up. He is rehearsing the leading part in the new Priestley play and she is rehearsing for the new Joe Cook show and after ten weeks in that she will go into the new Coward revue. This hasn't a title yet. I suggested calling it "Here's to Mr. Woollcott, God Bless Him," but Noel is curiously inhospitable to suggestions from others and he does make the good point that in England it would not mean as much as in the States. . . .

A. W.

The romance between Beatrice Kaufman and George Backer was known to everyone of their social acquaintance. It gave Woollcott the opportunity to remark that "seeing them together is like watching two plum puddings in heat."

Aleck's quarters in the Hotel des Artistes no longer suited him, and he moved into what was called the Beekman Campanile, a cooperative apartment building at the foot of Fifty-second Street and the East River. To look after the place Aleck had stolen help from the house at 412 West 47th Street. Jane Grant and Harold Ross had two excellent servants, Arthur and Marie Treadwell. Their son, Junior, was wooed by Woollcott and impressed into his service at an early age. Junior remained faithful to him throughout Woollcott's life.

The apartment on Fifty-second Street was on the third floor and faced the river. Next door to Aleck's rooms was the more spacious duplex of his dear friend Alice Duer Miller, the novelist and short-story writer. Mrs. Miller lived there with her husband, Henry, and when Woollcott gave a party that was too large for his quarters, he thought nothing of opening a door to the Millers' and allowing the overflow to move into his neighbors' apartment.

F.P.A. suggested a name for Woollcott's new place. Claiming he had dipped into Indian lore, he came up with what he described as an Objibway word, Ocowoica, meaning The-Little-Three-Room-Apartment-on-the-East-River-That-It-Is-Difficult-to-Find-a-Taxi-cab-Near.

Dorothy Parker came up with a two-word description.

"Wit's End," she called it, and the name lasted.

Sunday breakfasts became Woollcott's favorite form of entertaining. Eggs, sausages, French toast sprinkled with maple syrup, pancakes filled with various jams, jelly doughnuts were the main courses—the dishes preferred by the master. There were side offerings of salmon, kippers, and other nonsugary digestibles for those who wanted them.

The gatherings started at nine in the morning and lasted until late in the day. Peggy and Ralph Pulitzer lived in the Campanile. So did Margaret and Herbert Swope. Frank Sullivan resided a block away. The Lunts were in the neighborhood. A variety of visitors, from Charlie Chaplin to an undergraduate from Hamilton College, might be found there on any given Sunday.

Woollcott presided over these assemblies in a most unusual attire.

"His Sunday breakfasts or brunches were fantastic," Cornelia Otis Skinner observed. "Woollcott sat like a Buddha in his pajamas. They were mostly unbuttoned to show the Buddha half of his stomach, and he never rose when anyone came, and never rose to say good-bye to anyone."

If he looked like Buddha, he ruled with the iron will of Oliver Cromwell.

"You, madam, are married to a cuckold," he said to a woman opposite him.

The illustrator Neysa McMein was one of his closest female friends. When marriage was mentioned there were no less than half a dozen serious contenders for Aleck's hand. Among them were Miss McMein, Mrs. George S. Kaufman, Mrs. Paul Bonner, Miss Ruth Gordon, and Miss Eleanora von Mendelsohn.

"I am thinking of writing the story of our life together. The title has already been settled," Aleck informed Miss McMein upon her arrival at breakfast.

"What is it?" she asked.

"*Under Separate Cover.*"

Discussions and discourses regarding the possibility of Woollcott's marriages were frequent among his friends. No one took them seriously. In fact, one lady friend said—but not in front of Woollcott—"Aleck just wants somebody to talk to in bed."

From the days when he had been the drama critic on *The New York Times*, Woollcott was someone to listen to as well as read. Caustic or complimentary, he passionately loved the theater and the people within it. Whether he wrote flowery or sourly mattered little to his readers. What did count was that he held their interest. This was true in his magazine articles and in his conversation. His colorful speech, the outrageous way he used words, his loyalty and generosity to his friends, in and out of print, made him the monarch of an enormous group of writers, actors, painters, musicians, poets, and composers in New York as well as an acknowledged figure in England and the Continent.

There was more than food to be consumed at Aleck's breakfasts, more, too, than banter to be tossed back and forth. Games were played after the meal with regularity. Puns and anagrams, charades, cards, and—Aleck's favorite—cribbage.

Woollcott was so adept at cribbage and urged so many people to play it with him that his next-door neighbor, the stately Alice Duer Miller, rose from the board late one afternoon and denounced him.

"You, sir," Mrs. Miller said with quiet dignity, "are a cribbage pimp."

Aleck didn't always come out ahead, though. Following a marathon cribbage match with George Backer, he lost the use of his apartment *and* the services of Junior for three entire months. And Backer collected.

Russel Crouse remembered one of those Sundays with embarrassment and chagrin.

"Woollcott invited me over for one of those breakfasts. This was when I was a reporter on the New York *Globe*. I'd just bought a blue shirt with a sort of embossed fleur-de-lis. It was pretty wild and I thought, 'Gee, this is just the time to wear this.'

"It was a hot June day and a lot of English actors were standing around Woollcott's apartment saying 'Haw' and all that sort of thing. Then Sir Somebody-or-Other mumbled, 'What say we take off our coats?' I thought it was very un-British but when they took off their coats, I took mine off.

"The minute I did, Woollcott hushed the whole party.

" 'You people don't know Crouse very well,' he proclaimed. 'He's a loyal person, very loyal. As you can see, he goes to that country store in Findlay, Ohio, where he was born and buys his shirts.'

"Well, the river was there, right outside, and it was all I could do to keep from jumping. Woollcott must have known how I felt. He gave me a wink. Not only did I forgive him, but he made me feel like I had won the approval of the reigning potentate and his court.

"I'll have to admit I go along with Peg Pulitzer. Most people were flattered at being insulted by Woollcott. Being noticed by Aleck at all placed you a few rungs up the ladder to social success. Today, people seem to have a touch of that attitude of indulgence toward Truman Capote."

The reputation surrounding Woollcott by now was so intimidating that even people who *might* have had something to say often remained mute. Thornton Wilder, who would become the only man to win a Pulitzer Prize for a novel and two more for plays, presented himself at breakfast one Sunday. It was his initial meeting with Woollcott.

"And what class did you graduate with up at Yale?" Aleck demanded of him.

"1920."

"Ah," Woollcott answered. "I didn't know the numbers went that high."

Wilder smiled and Woollcott bestowed upon him a heaping plate of sausages and eggs.

The last word or even the last act did not always go to Woollcott. Charles MacArthur showed up at Wit's End one evening.

"Mr. Woollcott is out," Junior told him after he answered the door.

"Out? We have a date," MacArthur protested.

"Mr. Woollcott said you were late and that he considered it a broken engagement."

"Five minutes late for dinner and the theater and he says it's a broken engagement?"

"Yes, sir."

"I'll be right back, Junior," Charles MacArthur promised. Hurrying to the nearest grocery store, MacArthur bought dozens of packages of raspberry Jell-O and then returned to Wit's End.

Junior met him at the door.

"Yes, Mr. MacArthur?"

"Junior, I've got to go to the bathroom. Do you mind?"

"No, sir. You know where it's at."

Of course he did. Once inside, MacArthur locked the door, peeled off his overcoat, closed the drain to the bathtub, tore open package after package of raspberry Jell-O, and emptied them into the bottom of the tub. This done, he gleefully ran three or four inches of hot water, following with an equal amount of cold water. Then he opened the window, permitting the wintry winds to fill the small bathroom. When he had finished, Charlie picked up his coat, stuffed his pockets with empty Jell-O packages, unlocked the door, and let himself out, closing the bathroom door behind him.

"Everything all right, Mr. MacArthur?" Junior asked.

"Thank you. I feel much better," the playwright answered.

"I'll tell Mr. Woollcott you were here."

"You do that, Junior."

Six hours later an infuriated Woollcott stood in his bathroom looking down at a tubful of quivering Jell-O.

"MacArthur and his practical jokes," he fumed. "Son of a bitch had to make it red. Lime would have gone much better with this room. And it smells like a goddam fruit store!"

Junior grinned. "I have sinus trouble, Mr. Woollcott, but it sure looks pretty."

When Woollcott first moved into Wit's End, he rearranged the apartment to please Junior. The kitchen now overlooked the East River and Woollcott's bedroom faced the court. He was rewarded for this accommodating act by having Junior race in two or three times a week, exclaiming, "Mr. Woollcott, Mr. Woollcott! I think I see a body floating in the water!"

Aleck in his better moods comforted Junior by telling him that what he saw were logs floating downstream. When he was irritable he agreed that what Junior saw were the remains of slain gangsters.

Harold Ross and Jane Grant divorced, and Ross remarried. When he moved his new wife to a new apartment, he hired Mary Brown Warburton, one of the best decorators in New York, and decided to give a party to show off her work. The affair was held during one of those times when Woollcott and Ross were feuding. Aleck was not invited, but since Junior's father and mother worked for Ross and a great many guests had been asked to the event, Junior went over to help out.

The next day Woollcott determined to make no mention of the previous night. However, Danton Walker, his secretary, turned to the houseman.

"Tell me, Junior, how does Ross's place compare to Wit's End?"

"Mr. Walker, if you gotta know, it makes this place look like a shit house."

Woollcott inhaled deeply and all of his chins quivered.

"Very descriptive, Junior," he glowered. "Now please make another pot of your goddam coffee!"

Because the Depression was so gloomy, Woollcott and his crowd constantly held parties in order to lift their spirits. They gave progressive dinners where the guests ate the first course in one place, the second course in another, the third in still another. They amused themselves with treasure hunts, midnight suppers, and costume balls, which Aleck almost always attended dressed as Simon Legree. They held dances in their homes and in the midtown hotels. Incredibly, Aleck was an excellent partner on the dance floor.

Lilly Bonner, a great friend of Woollcott's, told her young son Paul how light Aleck was on his feet, and that he had a marvelous sense of rhythm.

"But how can you dance with somebody so . . ." He hesitated to use the word fat. "I mean, how can you get close enough?"

"Oh, he sort of puts you to one side," Mrs. Bonner laughed as she answered, "and off we go."

Gaiety did not always prevail on the third floor of the Campanile. A painful and touching episode illustrates that Woollcott's life was filled with more than jovial camaraderie and low and high jinks.

Anita Loos, author of the forever successful *Gentlemen Prefer Blondes,* wrote a magazine article in the Thirties giving her recollections of the Round Table.

Miss Loos had not cared for the Algonquin group and attacked Aleck in particular. The article seemed harmless enough because the Round Table existed no longer and its members had scattered. To her surprise Anita Loos received a telephone call from Woollcott inviting her to tea.

Although his words no longer appeared on the Op Ed page of the *World,* Aleck still wrote for *The New Yorker* each week and his articles filled the pages of national magazines. The tiny Miss Loos recognized Aleck as a force with whom one had to reckon, and she assumed the invitation to tea was to extract an apology for her story on the Round Table. She felt she had no alternative but to accept.

Arriving at Wit's End late in the afternoon, she found Aleck alone and amiable. No mention of her magazine article came from his lips. Instead, they spoke in generalities until Aleck interrupted to show her, with a trembling hand, a faded photograph of a scene from a production that had been done by the Charlatans. The character dressed in girl's clothes was the young Alexander Woollcott.

Suddenly, his emotions gushing, Aleck told Anita Loos that he had always wanted to be a girl.

Miss Loos didn't know what to make of the confession.

Woollcott grasped her hand in what she termed "an outlandish climax" and declared, "All my life I've wanted to be a mother."

For that moment he let down his defenses, hoping that if he told her the truth she would understand the conflicts within him that made him behave as he did.

"Now that you know me better," he implored tearfully, "do you think we can be friends?" He was trying desperately to have her empathize with him. To no avail.

The most Anita Loos could feel was pity. The least was a sense of bewilderment and revulsion.

She left as quickly as possible and confided the story to few people, doubting that anyone would believe it. Aleck regretted the incident deeply. Whenever he saw Miss Loos again, he tried to avoid her. When that proved impossible, he refrained from mentioning the events of the unhappy afternoon.

By 1931 Woollcott was ready to admit the existence of other continents besides Europe. A visit to Asia would provide him with a series of magazine articles.

Hamilton College, as it did so frequently in Woollcott's life, played a large part in his travels to the Orient. Henry Ke-an Yuan came from China in 1928 to study at Hamilton. Charles Brackett, the novelist and Hollywood writer and producer, claimed that Woollcott chose only those friends whose lives would make good magazine articles. Harry Yuan's father had been President of China from 1912 to 1916. As a result Aleck took the young man under his wing. He was horrified when Yuan was expelled from Hamilton at the end of his junior year—some minor matter of allegedly obscene Chinese ideographs being substituted for the answers to a final examination in a philosophy course. Angered by the failing grade he received, Harry Yuan began throwing rocks through the windows of an administration building. Dismissal followed. Yuan, however, was quickly accepted by Hamilton's rival, Colgate.

"An institution maintained solely for the purpose of educating students expelled from Hamilton," Aleck claimed.

Woollcott's letter to Yuan commiserating with him upon his removal from Hamilton was kindly received. Harry Yuan visited The Great Alumnus at Wit's End many times. When he returned to China, he wrote and invited Aleck to spend some time as his guest.

Woollcott immediately accepted the invitation. He took the train from New York to Seattle. At dockside, Aleck, who then weighed over 250 pounds, found time to banter with reporters.

"I wish to say emphatically," he declared, patting his enormous paunch, "that all rickshaw boys do not plan to go on strike when I land in China."

His first stop was Tokyo. He stayed at the Imperial Hotel (designed by his friend Frank Lloyd Wright); he made side trips to Osaka, Kyoto, and other Japanese excursion points. Chiefly, he was interested in Japanese theater, Japanese actors, and Japanese food. He found their customs quaint, their courtesy admirable, and their chopsticks abominable. He made notes on everything he saw and did for his magazine articles.

China overwhelmed him. Harry Yuan met him in Tientsin. He played poker with Mrs. Wellington Koo, visited the Peking Opera, the Great Wall of China, the many palaces and estates of his hosts. "As you see, they live just like the Swopes," Woollcott wrote home.

John Goette, a journalist and an expert in jade, attended a luncheon in China given in honor of Woollcott by John Thomason, Marine officer, author, and artist. Thomason came downstairs a little late, dressed in the white breeches, shining boots, and maroon blazer of the U. S. Marine polo team.

"At last, the gentlemen of the chorus," Aleck called out, irked at the tardiness of his host.

Woollcott came away with the distinct impression that he was seeing an era that was soon to pass into history.

He wrote several articles about his visit to China, but his best included the time when he got into a chair in his descent from the Great Wall, listened to the chair bearers grunt under his weight, and then overheard a young Chinese drawl in perfect English, "Ah, the Yellow Man's Burden."

Arriving in San Francisco, he went to Los Angeles, where he renewed his friendship with Charles Lederer, a Hollywood screenwriter who had been introduced to Woollcott by Charles Mac-Arthur. A persistent rumor in those years was that Lederer was the out-of-wedlock son of Marion Davies. Woollcott took to him at once, sensing a sensational magazine story.

By the time Woollcott realized that Miss Davies was Lederer's aunt and not his mother, he was so entranced with Charlie's humor that he sought him out.

"What're you going to give me for Christmas?" Woollcott demanded.

"Nothing," Lederer replied.

"I don't allow that," Woollcott persisted. "You have to give me something."

"I'm not going to give you anything because there isn't anything you want that I could afford."

Woollcott paused and thought for a moment. "A clock. I could use another clock at Wit's End."

"You have seven of them already," Lederer protested.

"Yes, but I'm clock crazy."

"As a matter of fact, I heard that said about you by a Chinaman."

Woollcott laughed all the way back to New York.

At home there was nothing to laugh about.

Woollcott's feud with Swope had begun with the former's departure from the *World*. Although Swope had not relished the idea of losing the most popular and influential drama critic in the nation, still he and his wife invited Woollcott to their palatial estate in Long Island.

Croquet was king on the grounds of the Swope country place, and Woollcott and Swope played and talked a great game. Banter, it must be understood, formed an integral part of croquet. Swope

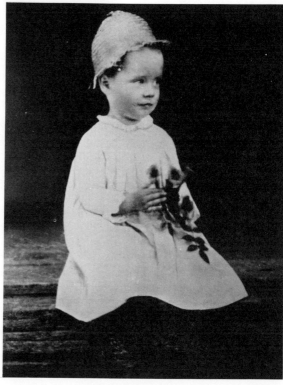

early Woollcott. Why the dresses?
All boys could have their diapers
changed more easily than if they wore
trousers.

3

Woollcott at seventeen. Why the dress? The following caption was typed by Aleck himself on the back of the original photograph: "Under the influence of some intuitive yearning and Rose Field—At the instigation of Ivy Ashton Root— And by The Grace of God— THE PHALANX DUSE OF 1905"

4

Woollcott at college. Why the dress? The founder of the dramatic society reserved the feminine leads for himself.

5

Woollcott at college: straight, sol and stiff-collared.

The elite drama critic: elegantly dressed and mincing daintily past a poster devoted to one of his retired leading ladies, Minnie Maddern Fiske.

Master of the island retreat, the Neshobe Club at Lake Bomoseen, Vermont.

Started in Paris, the Thanatopsis poker game moved into New York at the end of World War I. It found its first American headquarters in the Woollcott-Ross-Grant-Truax ménage on West 47th Street. After the Round Table came into existence, the poker game moved permanently into a suite in the Algonquin Hotel. Seen here in the very center as usual is Woollcott. Other card players at the table, ranging from left to right, include F.P.A., the humor columnist, the banker Henry Wise Miller, columnist Heywood Broun, socialite Gerald Brooks, Harpo, one fourth of the Marx Brothers, Raoul Fleischmann, publisher of *The New Yorker*, George S. Kaufman, playwright, director, and drama editor of *The New York Times*, diplomat and novelist Paul Hyde Bonner; the kibitzers standing behind the table are, left to right, Dorothy Parker, poet, critic, and short story writer, Robert Benchley, critic, humorist, and actor, composer Irving Berlin, Harold Ross, founder and editor of *The New Yorker*, Beatrice Kaufman, editor and wife of G.S.K., Henry Miller's wife Alice, novelist, short story writer, and social arbiter of Woollcott's merry world, executive editor of the New York *World* Herbert Bayard Swope, George Backer, journalist, builder, and political thinker, Joyce Barbour, an English actress, and Crosby Gaige, the theatrical producer. Bonner commissioned the painting and Will Cotten did it in pastel in 1929 when the stock market was still high and the card players were in the chips.

Katharine Cornell and
fleshy escort.

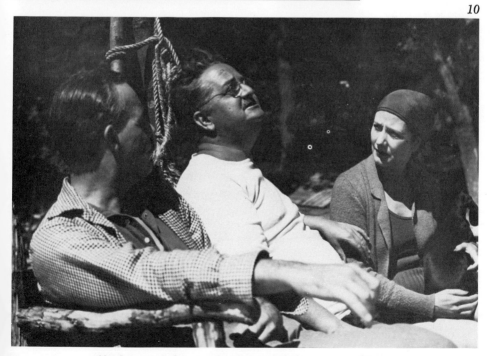

Alfred Lunt and Lynn Fontanne and the sun worshipper.

11

The Town Crier at his specially
constructed microphone.

12

HEAR YE   HEAR YE

Enjoy
Granger Pipe Tobacco
with Alexander Woollcott
the Town Crier

Every Tuesday *and* Thursday Evening
Columbia Stations

Hear the Crier.

13

The Town Crier with friends Harpo Marx and Dorothy Parker.

William Auerbach Levy's caricature became so famous Woollcott had it engraved on his stationery.

was.

Hamilton College's best-known alumnus and the son of the President of China who recently had been expelled from Hamilton.

Above his head hung a Russian poster, souvenir of the trip he arranged for Harpo. Words at the bottom made all of Moscow turn out: IN PERSON, MARX!

17

The Naked Woollcott.

18

Without fright wig, baggy pants, battered hat, and horn stands Harpo Marx. Without shame and with everything hanging out stands Aleck.

19

Joe Hennessey, his friend and
manager.

The Athlete.

The Actor.

Breakfast with Noel Coward.

Rehearsal with Moss Hart and George S. Kaufman.

Adrift on Lake Bomoseen.

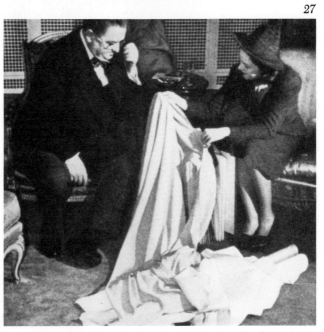

The couturier selecting the fabric for the dress
he designed at Bergdorf Goodman, New York.

While preparing his lectures, Woollcott frequently utilized not one but two pairs of eyeglasses.

Portrait by Mr. Charles MacArthur, courtesy Miss Helen Hayes.

At the opening in Boston.

As Sheridan Whiteside in *The Man Who Came to Dinner.*

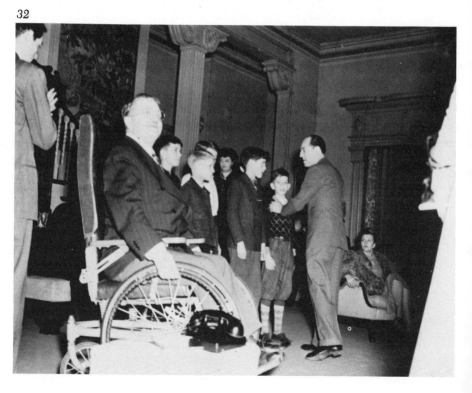

Skating on thick ice.

The result was the same as if it had been thin.

The summer of '42. Near the end.

and his former critic were so adept at both that they soon became known as the Katzenjammer Kids.

Luxury was a way of life for Swope. Servants of every kind were always on hand. If it was a repast at two in the morning, there was a chef ready in the kitchen. Upstairs maids, downstairs maids, gardeners, pastry chefs, chauffeurs, everybody at the Swopes' place worked with precision, thoughtfulness, and courtesy.

All of these arrangements had been organized by a man named Joseph Hennessey. Two inches taller than Woollcott, thin but what was known in those days as wiry, Hennessey was handsome, with brown hair, a self-effacing demeanor, and a scholarly, bookish mind. He was always there when needed, and when not needed he appeared to cloak himself in invisibility.

Hennessey was born in New York City in 1896. He completed DeWitt Clinton High School, along with the lyricist Herbert Fields and the novelist Paul Gallico. Not having the money to go to college, Hennessey enlisted in the U. S. Army and in 1916 became a trooper, riding with Black Jack Pershing into Mexico. Upon America's entrance into World War I, it was readily determined that mounted soldiers were not needed. Hennessey and his fellow cavalrymen were retrained from the martial use of saber and saddle to the more deadly use of the machine gun.

After serving in France, Hennessey returned to New York and opened a bookshop. Woollcott met him there, shortly before Swope hired him to serve as his general manager at Great Neck. As Swope and his wife were leaving for France one summer, both husband and wife felt they would enjoy their trip more if a man was placed in charge of the estate, someone who could look after their young son, Herbert, Jr. Swope gave Hennessey a large enough stipend to close up the book business and move out to the Swope country place.

There Woollcott renewed his acquaintance with Hennessey. Aleck was impressed by the efficient manner with which Hennessey operated all of Swope's domestic matters. Indeed, he was inspired to the point where he hired Hennessey away from Swope. And over the years Hennessey was to become Aleck's adviser, manager, and closest friend.

But Swope had recently moved from Great Neck to a larger house and grounds at Sands Point, and he felt like the woman who believed that while it might be appalling to steal her best friend's husband, it was unforgivable for the same friend to steal her cook. It was against this background that the great split between Woollcott and Swope took place a few months later.

Swope had lost millions in the stock market crash. He was half a million in debt to John D. Hertz, the Chicagoan who conceived the rent-a-car system. Upon learning that Hertz planned to move to New York, Swope gave a sumptuous dinner in his honor at the Lotus Club. Fifty of the foremost financiers in Manhattan were his guests.

When Swope proposed Hertz as a shareholder in the Campanile cooperative, matters grew ugly. Josh Billings, a Texan whose oil wells had run dry, owned a thirty-room triplex in the Campanile. Hertz, under the sponsorship of Swope, offered to purchase it. The rules of the Campanile stated that no one was allowed to buy into the building without the unanimous consent of the other shareholders. All shareholders agreed save one. Woollcott blackballed Hertz. Swope roared that Woollcott was anti-Semitic.

Their mutual friends paused and considered the charge. It was true that now and again Woollcott's humor employed the word "Jew."

Once when the Thanatopsis Club had met at the Colony Restaurant, Woollcott, Heywood Broun, and Harpo Marx shared a taxi home. No sooner had the driver lowered the flag on the meter than Woollcott and Broun got into a literary argument of such ferocity that Harpo wondered if they might come to blows. He attempted to intercede but neither man paid any attention to him.

Harpo's home was the first stop. He got out and said good night to his two friends. They ignored him completely as their argument continued unabated. Feeling miffed by his friends' behavior,

Harpo told the driver to take the two gentlemen in the back seat to Werba's Theatre, a burlesque house in the most distant part of Brooklyn.

Harpo's telephone awakened him two hours later.

"You Jew son of a bitch!" Woollcott's high-pitched voice bellowed over the phone. This was followed by a click. Aleck had hung up.

Anti-Semitism? Harpo, Woollcott's dearest friend, was Jewish. Groucho, Chico, Zeppo, and Gummo were Jewish. So were George and Beatrice Kaufman, George Backer and Dorothy Schiff, Moss Hart, Franklin P. Adams, Howard Dietz, Edna Ferber, S. N. Behrman, Art Samuels, Al Getman, Raoul Fleischmann, the Gershwins, Oscar Levant, Jascha Heifetz, Herman Mankiewicz, and Ben Hecht. Even his darling Dorothy Parker was half Jewish.

Baffled by Swope's charge, Aleck turned to the subject of one of his earliest books, Israel Baline, and declared, "Not only are some of my best friends Jews, but all of my friends are Jews." It was a slight exaggeration, but a point well taken. Incidentally, the name Mr. Baline chose for himself after his immigration from Russia was Irving Berlin. More to the point, Aleck's reason for barring Mr. and Mrs. Hertz was personal: he simply did not like them.

Letters between Woollcott and Swope grew more acrimonious as the month passed. Aleck felt badly about it. Wit's End no longer was a happy haven to place his weary head. He sold it to Noel Coward, the Hertzes moved into the Billings triplex, Swope felt satisfied on that account, but the feud between Woollcott and himself, having started, never ended. Each man found a reason for insulting the other, and while at various times one antagonist wished to make it up, the other did not. And when the other wanted to call a halt to their animosity, the first refused.

Howard Dietz later commented on the Woollcott-Swope feud. "Aleck was one guy who never cared what was said about him. Not because he had a thick skin, but because he could come back harder. I could be wrong. Maybe he was just covering up like most people."

And then, because he wrote some of America's better lyrics, Dietz said of Woollcott, "Arsenic on the outside, a peach underneath."

Although the theater still occupied a large amount of space in Woollcott's magazine copy, traveling and literature began to compete with it. In the autumn of 1932 he went to Russia. There, wrapped in a greatcoat and crowned with a caracul cap, Aleck was every Russian's idea of what a bloated American capitalist should look like.

Standing on a corner in Moscow, Woollcott noticed the timid approach of a Russian child. The small boy came up to Aleck and, after staring at the huge figure, reverently rubbed his hand over the Woollcott girth as if to pay tribute to all the good food that went into its creation.

Woollcott saw every play running in Moscow and Leningrad, met the leading actors and directors, and was feted with tea and raisin cake. As a gesture of gratitude for the hospitality shown to him, he gave each of his hosts and hostesses one of the most precious of all commodities in the Soviet Union: a roll of toilet paper.

His literary comments and criticisms were to be found in several magazines. A sense of discovery or at least early recognition pervaded his likes or dislikes of novelists. That his taste was good may be seen in Woollcott's drum-beating for Hemingway, Fitzgerald, and Faulkner. In a relatively short time he became the highest paid and one of the most widely read book reviewers in the country. His articles commanded $2,500 each.

The sense of power he knew and exercised in the theater was quickly grasped by Woollcott in the world of books. In short order he made a best seller out of an obscure English work, *Lives of a Bengal Lancer*. He followed this critical triumph by taking an even more obscure volume that had been sitting on the book shelves for six months after its publication date and building it into a best seller. James Hilton was the author and his book was called *Good-bye, Mr. Chips*. An earlier Hilton work was titled *Lost Horizon*, and Woollcott again touted it onto the best-seller lists.

Having made so many books into successes, wasn't it possible for Woollcott to write one of his own? Aleck had written at least six books, each one less popular than the one before. One of the most quoted remarks of the day was:

WOOLLCOTT: What is so rare as a Woollcott first edition?
F.P.A.:   A Woollcott second edition.

With the exception of a rather romantically written biography of Irving Berlin, Woollcott's works were compilations of his articles. Here and there one of the pieces stood out, but judged on the whole, the books had no great appeal for the reading public.

In 1934, when Woollcott was forty-seven years old, he brought out a new composite of his writings. It ranged from his travels to one of his favorite subjects, crime. Jack the Ripper and Lizzie Borden were balanced by essays on Eugene O'Neill, Father Duffy, Charles MacArthur, Benchley, and Parker. He included the account of the Chalice of Antioch, which may or may not have been the Holy Grail, and a hilarious tale of two vaudevillians who found themselves in Memphis, Tennessee, playing a matinee before an audience that didn't believe they were comedians and, as a result, sat stonily throughout their act. At the end of it, one of them stepped forward and advised the audience, "And now, if you will all just remain seated, my partner, Mr. Sweeney, will pass down the aisle with a baseball bat and beat the be-Jesus out of you."

Aleck neglected to tell what happened when word got back to the home office of the Keith-Albee Circuit in New York. Mr. Keith, a religious man, banned the Sweeney and Duffy act from vaudeville.

But no matter, the story pleased the publisher just as it stood. Aleck dedicated the volume to Beatrice Kaufman.

On the flyleaf of the first edition was the following inscription: "*While Rome Burns,* five hundred copies of this first edition have been printed on all rag paper and autographed by [the signature read] Alexander Woollcott."

On Copy 473, sent to a former captain on *Stars and Stripes,* there was an additional inscription reading: "This copy is presented by the author to Adolph Shelby Ochs, whom he salutes from force of habit." Woollcott expected this book to get the same reception as his previous works, but to the publisher's surprise and the author's delight, *While Rome Burns* became a runaway best seller. The rave reviews, the 290,000 sales—sensational for the bottom of the Depression—the enormous amount of mail it brought pleased Aleck beyond his fondest hopes.

After he had hammered away at his typewriter for twenty-five years, the keys he hit at last struck gold.

13 Playmates
on Their Playground

"ALECK HAD THE SOUL OF AN INNKEEPER," HARold Ross insisted. If that was true, the inn he kept was on an eight-acre island in the middle of a lake near Bomoseen, Vermont.

"It looks like a tea cosy in the summer and a birthday cake in the winter," Woollcott said in a fond description of Neshobe Island. The land was heavily wooded. Birches, maples, and evergreens were everywhere. The hills and cliffs rose out of the water and formed small valleys, quarries, and meadows in which wild flowers grew. The lake that surrounded the island had been scooped out of the harsh Vermont soil by the last glacier to come down the eastern portion of the continent. Bomoseen was still icebound in the winter. In the summer, however, the water of the lake was warm enough to encourage swimming, boating, and sailing. On this island Aleck slowly established a summer satrapy. Eventually it would become his year-round residence.

In 1924, the illustrator Neysa McMein and Aleck had met a young lawyer named Enos Booth, who had owned a small shack that was used mostly during the hunting season in New England. Suppose they went up there, Lawyer Booth had suggested, and looked it over with the possibility of using it as a vacation place? A car filled with Aleck and his friends made the five-and-a-half-hour motor trip north from New York City to the edge of a sparkling, spring-fed lake. A one-cylinder motor launch took them across the nine-tenths of a mile of water to Neshobe Island.

"Having the spirit of a social director and the discipline of a lion tamer, Aleck decided immediately that a club should be founded to take over the island," Howard Dietz remembered. "The initiation fee was a thousand dollars, and the annual dues were a hundred dollars per person."

The original members were Woollcott, Alice Duer Miller, Beatrice Kaufman, Ruth Gordon, Neysa McMein, Harold Guinzburg, George Backer, Raoul Fleischmann, Howard Dietz, and Ray Ives, an accountant and insurance man whose wife, Emmy, was an editor of *Vogue* magazine. Memberships were bought and sold, but the number could go no higher than ten.

Not all ten members were allowed on the island at once. Reservations had to be made in advance, guests could be brought—but all activities, meals, and arrangements were under the watchful eye of Woollcott.

At the beginning, living conditions were primitive. Cold water from a hand pump and an outdoor privy served as conveniences for Aleck's pampered New York guests. Baths could be had from pitchers and basins in their rooms or, if a more thorough cleansing was desired, the lake was cold but available. To look after the place and themselves, the islanders hired a local resident known as Bathless Bill.

"Bathless Bill was a combination woodchopper, bed maker, sweeper-upper, and consort to our cook," George Backer said. "They never married but they lived together in a back room and fought almost every night. She threw pots, pans, anything that was available. He, I'm afraid, threw an occasional punch."

There was no gas, light, or telephone on the island. Kerosene lamps served as illumination. At one end of the main room was a huge fireplace that was the sole source of heat for hot water.

Transportation to the mainland depended upon a red flag, which, when run up to the top of the pole, would summon William Bull and his motor launch. Bull and his son Howard were native Vermonters who operated an inn alongside the lake. The ferry to Neshobe was a sideline.

Their most delicate job of navigation was to get Harpo Marx's harp into the boat, across the lake, and onto the little pier that jutted out from the island. From there it was carried by hand up into the house, which was in reality an unpainted shack. Set in the middle of the cluttered room the harp looked like a jewel, and after dinner, on the nights he felt like it, Harpo would play for the distinguished guests.

Soon the club members divided into two groups, the Masses and the Classes. The Masses wished to continue the rustic way of life, while the Classes stomped for indoor plumbing, electricity, and high cuisine. When Woollcott decided to join the Classes, the Masses lost out. Those wishing to withdraw had their memberships snapped up by Harold Ross, Harpo Marx, Charlie Lederer—all Woollcott people.

If Aleck was the Master of the Round Table, he became the Absolute Dictator and Unquestioned Overlord at Bomoseen.

Dress was not especially important at Neshobe. Aleck was often seen in a pair of shorts worn well below his bay window.

"Heywood Broun," according to Margaret Pulitzer, "wore his underdrawers and in the back pocket he carried a bottle of gin which was pretty warm."

Dorothy Parker arrived one weekend carrying a large hatbox. In it was a lady's garden hat. Mrs. Parker, who had an exquisite figure, wore the hat and nothing else for the entire weekend.

Nudity was permitted. Inebriation was not. The same Mrs. Parker was packed off in disgrace for becoming drunk three days in a row.

Woollcott had developed a strong aversion to intoxication. A few years earlier, the son of a professor Aleck knew at Hamilton had been the butt of a hazing incident at the college. Drink-sodden boys had burst into a dormitory and thrown young Duncan

Saunders from his bed. Tragically, Saunders' head hit the fireplace and he died instantly. Thereafter, Aleck had little patience for those who took more than they could hold. His tolerance for drunkenness became low and on the island he would have none of it.

Noel Coward arrived in time for dinner one evening. Afterward he suggested that he read his new play to the vacationers. Aleck, in a teasing mood, looked about the common room they all shared and scowled at his favorite Englishman.

"Going to read your play, Noel? *Where?*" he asked.

Oscar Levant came to the island one afternoon and was horrified. "Open spaces!" he cried to Charlie Lederer. "Trees, leaves, bugs! Get me off of this place, get me off!"

Aleck shook his head slowly.

"There isn't anything the matter with Levant that a few miracles wouldn't cure."

Woollcott also disliked having married couples visit the island together. Not only was he jealous of their companionship, he knew he would receive more attention from them when they stayed without their mates. If Beatrice Kaufman was there, George must remain in New York. If he came, she should depart. If they both insisted on being at the island, Aleck asked them to sleep in different rooms.

Harold and Alice Guinzburg were too determined to be separated by Aleck, even for a night. Alfred Lunt and Lynn Fontanne were too dear to Woollcott to separate. But when Helen Hayes and Charles MacArthur received their annual invitation to spend two weeks with Woollcott, MacArthur would refer to the time as "jury duty."

With the regularity of a time clock Woollcott would get up at seven o'clock each morning, pound on everyone's door, and demand that all join him in a dip in the icy waters of the lake.

Breakfast was served at eight and Aleck, what with eating and talking and reading his own and everyone else's mail to all those assembled, managed to prolong the meal to ten or eleven o'clock. From then on, anyone could do what he or she wished, although there always had to be enough players for croquet.

Aleck took to mallet and ball regularly and with the utmost intensity. Book after book advises of Aleck's great humor while playing croquet. No volume documents it. Numerous friends relate how clever Woollcott was with words during these matches. All that remains is an example of his irascibility while playing.

"He was having an argument with an English nobleman about who was to go first in the croquet match," Howard Dietz recalled. "Woollcott finally became so exasperated that he said, 'All right, take a bite of my ass!'"

Another time Woollcott announced to his competitors on the course, "My doctor forbids me to play unless I win."

Aleck tried continually to hold down the drinking of hard alcoholic beverages until five in the afternoon. Dinner was at seven or eight. Then the games began, the same that were played at Wit's End. There were two additional games, both in keeping with Woollcott's personality. The first was called Murder, the second Cops and Robbers.

As guests drifted off to sleep, Aleck lured those still awake to listen to his stories of bloody murders or eerie ghost tales or any other narrative that might hold their interest. Alice Guinzburg, the publisher's wife, herself an insomniac, realized that Aleck, too, belonged to that sleepless group. But how, she wondered, did he have the energy to rise at seven each morning, romp down to the lake with his dogs chasing after him?

There was a pack of dogs constantly in residence at Bomoseen. Friends were always giving Aleck dogs as gifts and he would name them Harpo or Charlie or Alice after his closest friends. He was inordinately fond of a poodle, but he doubted her loyalty.

"Considered as a one-man dog, she's a flop," he said. "In her fidelity to me, she's a little too much like that girl in France who was true to the entire Twenty-sixth Infantry."

Otis Skinner had a house in Woodstock. His daughter, Cornelia, wishing to rehearse her monologues without an audience, would make the hour's drive from Woodstock to Bomoseen just so she could have the privacy of standing alone at the end of the island and shouting at the top of her lungs. No one ever interrupted her, but Woollcott sent the dogs down to listen after first warning Miss Skinner that if they didn't like what they heard they would bark.

One evening Woollcott went sailing with another actress, Margalo Gillmore. Halfway across the lake the wind failed and the sailboat was becalmed. Motorboats kept flashing by the small craft.

"I can see the headlines," Aleck told her. " 'Famous Critic Dies With Unknown Actress.' "

Harpo Marx pulled up to the boat landing in an old broken-down jalopy that he had taken to a mechanic to make look even more dilapidated. Woollcott was invited to inspect the automobile.

"What do you call that?" he asked.

"My town car," Harpo replied.

"What was the town?" Woollcott asked. "Pompeii?"

Work in progress was a way of life on the island. Ethel Barrymore came to study for a play and wound up by asking Aleck's opinion of her interpretation of the role she was to portray. Hecht and MacArthur finished their screenplay of *Wuthering Heights*. Lunt and Fontanne read poetry after dinner. Thornton Wilder, who felt there was too much mental electricity at Neshobe to work, was content to lounge and observe others.

Woollcott always kept at least one secretary in attendance at Bomoseen. From there he dictated three of his better-known letters of recommendation. He took fiendish glee in writing one letter and sending the supposed carbon to those who applied for his endorsement.

To the headmistress of an exclusive school for young women he wrote on behalf of George and Beatrice Kaufman's daughter, Anne. The real letter is lost. The false carbon exists.

I implore you to accept this unfortunate child and remove
her from her shocking environment.

To the Kaufmans' horror, Woollcott proceeded to list the series
of orgies practiced in the Kaufman home.

When Dorothy Parker and Alan Campbell sought to establish
a charge account with a New York department store, Aleck allegedly wrote:

Gentlemen; Mr. Alan Campbell, the present husband of
Dorothy Parker, has given my name as reference in an attempt to open an account at your store. I hope that you will
extend this credit to him. Surely Dorothy Parker's position in
American letters is such as to make shameful the petty re-
fusals which she and Alan have encountered at many hotels,
restaurants, and department stores. What if you never get
paid? Why shouldn't you stand your share of the expense?

S. N. Behrman got a similar surprise when he received a carbon
copy of Aleck's letter to a real estate firm.

I was astonished to learn that your company was even re-
motely considering accepting as a tenant such a notorious
drunkard, bankrupt, and general moral leper as my miserable friend Behrman.

Practical jokes were as plentiful as puns in Woollcott's day, and
people found them both acceptable and amusing. A typical example concerned Miss Pratt Williams, the sister of Aleck's radio
producer.

Woollcott was fond of the attractive southern girl and invited
her to spend her eighteenth birthday on the island. Along with
her brother Herschel, Pratt Williams loaded her little red road-
ster with baggage and drove north to Bomoseen. After she parked
her car on the mainland, brother and sister were ferried to the
island. A few hours later Franklin P. Adams and his wife, Esther,
arrived.

"Who has the car with the Louisiana plates?" Adams asked.

"Rose Long," Aleck answered at once and pointed to Pratt Williams.

That was the summer Senator Huey Long of Louisiana splashed into New York City, consuming vast quantities of rum fizzes, and spoke enough about Sharing the Wealth and Soaking the Rich to be considered possible Presidential timber.

After Aleck had introduced her as The Kingfish's daughter, he took Pratt Williams aside and warned her. "If you dare let on for a moment that you're not Rose Long, I, personally, will have your gizzard out with my stiletto tonight!"

Woollcott then went on to elaborate the hoax. Telephoning his secretary in New York, Aleck instructed him to send telegrams of parental assurance addressed to Miss Rose Long, Neshobe Club, Lake Bomoseen, Vermont. All were signed Father or Daddy. He even had Leggett Brown send a personal telegram to Mr. Alexander Woollcott in which he thanked his daughter's host most profusely for the care and courtesies shown to "my little girl."

For five days Pratt Williams, complete with southern charm and New Orleans patois, played Rose Long.

Finally, at dinner one evening, Aleck led the conversation around to the politics of Senator Long. Long was not a favorite of Aleck's guests, and Woollcott insidiously egged on his friends to speak in a more and more offensive fashion of the pride of the South.

Alice Duer Miller, unaware of the hoax, but *grande dame* that she was, arose majestically from her place and said, "I will not allow you to speak in front of this child about her father this way."

Seizing Pratt Williams by the hand, she marched her out of the dining room. A week later Franklin P. Adams found out about the joke and wrote Miss Williams. "You dirty little Southern rat fink," his letter began, "I hope for the rest of your life you have warm orange juice for breakfast."

However irate Adams may have been at the practical joke, Aleck was vastly amused by it. "Not only was it good sport," he said later, "but unlike most practical jokes it harmed no one. As usual, my sense of timing and my sense of the dramatic were superb."

By the time Woollcott wooed Jo Hennessey from the Swopes, Neshobe Island was a going concern. Jo simply made it run more smoothly. The fact that he had known Woollcott socially before he had gone to work for Swope made it easier for both men as Hennessey took up the managerial reins of Woollcott's life.

Someone had told Woollcott of a poor poet living in the woods an hour's drive from the island.

"You know poets, Jo," Woollcott told him, "they're always on the brink of starvation. Pile up the car with everything we have— hams, bacon, eggs, bread, a few bottles of wine. We are nothing if not generous."

Hennessey did as he was asked, and together he and Woollcott set off in search of the impoverished maker of verses. They found the cottage without much trouble. It was a bit larger than they had anticipated. They were stunned, however, when they rang the doorbell and were greeted by a French maid in an afternoon uniform.

"Archibald MacLeish's country home was almost as beautiful as his wife," Hennessey said gallantly. "What neither Aleck nor I knew was that MacLeish's father owned Carson, Pirie, Scott, the second largest department store in Chicago. MacLeish was very polite in accepting the food. He thanked us properly and we stayed a moderate amount of time and then went back to the island."

"No reason why he shouldn't be living well," Aleck mused on his way home, "but damn it, there's as much chance of finding a rich poet as of finding a naked Santa Claus."

During the winter of 1938–1939, the twenty-one years of guerrilla warfare between Aleck and Harold Ross broke out into full combat. Woollcott left *The New Yorker* (Ross could never make up his mind whether he had fired him or Woollcott had deserted). "Shouts and Murmurs" no longer appeared in the magazine; Woollcott's last contribution was a profile of his old Hamilton schoolmate, now a highly successful practitioner of the law, Lloyd Paul Stryker. It ran in mid-January, 1939.

On March 18, and for two successive weeks, one of *The New Yorker*'s best writers, Wolcott Gibbs, ran a profile called "Big Nemo." Aleck was the subject. At the time it seemed outrageous. Woollcott's friends cursed, sighed, and some even canceled their subscriptions to the magazine.

Gibbs opened his piece by writing that "a lady who loves him once said that Alexander Woollcott has eight hundred intimate friends. This may easily be true, because he leads a social life that might have seemed exhausting to Catherine of Russia."

Gibbs continued with a column of quotations ranging from Charlie Brackett's description in his novel on Aleck—"a competent old horror with a style that combined clear treacle and pure black bile"—to half a dozen less damaging but hardly complimentary comments.

"The rest [of the eight hundred]," Gibbs wrote, "have usually contented themselves with describing him simply and passionately as a monster, or at the very least as a man of absurdly mixed ancestry."

The nadir of the three articles arrived when Gibbs quoted Woollcott's old enemy, George Jean Nathan, in the magazine *Smart Set* on the subject of Aleck's abilities and techniques as a drama critic:

This style is the particular bouquet I invite you to sniff. . . . It never strikes a mean; it is either a gravy bomb, a bursting gladiolus, or a Roman denunciation, unequivocal, oracular, flat, and final. . . . A style, in brief, that is purely emotional, and without a trace of the cool reflectiveness and contagious common sense suitable to criticism.

For years friends, enemies, and observers of Woollcott have quarreled over "Big Nemo." As late as 1965, the eminent theatrical commentator Maurice Zolotow wrote: "Had the profile balanced its sarcasm with humor and a recognition of Aleck's virtues, it might have been digestible to his circle. But it was as slanted and as nasty a piece of magazine biography as I have ever read."

William Shawn, the current editor of *The New Yorker,* recently said, "I can't stand pieces that have any element of cruelty in them, and I think it's possible that the Woollcott piece had some. Even though it was no doubt truthful, and even fair, by ordinary standards. Perhaps I couldn't bring myself to publish the same piece today."

Alfred Lunt and Lynn Fontanne were of that opinion. They had canceled their copies of *The New Yorker* and though they missed them, they believed their loyalty to Aleck took precedence.

They imagined they were hallucinating, therefore, when they arrived at Bomoseen in the summer of 1939 and found Aleck studiously thumbing through *The New Yorker.*

"Oh, I've never stopped having it sent," Aleck said. "As a matter of fact, I'm making suggestions now about some future articles."

In the mid-Thirties chaos suddenly took hold of the part-time residents of Neshobe. More properly, the summertime vacationists discovered that someone was laying the foundation for a house on the highest ridge on the island. Who was the culprit? Enos Booth. And who had drawn the legal papers creating the exclusive Neshobe Island Club? The same Enos Booth.

Aleck, who had always loathed most lawyers, realized that he would have to deal with what he believed was a trespassing advocate. Actually, Mr. Booth wasn't trespassing because when he had drawn up the papers for the Neshobe Island Club, the lawyer had cunningly in an inconspicuous paragraph granted himself the right to build a house on the highest ridge.

Whoever really reads the fine print of a contract?

"One listens to one's lawyer prattle on as long as one possibly can stand it and then signs where indicated," Aleck said later.

To make sure that the island would always belong to him and

his friends, Aleck bought the parcel from Mr. Booth. He then sought out the holder of the mortgage to the place. By a small coincidence the mortgage was held by the first Mrs. Marshall Field, wife of the owner of the *largest* department store in Chicago. Always a wizard with older women, Aleck negotiated until he owned half the acreage and the Neshobe Island Club owned the other half.

Bouncing up to the top of the ridge, Aleck looked at the foundation Lawyer Booth had laid. Then he asked Jo Hennessey if he would build a stone house on those foundations.

The house that Hennessey constructed was much different from the first house on the island. The original had been a clapboard shack that had slowly undergone a series of improvements. It had no insulation against the cold and wind of the Vermont winters.

Not only was the new house windproof, it was much bigger, even luxurious when compared with the building below it.

"There was a large living room with a dining L," Jo Hennessey remembered, "a kitchen, two maid's rooms, and a bath. And there was a library, four bedrooms, and three baths."

Into it Woollcott moved the most precious of his possessions: books, plays, sketches of actresses, memorabilia of the stage from New York and London, as well as the first manuscript he submitted to a magazine, along with its rejection slip. At the time of its writing he was eight years old.

He had at last come full circle to his early days at the Phalanx. Once again he was living with a group of people. True, these people were much different from the Bucklins, the Searses, and the family that inhabited the Phalanstery near Red Bank. Many of the famous were summoned by Woollcott to Bomoseen—novelists, scientists, politicians, statesmen, poets, playwrights, nobility from England, France, Russia, and the rest of the Continent—and they all came because it was Woollcott who did the inviting.

Bomoseen ensured its distinguished visitors against boredom and protected them from the prying eyes of the public. It boasted the finest food and the best conversation and Aleck Woollcott to plan it all for them.

Aleck sent out bills to those visitors who could afford to pay, and dunned those who didn't. Charges for food and lodging: $7.50 per day.

With an ever-increasing sense of happiness, Aleck took to filling in the schedules of his guests before they had even arrived on the island.

"What looks like an entertaining aggregation will be coming and going throughout the week!" he wrote Harold Guinzburg. "But from the 24th on until Labor Day there is at least a threat of our being too crowded for comfort. Of course, I could always make room for you in Beatrice's bed, and I suppose you won't mind eating in the men's toilet. You could defeat this ugly prospect by getting here first and helping me repel invaders, but between now and the 24th I can offer you Neysa, Harpo, Lederer, Beatrice, Irene Castle, Dr. William Mann [head of the Washington Zoo] and the Lunts. The Lunts will occupy my house on the top of the hill. Perhaps you could arrange a design for living with them."

Eventually, his preoccupation with the Neshobe Club and the people who visited him made him benign and solicitous. Even his friends began to refer to him as a mother hen.

Woollcott spent more and more time on the island. When the summer people left, Aleck stayed on and watched the frost turn the green leaves to yellow, orange, and red. His love for the city grew smaller as his passion for the island increased. It seemed nothing could lure him away from it, nothing except the one magical word of the Thirties: radio.

14 The Voice in the Living Room

*T*HE GREATEST INSTRUMENT FOR THE DISSEMINA-
tion of information and entertainment since the invention of
movable type is what the British refer to as the wireless, the Germans dub *Telefunken*, and the Americans call radio. An Italian
physicist named Guglielmo Marconi invented it in 1894.

By 1912 a young American, David Sarnoff, seated beside his
receiving set, picked up the distress signal of the White Star liner
Titanic. The S.O.S. heralded one of the greatest disasters in mari-
time history, sending 1,513 people to an icy end and Alexander
Woollcott to Halifax, Nova Scotia, to cover the story for the
Times.

With shellfire cutting telegraph lines, both sides employed Marconi's invention with increasing frequency during World War I.

Following the war, America took to radio as no other nation.
The first commercial station began broadcasting from Pittsburgh
in November, 1920. It was and still is called KDKA. A country
filled with tinkerers and gadgeteers set about constructing crystal
sets. In 1922, America spent 66 million dollars for radio equipment. The next year the figure jumped to 136 million dollars. By
1925 it swelled to 430 million.

The young man who had received the *Titanic*'s distress signal
became president of the Radio Corporation of America, a business

that made and sold radio sets and vacuum tubes. To encourage sales of both products, even though it might mean a financial loss, David Sarnoff began the National Broadcasting Company. To the stockholders' glee, NBC began to make millions.

Financial promoters quickly interested themselves in radio. Scores of loosely connected networks sprang up throughout the country. The Mutual Network's New York station carried the call letters WOR.

Radio is not at all similar to the theater, a dramatic medium with which Woollcott was familiar. Neither is it similar to the world of books, in which he had been immersed for many years. In the theater, if a producer does not have a play he likes, he produces nothing. If a publisher does not care for a book, he does not bring it out. In radio there are a given number of hours to be filled each week, whether those hours are to be divided into fifteen- or thirty-minute segments, whether they are commercial (paid for by a sponsor) or sustaining (paid for by the station). Unlike a dark theater or a quiet press, radio allows no dead air on prime time—6 P.M. to 11 P.M.

In 1929, the program manager of WOR looked for a way to fill a half-hour; something different, intelligent, compelling, inexpensive. What he found was Alexander Woollcott, who it would seem had been waiting for such a chance all of his life. Woollcott, one of the best raconteurs in New York, knew how to tell a story. The years he spent watching plays had taught him how to utilize his voice for drama. His memory housed a vast library of what radio calls "material."

Woollcott's timing in going on the air was perfect. Radio in 1929 shifted from low to high gear. In contrast, America shifted from boom to bust. About all people could find money for were those wooden boxes with tubes and wires inside, and an array of knobs and a horn that radio technicians called a speaker on the outside.

Radio was free, which was just about what America could afford. The voice that came into everyman's living room entertained him and his family from dinner until bedtime. It was a medium that made use of the imagination of its audience as no other medium had done before. Seated around the room that contained the radio, the audience heard only voices, music, and sound effects. Unlike the theater, the screen, or the printed word, radio permitted the imagery conceived by the individual listener to be as colorful, amusing, touching, or meaningful as his own mind could envisage.

The bulk of the performers for radio came from vaudeville, and vaudeville's years were broken into four thirteen-week cycles. Because no air conditioning existed, summer heat kept patrons from box offices. There existed as a result a summer hiatus of thirteen weeks. Radio followed this practice by and large with the exception of people like Alexander Woollcott.

Early radio comedy names included Amos 'n' Andy, Ed Wynn, Fibber McGee and Molly, Jack Benny, Burns and Allen, Eddie Cantor, and Jack Pearl. Paul Whiteman, Ted Lewis, Ben Bernie, Rudy Vallee, and Guy Lombardo were among the first orchestra conductors of the Twenties. Floyd Gibbons reported the news. Grantland Rice and Graham McNamee broadcast the sports. With the exception of Rice, McNamee, and possibly Gibbons, everyone else employed large staffs of writers. Woollcott alone wrote for Woollcott. He therefore insisted on appearing for only twenty-six weeks. The work was taxing, and the remaining twenty-six weeks gave him time for world travel and rest at Bomoseen.

For his first appearance in the fall of 1929, the forty-two-year-old Woollcott was not carried by the entire Mutual Network. He was heard only on WOR.

Harold Ross telegraphed Aleck his congratulations: "YOU WERE WONDERFUL. I LOST MY DINNER."

On his initial program Woollcott had as his support the leading players of *The Little Show*: Fred Allen, Clifton Webb, and Libby Holman. Those appearances took place in the days before the formation of the American Federation of Radio Artists when performers could be paid with a small gift, a dinner, or even a thank-you note. Certainly a man of Aleck's influence in the New York theater, to say nothing of his personal connections with the stars themselves, could provide guest after guest of such magnitude that Alexander Woollcott quickly was snapped up by a local sponsor.

The Colonial Radio Company signed him commercially for thirteen weeks. After Colonial bowed out, the Gruen watch company took over.

Woollcott on radio behaved differently from Woollcott at the Round Table or Woollcott at the island or at dinner parties. He was not a wisecracker; he was not flip or cutting. Instead, he treated his listeners as he would speak in confidence to his dearest friends. New York, New Jersey, and Connecticut audiences were enchanted by him. What he needed was less than a handful of elements: a first-rate title for his program, a national network, a sponsor, and a man who believed in him.

William S. Paley was the man who believed in him. Born in Chicago, educated at the University of Pennsylvania, Paley came to New York and took over a small radio station that eventually became the Columbia Broadcasting System, the largest and most successful competitor of the National Broadcasting Company.

By the early 1930's NBC had most of the comedians, all of the big orchestras, beginning with Arturo Toscanini and the NBC Symphony, and the big dramatic hour, "The Lux Radio Theatre, produced by Cecil B. De Mille from Holllllllywood."

Paley wisely concentrated on three areas: experimental drama, semiclassical music, and news. "The Columbia Workshop" attracted a roster of writers that eventually made radio into an art form: Norman Corwin, Charles Jackson, Erik Barnouw, Morton Wishengrad, Norman Rosten, Arnold Perl, Marc Blitzstein, to say nothing of Carl Carmer, Stephen Vincent Benét, and Archibald

MacLeish. Paley's newsroom included Edward R. Murrow and Elmer Davis. With increasing frequency the "Workshop" writer teamed up with people in the newsroom, and the radio documentary was brought to a high peak. André Kostelanetz, his wife, the soprano Lily Pons, and the violinist Albert Spalding turned America on to Tchaikovsky, Bizet, Verdi, and Gershwin.

With these programs and stars, Paley turned CBS into a national network that not only threatened but eventually matched NBC in prestige. On his way toward becoming a radio tycoon, Paley paused long enough to pick up a treasure named Woollcott.

"I saw in him a unique personality," Paley said. "He had a quality that I felt would appeal to a mass audience and indeed he did."

Paley put Woollcott on sustaining, where he reviewed books, told a few stories, and invited a guest or two to share his microphone. The opportunity to show off Aleck before a commercial audience came during a two-and-a-half-hour broadcast of a national auto show. CBS arranged for Woollcott to be the master of ceremonies for Chrysler. This pleased everyone except Aleck.

"They have no right to sell my body," the nasty-tempered Woollcott complained loudly. CBS executives streamed into Wit's End to placate the unpredictable artist. Assistants to vice-presidents, vice-presidents, senior vice-presidents, vice-presidents in charge of programming attempted to stroke Woollcott. To no avail. Larry Lowman, one of the bigger wheels at CBS, tried and failed. At last William S. Paley went to visit Aleck and came away with nothing but insults.

If wisdom and power failed to move Woollcott, perhaps beauty and charm might. Ann Honeycutt, young and attractive, served as script editor at CBS. In desperation, CBS sent her to convince Aleck to do the Chrysler job.

"I came to work in very bad shape that morning," Miss Honeycutt remembered. "I had been out all night and somebody said

I had to go over and see Woollcott. I tried to pull myself together and I finally got a cab. A block away from Woollcott's the cab stopped for a light in front of a florist's. I paid the driver, got out, and bought some flowers—roses, maybe. It was the sort of thing that would have come only to a hung-over mind. I walked to Wit's End and Woollcott answered the bell himself. I told him who I was and where I was from."

"I will not talk with anyone from CBS," Aleck told her sharply.

Ann Honeycutt looked at him wearily. "Well, they told me to come over and these flowers are for *you* from *me*." With that, she thrust the flowers into his arms. If he was astonished, Woollcott didn't show it. Instead, he invited her in.

"I don't care if you do the show or not," she told him. Intrigued because everyone else from the network had come pleading and this girl had not, Aleck invited her to sit down. She did, but not before she muttered that she was not interested if he did the broadcast and that she just came over because she had been ordered to see him.

"What's the matter with you?" Woollcoott asked. "You're so cranky."

"I had a very bad night," she replied. "I was out till all hours and I was drinking."

"That's awful." Aleck suddenly became sympathic and understanding. "What did you do?" he asked softly, the old gossip within him coming quickly to the surface.

"It was one of those nights when there was almost nothing that I *hadn't* done," Miss Honeycutt said frankly. "And this recitation of sins got me in. He loved that kind of thing. I didn't know it at the time, but that really kept me there. I had a few ideas about the show and we talked about them, and finally he stopped."

"I suppose you'd like to have a drink in your dreadful condition," Aleck said.

"I would, yes. That would be fine."

"You want to take a nap?"

"I wouldn't mind. I *am* tired."

He gave her a drink, took her to his bedroom, closed the door, and Ann Honeycutt slept. A few hours later Woollcott awakened her.

"Here is something I think might work on that show we talked about," he told her.

"My sins had paid off," Miss Honeycutt said." I went back to the Columbia Broadcasting System refreshed, with the script in my hand, and I was the heroine. The show was a success, and after that I adored Alexander Woollcott from the eyebrows up."

As a result of his work for Chrysler, offers poured in for Woollcott's services on the air. Soon Aleck designed a special form for his own program.

The idea of calling the show "The Town Crier" and ringing an old town crier's bell to open the program came from an advertising man named Paul Davis. Woollcott, knowing a good thing when he heard it, bought the idea for a single sum. The bell would be rung by a sound-effects man (or, when Woollcott chose to honor someone special, he would allow that person to ring the bell), the announcer would call out, "Hear ye! Hear ye! Hear ye!" and Woollcott would say, "This is Woollcott speaking."

The bullring in which Aleck started work, in which he played all of the roles from the matador to the toro, from the picador to the trumpeter, was called Studio One. It was on the top floor of what was then the CBS Building at 485 Madison Avenue in New York City.

Immediately to the right of the elevator there was a short flight of six steps. The door at the top of these stairs opened into a large, well-lighted, high-ceilinged room of approximately 60 feet by 90 feet.

In contrast to the backstage areas of the theaters Woollcott knew so well, Studio One was not dark, cramped, dusty, and drafty. It was clean, so clean compared with a theater that at first glance it might have given an impression of being antiseptic. It was, however, highly functional. Unlike any house on Broadway, Studio One had a constantly comfortable temperature summer and winter. It was pleasantly warm during the cold months and completely air-conditioned in the summer. People who worked in radio hurried gratefully to the studios during June, July, August, and September. Years before movie houses were air-conditioned and a decade and a half before cool air was introduced into the legitimate theater, radio provided that comfort for its workers. William Paley saw to it that no studio in the country was better equipped than Studio One.

In place of the theater's stagehands who slouched about, frequently unshaven, slovenly dressed, secure in the knowledge that Local Number One would keep their jobs open for them, the technicians in radio were generally young, attractive, well-dressed college men. They shared two attributes: a pride in their work and a refusal to wear vests. In the radio studios of America, the three-piece suit became obsolete.

These technicians included a director, an assistant director, an engineer, sound-effects persons (CBS was the first network to put a woman in charge of a sound-effects crew), a musical conductor, and an orchestra.

The director functioned in much the same fashion as he did in the theater. The assistant director had the responsibility of timing the show. Every ten seconds he would glance at his stopwatch and jot down the time on his script. In the theater a play lasted until the final curtain was lowered. In radio a half-hour program was over in exactly 29 minutes and 20 seconds. Not 30 minutes, not 29 minutes and 5 seconds.

Precision is what radio demanded. "Five, four, three, two, one, take it," the assistant director would say softly in the control room.

At the count of "Five," the director, standing beside his assistant, would raise his right arm. When the words "Take it" were spoken, the director's arm would be extended, his right index finger would point through the soundproof glass that separated the control room from the studio, and the program would go "on the air."

Hand signals for speeding up or stretching the rate of speech were easily given and understood. The now familiar gesture of "on the nose" began in the control rooms of radio.

Studio One, like all radio studios, was windowless. Its ceiling and walls were covered with an off-white asbestos tile that was perforated with holes every square inch. These served to sound-proof the studio from outside noises. On one side of the studio were large wooden vanes that turned into the studio or away from it, depending how "live" the engineer and the director desired the mix of voices, sound effects, and music to be. Opposite the live end of the studio was the "dead" end. This was a wall hung with rich gray-velour draperies that drank in sound and absorbed or deadened it. The rugs on the studio floor were also gray. The only other color was a pastel blue. Psychologists had discovered that people working in rooms with muted colors were less likely to grow temperamental than those who worked in studios decorated in primary colors.

The CBS house orchestra sat at the far end of the studio, oc-cupying about two-thirds of the floor space. The remaining area was given over to the microphones and the sound crew. Actors stood in front of the microphones and read from mimeographed scripts.

Because Aleck was such a heavy man, CBS engineering devised a table microphone for him that did not interfere with his bifocal vision. While others stood, Aleck always read his scripts sitting down.

At the near end of the studio was another small flight of stairs. At its top was a door that led into the "client's booth," a 12-foot-by-14-foot room with chairs and a speaker that carried in every-thing from the studio. Theoretically, this small room existed for the convenience of the sponsor and his advertising agents. In practice, friends of Aleck utilized it to watch and listen to the antics in the studio. Behind its soundproof glass wall they could talk, laugh, smoke, and, if they chose, pick up the telephone and make outside calls.

Adjoining the client's booth was the control room. At the desk on the left sat the assistant director, his eyes darting constantly from his script to his stopwatch. In the center of the control room stood the director. To his right sat the engineer. Before him was a console with dials and needles and electronic equipment complex enough to send the sounds and voices from Studio One almost instantaneously from the network transmitter to the radio sets in America's homes.

By the time Woollcott arrived at CBS his respect for the director, the engineer, and the assistant director was such that he familiarized himself with every aspect of their work. He quickly realized that those technicians could assure his success. The result was that he not only respected but quite frequently catered to them.

He made certain he had the best crew in radio. His producer was Herschel Williams, a bright young man from New Orleans who had attended Yale. His director was another Yalie, Earle McGill, who became president of the Radio Directors Guild. His announcer was Paul Douglas, who was to star eventually in Garson Kanin's Broadway comedy *Born Yesterday*.

Paley put Woollcott on sustaining in 1933. A year later, to Paley's satisfaction, the program was sold commercially to the breakfast-food product called Cream of Wheat.

The advertising agency was J. Walter Thompson and the man on the Cream of Wheat account was Paul Harper. Harper had the great fortune to have participated in World War I and was, therefore, acceptable to Woollcott immediately. The advertising executive soon made clear the policy of his account to Woollcott's producer, Herschel Williams.

"Remember, this is a Middle West client," he cautioned Williams. "They have rather pristine views and the program is going to be broadcast at seven P.M. Sunday evening. This is going to have a family audience and we musn't overstep the bounds of good taste."

Williams understood. Without too much difficulty he wangled an invitation for himself and Harper to Bomoseen. On the island Aleck was as sweet as the syrup he poured over his pancakes each morning. For two thousand dollars a week, which is what Cream of Wheat guaranteed him for twenty-six weeks, he couldn't have been more agreeable.

Harper was not lulled into a sense of false security. He had read the Woollcott story in *The New Yorker* about the blonde at the cashier's desk of a southern restaurant who was seeking to pay her check with a five-dollar bill when it was rejected as counterfeit. Milady paled visibly. "Counterfeit!" she cried. "My God, I've been raped!"

He knew all about Woollcott's continuous feud with Harold Ross when Aleck was writing "Shouts and Murmurs." Woollcott had tried running improper misprints from newspapers that he supposedly had kept in his wallet. The first story, Herschel Williams recalled, had to do with a "Mr. John McCreedy, a prominent young engineer from Wichita Falls, Kansas, who was seriously injured last week while working on a bride four miles west of the city."

Woollcott howled gleefully. He claimed he had inserted that story only to catch the always-quick pencil of Katharine White, his editor on *The New Yorker*.

The other story he "cleaned out of his wallet" had to do with a clipping from a Flint, Michigan, paper that said: "The Hurley General Hospital has instituted a new system for recording the patients who come in—and the doctor's first diagnosis. Here, for example, is a card and on the front is the patient's name, the patient's address, and what the patient says is wrong with him. In this case, the patient said, 'I have piles.' On the opposite side where the doctor makes his initial comment it read, 'I'll say he has piles!' "

Aleck appeared just the tiniest bit interested in the unerring accuracy of Mr. Harper's information. He solemnly promised no such stories would be told on the air.

The advertising executive was still uneasy and sent Williams, Aleck's producer, to Minneapolis, Minnesota, the home of Cream of Wheat. Dan Bull was the president of Cream of Wheat. After the inevitable tour through the plant, Mr. Bull sat Mr. Williams down in his office.

"I don't want any of Woollcott's off-color stories," the breakfast-food magnate intoned. "The first off-color story, we're through. Look at the contract we have with Woollcott. We have the right to cancel. Do I make myself clear?"

He did.

Prior to his first broadcast, Woollcott invited his producer to Wit's End and insisted upon reading his script. The bell was to ring, the announcer was to call out "Hear ye" three times, and then it was "This is Woollcott speaking." His opening gambit was the story of Liza, the black girl from Charleston, South Carolina, who was the Raggedy Ann of the neighborhood. She was worse than ugly, she was plain. Liza did have the good sense, though, to disappear from Charleston and go north. A few years later her family received a telegram saying that she was coming home and that they should meet her at the North Charleston station. The family did as they were asked, and when the train pulled in, Liza got off, all dressed up in a purple dress and hat with feathers on it. "My God, Liza! What happened to you?" the family wanted to know. "Ain't you heard?" Liza responded. "I's been ruined."

Herschel Williams sat in front of the pajama-wearing Woollcott and thought of only one thing. Oh, my God, there goes the Cream of Wheat contract!

Woollcott was watching his face closely.

"What's the matter?" he demanded. "Don't you think it's funny? Don't you think it's appropriate? I'm like Liza. For the first time I have an opulent patron behind me."

Williams thought of Dan Bull's face.

"Woolk," he hesitated.

"Yes?"

"That's a very old story."

"It is?"

"It's been around a long time."

"I never heard it before."

"That doesn't make it any younger. Tell you what," Williams said tentatively, "all you have to do is change one word in it and it'll be absolutely fresh."

"Oh?"

"The word is 'ruined.' Change it to 'sponsored.' 'Ain't you heard? I's been sponsored.'"

Woollcott agreed. The change was made. The show went on. And the first reaction from Minneapolis was a purring sound.

Not all of his broadcasts were as simplistic as the first. As the Town Crier, Woollcott drew upon material ranging from passages in the Bible to scenes from Shakespeare. His old favorites, Lizzie Borden and the Hall-Mills murder case, were discussed with as much fervor as the Stanford University professor who was accused of killing his own wife, tried, found guilty, and sentenced to the gas chamber. Woollcott took up his cause and secured a new trial for the previously convicted man. The second time around, the jury voted to acquit the professor.

If he wallowed in crime, he was a champion of philanthropic works. Woollcott was one of the first radio personalities to adopt a charity and fight over the airwaves for its success. Because his eyesight had been so poor from his early childhood and because he read continuously and wrote almost as much as he read, Aleck always secretly believed he was on the verge of blindness. Seeing Eye Dogs for the Blind, with headquarters in Whippany, New Jersey, was a cause close to Woollcott's heart. Anytime he could get in a word for the dogs or for the blind he would. The same held true for the still hospitalized soldiers of World War I, for the actors and actresses he liked most, and for plays—new or old.

Aleck took quickly to the technique of broadcasting. He spoke with a sense of urgency and determination. The accent he used had been acquired in Kansas City, where he had spent some of his earliest years. He employed the hard *r*'s and the flat *a*'s of the Middle Westerner. His tone was tenor.

After a few voice lessons he learned how to play to a microphone, how to lean toward it and whisper a word or a sentence to give what he had to say a sense of intimacy. In a short time Woollcott mastered his craft.

The foremost people of the day considered it something of a prize to be invited by Woollcott to share his microphone.

"Aleck was a stagestruck show-off," Helen Hayes recounted. "He was an awful bully but a darling one, too. He was as generous as he was demanding. Just before my daughter, Mary, was born, he decided that I should go on the air with him. Now, I'm a short woman and one who showed her pregnancy very, very vividly and sharply. I looked like a watermelon when he decided that he and I would do the balcony scene from *Romeo and Juliet.*"

Knowing that he might not make the greatest of all Romeos, Woollcott decided to hedge his bet by playing not only Romeo but also the Nurse.

"Well, there we were in the studio," Miss Hayes continued, "me out to here and Woollcott having a pretty big stomach himself— this Romeo and Juliet could never possibly have reached within arm's length of each other. But there we were doing it. He was an absurd Romeo. Aleck just liked to read the lines. As the Nurse, of course, everyone agreed he was much better."

By "everyone," Miss Hayes referred to the theatrical community. For the rest of the nation, it was good programming to have the First Lady of the American Theater appear opposite the Town Crier.

* * *

Not treated as well as Miss Hayes was the pianist and wit Oscar Levant. Scheduled to play a short piece by Brahms on the Cream of Wheat show, Levant arrived at the studio at 485 Madison Avenue and was asked if he might shorten his work by thirty seconds, because the program was running long that night. Levant agreed. Shortly thereafter he was asked by Woollcott if he could cut another twenty seconds. Always ready to oblige, Levant made the second cut. It was only when Woollcott asked him if he'd mind terribly much making another cut that Levant answered, "I won't mind, but you'll hear from Brahms in the morning."

To Margaret Mitchell, author of *Gone with the Wind,* Aleck wrote about a letter he received from a Birmingham matron, a Mrs. Vance, whose cook had listened to a Woollcott broadcast. At its conclusion, Mrs. Vance related, the cook pronounced, "There's voodoo in his voice but glory in his tales."

Woollcott wrote Margaret Mitchell, "I am arranging to have this embossed on my professional stationery."

For years Woollcott had been one of the easiest touches on Broadway for impoverished playwrights, producers, and especially actors. It was natural, therefore, that a hard-luck story coming through the mail from a pair of his listeners should capture his attention. The typed letters with no return address claimed there were two elderly maidens living in Troy, New York, who were starving. A long series of one-way correspondence resulted in their confession that they believed Woollcott was the greatest person on American radio. Being Woollcott, he was able to recognize the truth when he saw it. Then came a pathetic letter from the two sisters. They wrote that one was on the verge of death and would meet her Maker happily if only she could hear Woollcott read the great Twenty-third Psalm.

It was almost too touching. But being a sentimentalist, Aleck, with the entire CBS house orchestra backing him, did indeed read the psalm.

The next letter was filled with gratitude and sorrow. The ailing spinster, propped up on her pillow, had heard him read the Twenty-third Psalm, and with a smile on her lips expired in the arms of her sister.

Woollcott was overwrought. Someone had to help this poor, bereft woman. But since there was no address on the envelope, he appealed over the air for her to contact him. To no avail. Jo Hennessey was dispatched to Troy and nearby towns with instructions to make a thorough search. Eventually a final letter came. The surviving sister had also passed on. The letter bore the signature only of "Nurse." Being an old newspaperman, Woollcott knew that death certificates had to be signed and registered. Hennessey was ordered to intensify his search. After months of the most detailed investigation, Hennessey reported what Woollcott had begun to suspect: that the entire matter had been a hoax.

There were several suspects, but the more Woollcott considered it, the more he remembered Charlie MacArthur and the bathtub filled with raspberry Jell-O. No one ever found out. MacArthur went to his grave denying any part in the scheme.

MacArthur, however, did pull enough pranks to be considered the prime suspect. Many of Charlie's days were occupied concocting such elaborate harlequinades. His collaborator Ben Hecht complained of the amount of time MacArthur spent away from the typewriter.

"Any writer who makes critics his cronies," Hecht said, "is almost certain to quit writing. MacArthur had more critic pals than any other writer in town. He didn't quit, but he went in for long hesitations."

No matter what Charlie did, Aleck forgave him. His warm charm and gentle wit served as his passport to anywhere.

"I'm rehearsing in Bernard Shaw's *Caesar and Cleopatra*," Helen

Hayes said to MacArthur, whom she'd just met. "We're opening at the new Guild Theatre. I'm playing Cleopatra."

"I wish I could play the asp," Charlie answered.

Early in the Thirties, after Woollcott had turned to radio, the Round Table at the Algonquin ceased to exist. It wasn't because of Woollcott, to be sure. So many of the others had scattered. The Marx Brothers had gone to Hollywood. So had Benchley, Parker, Lardner, and, from time to time, Kaufman and Sherwood.

Aleck was unable or at least unwilling to eat lunch alone. He had to have company and he wanted to have a clublike atmosphere such as Frank Case had provided. George Backer, who was then building the Berkshire Hotel, catty-corner from the CBS Building, volunteered to put in a restaurant. Aleck accepted his offer immediately and specified that the place should be a private club, away from the probing eyes of columnists and reporters and the popping eyes of tourists.

True to his word, Backer had Norman Bel Geddes design an absolutely magnificent dining room. It was narrow but it had a very high ceiling from which stars appeared to twinkle. To compensate for the lack of width, the largest mirror in the world was constructed for one of the long walls. It was blue in color. As it was being lowered into place, it cracked and a new blue mirror had to be manufactured and polished. The cost of construction rose from high to astronomic. Instead of the usual restaurant chairs, the room was outfitted with voluminous armchairs with seats ample enough even for Aleck's broad bottom.

When it was completed, Harold Ross looked it over. "This will be a beautiful swimming pool," he said, "as soon as they put water in it."

Hawley Truax was invited to inspect it. "Ridiculous place!" he complained. "There's hardly elbow room in here."

"A capital name," Woollcott exclaimed. "First rate. We'll call this the Elbow Room."

And so they did. Jo Hennessey was put in charge. The club was so exclusive that within six months it went broke. It reopened shortly thereafter under the name of the Barberry Room. This time it was a public restaurant under the management of an experienced boniface named Moriarity. It was highly successful so long as Woollcott was present. After he left, it slowly went the way of many New York restaurants: into debt and out of business.

Alexander King, editor, author, storyteller, and television personality, had known Woollcott in an early day. He spoke of him, referring to the Elbow Room period.

"I used to illustrate the drama page for Aleck Woollcott on the New York *World*, and in the course of events he introduced me to George Kaufman. Kaufman treated me with as much deference and courtesy as if I'd been a great man, and I was strictly nobody from no place. Kaufman, of course, was surrounded by great successes that he himself had written—hit play after hit play. Aleck, of course, was a dowager from Jersey. These men—I'm particularly interested in noting—practiced something that has gone out of existence since then. They promoted people and helped them. I remember shortly after Orson Welles arrived in New York. I was living in Woollcott's apartment because it was summer and my family was in the country and I had no place to stay. Orson Welles suddenly showed up, looking terrible. Woollcott immediately dressed him from head to foot; he gave him all the clothes he could spare. Then he took him out and got him shoes, which were hard to find because his feet were so big. Then he introduced him to Katharine Cornell. Orson toured the next season with Cornell.

"But this behavior was not unusual. He did the same things for me and for endless other people. The group that used to congregate first around the Algonquin and then the Elbow Room had the reputation for having a little bit of heartless wit, which may be, but they were all constantly writing letters for young people, both boys and girls, saying, 'He's good,' 'She's marvelous,' 'You must use him.'

"That's how I met Crowninshield—through Aleck Woollcott.

Frank edited *Vanity Fair* at that time. And Crowny did the damnedest for me right away, except there wasn't anything I could really do for him. Also, I couldn't write the special type of prose that was needed on Condé Nast publications. So he said, 'I'll tell you what. If you could master how to write the captions for *Vogue* fashions, they pay very well and it would be a steady dollar.'

"So I got a bunch of photographs and went over to Woollcott's house. Aleck wasn't home but Kaufman was there. You know how gaunt he was, like a buttoned-up friar. But nevertheless full of amiability, and I disclosed my uneasy heart to him. I gave him a photograph. It was a large yellow beret worn by a lantern-jawed model who was six feet two inches tall and weighed about eighty-five pounds. He looked at it and without a pause scribbled underneath:

" 'Only the Dalai Lama sitting in state at Koombum had the luxurious certainty that his tam-o'-shanter of yellow suede was draped with the elaborate indifference of final authorities. But now Cecil Veine, a French magician of haute couture, has made this jewel accessible to the discriminating modiste of the Western world.' And he said, 'Now, here's your sample.'

"And with that, Woollcott came into the room, and Kaufman told me to show it to Aleck. So I handed him the page and watched those big owl eyes of his sweep across every word.

" 'It'll do,' Woollcott finally said.

" 'You really like it?' Kaufman asked him.

" 'A plethora of swollen adjectives!' Aleck beamed. 'I'm ready to buy one for myself.' "

Woollcott knew words the way a diamond buyer with a loupe in his eye recognizes a new stone. In one of his broadcasts he employed the word "pubescent." To his horror, mail poured in by the sackful complaining that he had used an off-color or even obscene word on the air.

One long-distance call after another came from Cream of Wheat in Minneapolis. Being an expert at talking, Woollcott was able to convince the angry Mr. Bull that the word in question was not at all questionable. Having done that, he turned to the mountains of fan mail. Other stars frequently sent out mimeographed letters through the networks' press departments. Woollcott was a highly personalized performer and his own conscience demanded that he answer every letter himself.

Since 1928, Woollcott had had a private secretary. The first had been Danton Walker, who later became a successfully syndicated columnist working out of the New York *Daily News*. His successor was Leggett Brown. With the "pubescent" affair, Brown simply could not take the amount of dictation Aleck gave. Mr. Paley provided an entire staff of shorthand artists, and Aleck, like Julius Caesar—but wearing a dressing gown instead of armor—dictated to as many as three secretaries at once.

The matter having been cleared up to everyone's satisfaction, Woollcott proceeded, happy in the knowledge that when he spoke, people listened—intently. Further proof came when he asked listeners to donate unused eyeglass frames for the Seeing Eye Dog charity. The first mail brought 3,700 pairs of spectacles!

He might have continued broadcasting about Christmas, and the various battles of World War I, and Mr. Justice Holmes, and Elizabeth, the girl who would one day become Queen of the British Empire, and the Lunts, and Kit Cornell, and Helen Hayes as Victoria Regina; he might even have slipped in an occasional word or story broaching upon the *double entendre,* but it was something as simple and clear-cut as a former house painter and a former newspaper editor that proved his undoing.

In 1936, during a broadcast, Aleck took a hard look at fascism. Without knowing of the rampant isolationism in the Middle West, he soundly condemned Adolf Hitler and Benito Mussolini. The next day Cream of Wheat canceled his contract.

At first Aleck was stunned. Then he became furious. He had only done what they had been paying him to do: speak his mind.

"My dear Harper," Woollcott blasted the advertising agency man, "I have said enough to make clear what a blank check I would be signing if I recklessly promised to omit all controversial material. These elements lend the series salt, provoke discussion, whip up attention, and enlarge the audience."

No amount of palaver could persuade Dan Bull to rescind his cancellation order. Woollcott might have offended certain minority groups who were buying Cream of Wheat, and the sale of that product meant more to Bull than the opinion of Alexander Woollcott.

Aleck's career appeared to be finished.

Not exactly. The final arbiter of whether Woollcott went on or remained off the air was not Dan Bull but William S. Paley. Paley had signed Aleck to his original contract, and Paley decided that the American public should hear more of Woollcott. Moreover, William S. Paley had a sales force to find another sponsor for "The Town Crier."

It didn't take long.

The next fall Woollcott reappeared on radio without a sponsor. By Thanksgiving, CBS sales were deep in negotiation with the Liggett & Myers Tobacco Company. Shortly after the New Year, the tobacco company presented "The Granger Program," starring Alexander Woollcott as the Town Crier, broadcast over the Columbia Coast-to-Coast Network. It was aired at seven-thirty in the evening and rebroadcast for the Coast at 12:30 A.M. The contract also specified a full thirty-nine weeks. Even more gratifying were the figures. Woollcott was raised from two thousand to three thousand a week.

Granger was a pipe tobacco and soon many of Aleck's friends began sniping at him. They said that because of his sponsor he had taken up smoking. This was a familiar complaint. When Aleck had endorsed Muriel cigars, F.P.A. ran a short paragraph in "The Conning Tower" concluding with "As he was not a smoker, I considered it dishonest." That Adams, who had spent so much time in

Aleck's company, should have considered him a nonsmoker was incredible. Aleck had begun smoking cigarettes at Hamilton. He went on to cigars shortly after he joined *The New York Times* (witness the box of expensive Havanas the Shuberts had sent him as a peace offering after their battle to bar him from their theaters). There are in existence dozens of photographs of Aleck smoking one weed or another, but because he endorsed products for money, people carped. At times they were right. He endorsed Seagram's whiskey and it is questionable that he drank it. He endorsed the Chrysler Air-Flow automobile but never drove one. That is not to say that Jo Hennessey or some other friend might not have driven it for him.

Aside from these minor vexations, Woollcott was an even greater success for Granger pipe tobacco than he had been for Cream of Wheat. Over six million Americans listened to his broadcasts. The programs originated from almost any part of the country that Woollcott happened to be in, and always they were live. Magnetic tape had not been invented and acetate recordings were prohibited from use by contract with the American Federation of Musicians.

Any subject that came to his mind Woollcott turned into a radio broadcast. Any topic, even one as pedantic and dry as the use of English grammar, became an exercise in wit and humor.

I'm delighted with a story James Hilton told me the other day about a history exam at Oxford. In answer to the question "What do you know about The Lombard League?" one of the students correctly wrote down just the word "Nothing." For that, the examiners were about to give him a zero when they had the grace to realize that the real error lay in the sloppiness of the question. So they gave him full credit.

I was delighted by that story because in matters of speech, it's not elegance that interests me but exactness. Precision. Surgical precision. I suggest that those of us whose trade is in words, whether put down on paper or tossed onto the patient air-waves, and all those whose job it is to teach that trade might better concentrate on the really grievous injury done our medium every day by those who so ignore the primal eldest meaning of a word that eventually it loses its sharp edge as an instrument, its exact value as currency. Let me give a few illustrations—all in the pattern of the old story about Noah Webster, the man who wrote the dictionary. Of him it used to be told that his wife once caught him in the pantry in the act of kissing the cook. "Why, Mr. Webster," she said, "I'm surprised."

"No, my dear," he replied, "I'm surprised; you're amazed."

. . . I find that many of our newspapers no longer seem able to distinguish between "prone" and "supine." Your vocabulary is impoverished every time you forget that a man is prone when he lies face down, supine when he lies on his back. A few weeks ago in one of our better New York dailies I read a description of a well-dressed woman lying prone on her back on Fifth Avenue. I'd like to have seen that. Must have been quite a sight. . . .

A more typical Woollcott broadcast appealed to the emotions of his listeners. In the program partially quoted below, the Town Crier included Joyce Kilmer, author of "Trees"; "Wild Bill" Donovan, colonel of the "Fighting Sixty-ninth" Regiment and later, in World War II, head of the Office of Strategic Services; Al Smith, governor of New York and candidate for the Presidency; and Gene Tunney, undefeated heavyweight boxing champion of the world. The phrase "name-dropper" hadn't come into the language during Woollcott's time, but he was a prime practitioner of the art.

. . . 1918. A hot July day in the valley of the Marne. The New York regiment of the Rainbow Division had been up to its neck in the bloody business known as the Battle of the Ourcq. In a field hospital behind the lines I picked up the rumor that a certain sergeant, who like myself went into the army from the staff of *The New York Times,* had just been killed in action. A poet he was. Young fellow named Kilmer. Sergeant Joyce Kilmer. The rumor ran from man to man. I scouted through the little patch of woods where the tired and tattered remnants of the regiment had fallen back to rest. Yes, Joyce had been killed as he followed Wild Bill Donovan up the slope to the other side of the creek. Did I want to know more? If so, I'd better ask the padre. He'd just come in from burying Kilmer. They pointed to a clearing where a tall priest stood, clad in olive-drab, his trench coat muddy, his face beneath the helmet gaunt and drawn with a great weariness. He was talking with a half dozen soldiers who'd just reported for instructions. It was my first meeting with Father Duffy, chaplain of the Old New York Sixty-ninth. The beginning of a friendship which I count as one of the great and enriching privileges of my life—the kind of unearned increment we seem to owe to chance. Something of how he looked that day, what he wore—trench coat and all—how he felt, you'll be able to see from the heroic statue which will be unveiled in Times Square on Sunday afternoon. Sunday, May second. That was Father Duffy's birthday. He'd have been sixty-six. He died five years ago. Since then, to many of us—devout Catholics and hopeless heathen alike—this city, so peculiarly his, has seemed a colder place in which to live and work.

When your Town Crier was appointed to the committee which had this memorial in charge, I shied at the prospect of a bronze Father Duffy in Times Square, of all places— that flamboyant crossroads which, year in and year out, hasn't one moment of quiet in any hour of the twenty-four. Father Duffy, helmet on head, breviary in hand, forever amid a whirl of taxicabs and sight-seeing buses, orangeade stands and neon lights, burlesque houses and comfort stations—all the aural and visual yawp of the country's greatest midway. I'm afraid it was my own notion that his statue— if there had to be one—should stand apart in some green and tranquil sanctuary. But now I realize that the men on the committee who outvoted me—Al Smith, Bill Donovan, Gene Tunney, all of them—were wiser than I was. This is what Father Duffy himself would have liked—I'm sure of that now—his statue in New York of all places on earth and, if in New York, then at this spot of all spots, where every-thing round him would be rowdy and cheerful and com-mon—common as humanity itself. And on next Sunday when those who loved him gather there to make a fuss about him, all traffic on Broadway for five blocks will be suspended. My, how that would have tickled him! After all, Times Square was in his parish. Born in Canada? Yes. Schooled in Ireland? Of course. At Maynooth. But just the same he was the first citizen of our town. For most of us New York is too large. It wasn't too large for Father Duffy. Somehow he gave it the homeliness of a neighborhood. It was uplift-ing just to walk down the street with him. No matter what street, he was like a curé striding through his own village. Everyone knew him. On all sides, such pleased faces. At the sight of him the cop at the corner would light up like a Christmas tree and stop all traffic from curb to curb for Father Duffy. The fat banker who paused to speak to him, the checkroom boy who took his hat—he'd call them both by their first names. And were they proud? You see, what Father Duffy did was to make New York into a small town.

New York. In France he liked nothing better than to sit in a shell hole with Clancy and Callahan and Kerrigan and talk about New York. I've stood beside him ankle-deep in the Argonne mud and, above the noise of the rain pattering on our helmets, heard him think aloud how Fifth Avenue must be gleaming in the October sunshine. For him the most electric moment in all the war (I've told the story many times) came on a June night in Lorraine when the troops of the Old Sixty-ninth discovered that the green outfit relieving them was also from New York. The Seventy-seventh Division. The war had picked up both by the scruff of the neck, carried them across the world and dumped them in the French mud. And here they were, passing each other on the road. The excitement as old neighbors would identify each other in the moonlight. Father Duffy told me how he saw two brothers meet. All they could do was take pokes at each other and swear enormously. Much more of this would have caught the ear of the enemy artillery. Somehow order was restored and the march went on. No more mingling. Pipe down, everybody. So, with talk forbidden, these passing regiments found another means of communication. They hummed to each other—very softly.

"Give my regards to Broadway . . ." The rhythm did the trick.

"Remember me to Herald Square . . ." No need of words. The tune spoke for them.

Not all of Woollcott's broadcasts were filled with sentiment. Aleck came into the studio one afternoon ready for rehearsal. He intended to discuss his favorite topic: murder. After nodding hello to his director in the control room, Aleck walked to his microphone, blew into it twice to satisfy himself that it was "live," or on, and then began reading his script.

It concerned the latest, juiciest scandal to hit the front pages of the newspapers. The Broadway singer Libby Holman had been accused of killing her young husband, heir to the Reynolds tobacco fortune.

Four sentences into the script, his director, Earle McGill, hit the talk-back lever that made his voice audible in the studio.

"Hold it, Mr. Woollcott," McGill's words boomed out.

"What is it?" Aleck asked.

"As an ex-newspaperman, Mr. Woollcott, don't you think what you're saying might be libelous?"

"As an ex-newspaperman, I can tell you here and now that almost anything in a periodical that comes out of a coroner's office is considered to be in the public domain. Shall we continue, Mr. McGill?"

"No," came the voice from the control room.

"Would you be kind enough to explain why not?"

"We're sponsored by Granger tobacco. Taking a crack at the dead son of another tobacco company is not particularly good taste."

"Taste! Taste!" Aleck stormed. "What do you expect of me? It's like asking a color-blind man to match samples!"

After another five minutes of fuming, a typewriter was brought into the studio, and Aleck tapped out a more suitable story for that night's broadcast.

While his mind was a repository for countless stories, he guarded them jealously. Buttonholing Alexander King one night, he complained, "I give up on you. You go around to those terrible parties and you tell a whole new flock of stories. Such wastefulness! How can you be so idiotic? I've been living on four stories for the last thirty-two years and it's only now that they're beginning to listen to me. And waiting, expectantly, for the punch line. Every year I revive the same stories for the different holidays. At last, I've gotten them all broken in."

By now radio had made Aleck into what broadcasting could then do with relative ease: it turned him into a national celebrity. With hardly a glance backward he crossed the line from being a critic to being a showman. His collection of evening capes grew larger, the brims on his black slouch hats grew wider. He became both a personality and a star, and he took to each role with satisfaction. He also took the $3,500 a week CBS paid him without any fuss. His colleague the highly gifted John Mason Brown wrote of him:

As a drama critic or book trumpeter, as charity lover or prestige destroyer, as sentimentalist or "old meanie"—he is a figure not one in a million but one in one hundred and thirty million . . . if Mr. Woollcott has made it practically impossible for anyone in these United States not to have heard of him, the reason is, of course, that he has long since become part of the public domain—practically an annex to Yellowstone National Park. . . . Anyone who has ever heard Mr. Woollcott on the air or enjoyed the rare privilege of hearing him speak in person must be familiar with the Town Crier's voice—that voice which can persuade you there are truffles on his tonsils. There is not a bridge builder in the country who has his gift for suspense.

Even Sigmund Romberg forgave Woollcott for the two devastating lines about him. Romberg had his own radio program on NBC. Since his English was as thick as the goulash he loved, Romberg employed Deems Taylor as his narrator. One evening while Woollcott was broadcasting, Romberg, Taylor, June Walker, an actress who was that week's guest, and the entire NBC Symphony Orchestra marched over to CBS, entered Studio One, and serenaded Aleck.

Not to be outdone, a week later Woollcott led his entire array of guests along with the CBS house orchestra to "The Romberg Hour" to reciprocate.

The visit was highly successful. Woollcott had worked on it for six days. Toward the end of the hour, Deems Taylor, using terribly elaborate language, thanked Woollcott most profusely.

Aleck accepted the thanks and added his own. But Taylor was not satisfied. He came back with more verbal bouquets for Woollcott's time, the generous contribution of his talent, the thoughtfulness of his visit . . .

Woollcott, by now an old radio hand, watched as the sweep hand of the studio clock came within five seconds of the closing of the Romberg show.

"Deems, dear," Aleck cut in, "I may throw up."

A shorter and more tightly phrased sentence would, within a few years, provide a first line for a character to be named Sheridan Whiteside. Until then, "I may throw up" was one of the more startling statements of radio in the Thirties.

In Milwaukee, in Louisville, in cities scattered across the United States, there are homes in which the occupants proudly display an old town crier's bell, presented to their fathers and mothers or grandparents or great-grandparents. The bells are souvenirs left or sent by Alexander Woollcott in return for a night's lodging or a banana cream pie that led him on to three helpings.

In the bookshop and home of Jo and Helen Hennessey in Saratoga, New York, there are two bells on the floor upstairs and at least one bell downstairs.

On the top floor of the Columbia Broadcasting System Building in New York, in the office of the chairman of the board, mounted on a pedestal, under glass, with a soft light shining down upon it, is a gold-plated bell.

"That's the original Town Crier's bell," William S. Paley says. "That's the one Woollcott used."

It still shines brightly.

15 Inner Circle

RADIO SUCCEEDED IN SHOWING THE WORLD WHAT Woollcott really was. The single dimension of sound penetrated the carefully disguised defensive layers of his character. Instead of the acid-tongued, sarcastic personality he tried to palm off on an innocent public, radio exposed him.

The wicked Woollcott was a fraud. The true Woollcott was a sentimentalist.

This honeyed quality was not affected merely for the airwaves. Secretly it made up a large part of Aleck's inner nature.

Family always meant much to him. The nearness of communal living at the Phalanx made him forever emotionally close to all of his kin except his father. Particularly dear to him were his brother Billy and his sister, Julie.

With Billy and Billy's daughters, Aleck was to have a long and warm relationship. Julie, however, died in 1928, and the grief he felt as a result of her death was deep and lasting. Having cared for her up to the end, Aleck was so distressed that although he was able to take her ashes out to the Phalanx and bury them himself without ceremony, he found it impossible to write of Julie's death to her childhood friend in Kansas City. When at last he did manage to compose a letter, it carried not only the sad news of his sister but also similar word of his benefactor.

In September Dr. Humphreys died. You remember I was named after him. He was a person of circumstance and Trinity was so crowded for his funeral that I had to stand in the back of the church. In the shadow of the pillar there I watched the procession following the coffin out into the afternoon sunlight—Aunt Eva, bent and old but able to make the journey, and behind her young Eva and her husband and a swarm of grandchildren. And I knew that there were great-grandchildren stowed away in sundry nurseries. And I knew, too, that I could stand in the shadow of that pillar for a hundred years without seeing the end of the procession, without seeing the end of the chapter written by that rich and fruitful life. It is so different when a childless woman dies. Julie's chapter is ended. She was perfume, scattered now on the ground. And there is just a small company of us—you, dear Lucy, and a few others—for whom the fragance of her lingers in the air . . . so one by one the lights go out.

He never forgot Julie. Nor Alexander Humphreys' gift to him of three thousand dollars to tide him though Hamilton. Nor the charge that if he could, Woollcott might pass the money on to a similarly distressed student. Over and over during the years of his life, Aleck quietly financed people through prep schools and colleges.

At first he promised himself to pay for *two* young men and *two* young women through their undergraduate days. But then, having accomplished this, he expanded his generosity. To make a public display of what he had done was unthinkable to Aleck. His giving was hidden, always silent. Other good deeds were handled in similar fashion: softly, discreetly. How would it look to have the deadliest viper in Manhattan turn out to be an overweight, myopic lemon soufflé?

Not wishing to enter into an empty marriage and unable to

have children of his own, Woollcott decided to have two families, one he inherited from the blood of the Bucklins and the Woollcotts, and the other of his own choosing. His friends could be counted in the hundreds, his intimates by the score, but his second family was smaller. It consisted of three men, the oldest of whom was Jo Hennessey, whose influence on Aleck was continuous and ever increasing in importance. The second was Frode Jensen and the third was Richard Carver Wood.

Frode Jensen was a Danish boy with a traditionally stern stepfather. After a rather severe cuffing, Frode ran away to sea at the age of thirteen. After crossing the Atlantic eighteen times as a cabin boy, he decided to continue his education in America. He finished high school and went to Hamilton College, where he lived in the belfrey of the chapel, riding the rope that rang the bell to awaken the students and to summon them to class, to chapel, and to bed. In the days when football was a sport and not a business, Frode Jensen, though of medium height and in the welterweight class, was elected captain of Hamilton's football team.

He had the classic Scandinavian features: blond hair and blue eyes. He also had an engaging smile, an optimistic personality, and boundless energy.

Woollcott met him in 1933 and gave him the "Call me when you're in New York" invitation that he offered so many Hamilton men. When Jensen neglected to do so, Woollcott thought little more about him.

In the spring of 1934, Aleck entered Columbia-Presbyterian Medical Center for a two-week stay to take off weight. While he was there he learned about Frode Jensen, a student in the Columbia Medical School who had been graduated from Hamilton.

Woollcott was then a member of the board of trustees of his Alma Mater, and almost every alumnus could claim his attention. Gossip and small talk, which are almost as essential to hospitals as medicine, had it that a Hamilton graduate was working his way through the College of Physicians and Surgeons. He ran the elevator, he made change at the cash register in the cafeteria, and he translated medical documents from the Scandinavian into English. He also coached baseball, football, and basketball at a local prep school.

"How long do you think he'll last on a schedule like that?" Aleck asked a few of the interns.

"Oh, he'll be quietly dropped at the end of the year," came the response.

Lying in bed, staring up at the ceiling, Woollcott decided that he would begin to repay Alexander Humphreys in his own coin. He summoned Frode Jensen to his bedside, not once but several times. Eventually, Jensen appeared.

"He was in a room in the Harkness Pavilion," Jensen remembered. "It was so cluttered with flowers and books and cards and candy that it looked like he'd lived there for twenty years. Stacks of first editions of *While Rome Burns,* which had just come out, were waiting for their author to autograph them. It was late afternoon, just before they served dinner. Woollcott was asleep, lying on his back, looking like a great beached whale. His glasses were on the side table. I coughed discreetly and Aleck stirred.

" 'Who's there?' he called as he awakened. He began frantically searching the side table with both his hands. I realized then that without those thick tortoiseshell glasses he was almost blind. A nurse came into the room with a tray and I took the opportunity to withdraw without speaking to him.

"He sent me notes and messages through members of the staff to contact him. Finally he got me on the telephone in my room."

"This is Woollcott," he said.

"Yes?" Jensen replied.

"You don't answer letters, you have no courtesy in your bones. Now, damn it, I'm leaving this hospital and I want to see you next Sunday morning at my apartment or else!"

Jensen went to Wit's End.

"It was one of those Sunday breakfasts that Aleck was noted

for. If my memory serves me right, when I walked into his large living room Woollcott was at the opposite side from the door, stretched out on a couch in his pajamas and robe. Seated about were Alice Duer Miller and Helen Hayes and a number of theatrical and literary celebrities.

"I walked across the room very quickly and put my hand out."

"Young man," Aleck shouted up at him, "how dare you cross this room without first meeting the people in here? Now you go right back to that door and start over again."

Jensen would have gladly disappeared if he could. Woollcott had him enter again and then introduced him to every person in the room. Finally, the young medical student stood in front of Aleck.

"Junior," Woollcott told his valet, "give this fellow something to eat. He doesn't get very much where he's at."

After the other guests had left, Woollcott took Jensen on a ride through New York. The car, driven by a chauffeur, first went through Central Park, then over the Brooklyn Bridge to Billy the Oysterman's, where the two men repaired for drinks and dinner. Aleck told Frode his life story. Frode was telling his own tale to Aleck when suddenly Woollcott interrupted him.

"How would you like to give up all of those jobs?"

"How would I get through P. and S.?" Jensen countered.

"Someone once paid for my way through school. Suppose I pay for yours?" Aleck asked.

"Why would you do a thing like that?"

"Because I feel I owe it and I want to make good on that debt," Woollcott replied.

"But what would you expect of me?" Jensen inquired.

"Not a single thing" was the answer. "Just that you study medicine full time and become a good doctor."

"Can't I even run the elevator?"

"You can't even run the water for my bath. From now on, it's *Gray's Anatomy* and nothing else!"

Although somewhat startled by the older man's generosity, Jensen agreed. In time Dr. Jensen became a first-rate diagnostician. He also became Woollcott's personal physician, and, like so many of Woollcott's companions, named his children after Aleck.

Woollcott considered him the son he never had. There was even some discussion that Aleck would adopt him legally. But legal steps were not necessary. Frode Jensen took his place beside Jo Hennessey as Aleck's nearest and dearest friend.

"He was the best investment I ever made," Aleck said.

Richard Carver Wood was another Hamilton man. He had studied and trained to become an architect just at the time when the New York Stock Exchange plummeted into the Depression. People were more concerned with meeting mortgage payments than paying for the construction of country houses. Instead of joining the breadlines, Wood turned to the camera with striking results. A series of his photographs was exhibited at Hamilton during Graduation Week of 1935. Woollcott saw them, approached the young man who took them, and casually suggested that he pay a visit to Wit's End when he came to New York.

Wood did as he was bidden. Instead of being met by the acrimonious bear he had been told about, he was greeted by an amiable, kindhearted Humpty-Dumpty who seemed extremely enthusiastic about Wood's future as a photographer. To Woollcott's home, to his radio studio, to Bomoseen, to Genesee Depot, Wisconsin, where the Lunts lived, to many of the cities and towns where Woollcott lectured went Wood and Wood's camera. With enormous effectiveness he photographed Irene Castle, George Abbott, Noel Coward, Howard Dietz, Katharine Cornell, the Kaufmans, Moss Hart, Laurence Olivier, Vivien Leigh, Ruth Gordon, Harpo Marx—the entire file of faces in the Woollcott parade.

Because Wood knew how to operate a camera, Woollcott assumed anyone that mechanically minded would know how to operate an automobile. Naturally he was correct, and when Jo Hennessey was unable to drive Aleck to a lecture date or a vacation in Florida, Wood became Woollcott's chauffeur.

As official court photographer to Alexander Woollcott, Richard Carver Wood rode out the Depression quite nicely. Woollcott ordered thousands of photographs from him and sent them to acquaintances or correspondents. The contacts Wood made through Aleck proved invaluable. Through his association with Woollcott, Wood made a motion picture about Helen Keller with Katharine Cornell and Nancy Hamilton. It was called *The Unconquered* and in 1955 it won the Academy Award for the Best Documentary of the year.

Following Julie's death, Aleck's closest association with his family came through his brother Billy. His contact with Billy was a lifelong matter. Although there were personality differences between the two, they shared many similar traits.

Seven years older than Aleck, Billy was taller and stronger. Both men possessed a sharp wit, but Billy was warmer and less caustic. H. L. Mencken and Billy Woollcott both made their homes in Baltimore. They belonged to the same club. Mencken claimed that he was often ready to "butcher" Aleck, but when Aleck paid tribute to him on the air Mencken became enchanted with the Town Crier.

While visiting the Baltimore Woollcotts one year, Aleck was told of a remarkable spiritualist who had captivated the local populace by communicating ever so clearly with those dear departed who had passed over and were waiting on the other side. Woollcott refused to believe any of these fanciful stories, let alone attend one of the séances, but when he learned that the medium was in nightly contact with a long-departed Broadway character actress his interest perked up.

"Take me to this person," he commanded. "We'll see rather quickly how accurate she is."

The next evening the lights were darkened in the spiritualist's parlor. Those in attendance formed a circle by holding hands and Madame went into her trance. In a short time she announced she was in touch with the spirit of the old actress. Did anyone in the room wish to ask a question?

"Are you happy?" a voice from the circle inquired.

"Very happy," came back the message through the medium. "She wants all of us to know she is surrounded with friends and sleeps each night on a bed of flowers. Any other questions?"

"Ask her who was the author of her biggest hit," Aleck suggested.

"A man here wants to know the author of your most successful play," the spiritualist murmured.

A lengthy pause ensued.

"Unfortunately, it's been so long ago," Madame said as she transmitted the message, "that she is unable to recall."

"Fraud!" Woollcott cried out as he stood up. "Fake! An actress never lived who didn't remember the name of the playwright who wrote her biggest hit! I'm leaving!"

Touring stars of the New York stage were under strict orders from Aleck that when they played Baltimore they had to visit his brother Billy, his wife, and his four nieces, Nancy, Joan, Barbara, and Polly.

As usual, the actors did what the critic suggested. Leslie Howard called, was invited to dinner, and afterward, during the cordials, did Joan's arithmetic homework. Among the other stars to visit the Baltimore Woollcotts were Ethel Barrymore, Madge Kennedy, Harpo Marx, and the Lunts.

At Christmastime Aleck sent hampers of *pâté de foie gras*, brandied peaches, and imported cheeses to his nieces. "Baskets to the poor," the girls dubbed them, although their father surely was not impoverished. William Woollcott had become foreman of a factory that manufactured what Joan persisted in referring to as "mucilage," but which the other girls knew to be glue.

Uncle Aleck lent his name to an advertisement endorsing Chrysler automobiles. His nieces promptly clipped the ad, stuck it to a piece of paper, put lace hearts and Cupids around it, and wrote out a verse:

Buy stocks on margin if you must
But don't trail the family name in dust.

Sometime later Aleck wrote Billy and casually inquired if his older brother knew which one of his nieces had sent him that "charming valentine" and if she could be named he "would gladly break her goddam neck for her."

Gifts from grumpy Uncle Aleck ranged from books to pocketbooks, often with twenty-dollar bills inside the change purses. Then came the time when his nieces were old enough to travel to New York. The girls came in pairs, Nancy and Joan making up the older set, Barbara and Polly comprising the younger group.

The older twosome made the journey first. They would always be met at Pennsylvania Station by Ruth Gordon or Beatrice Kaufman or Lilly Bonner or another of Uncle Aleck's female friends. They would stay at Uncle Aleck's New York apartment, squeeze in as many plays as time would allow, be ushered backstage by their uncle to meet the more outstanding players, and consume enormous luncheons and dinners. To cap it all, a shopping spree was always planned for the girls at Saks Fifth Avenue or Lord & Taylor. They could have anything they wanted—compliments of Uncle Aleck.

Lugging the loot piled high in their arms, they would be seen safely aboard the train back to Baltimore. All four girls considered these visits to New York "as a marvelous sort of orgy."

The magic of these trips that appeared so casual was in fact planned with the greatest care by Aleck. One of his favorite public attitudes was his supposed hatred of children. This was all a pretense. He was fond of many of his friends' children and particularly showed great love for his brother's daughters. When it was time for the younger pair to come to New York, he even included one of them in his jokes.

"This is my niece Polly who plans to be a prostitute," he said to his assembled friends at Wit's End. Polly had just turned fifteen and was disconcerted by the laughter brought on by her introduction.

As the girls grew older, their uncle was able to do more for them. He put them through college, wrote letters, made phone calls, and badgered friends into giving them jobs on newspapers or auditions for plays in the theater. He was pleased when they married and he beamed proudly at the arrival of their children.

The nieces' feeling for Aleck was best summed up in a dinner conversation involving Mr. and Mrs. Irving Berlin, Woollcott, and Polly.

"What do you think of your uncle?" the composer asked the youngest Woollcott niece.

"I'm not sure," Polly answered after a moment's reflection. "There is one thing, though. He's Christ Almighty magnificent."

Recalling the incident, Woollcott said, "I have reached the age where I enjoy these restrained tributes."

16 We Are Happy to Welcome a Man Who

*H*AVING MADE HIS NAME AND VOICE RENOWNED throughout the land, Alexander Woollcott chose to make his person familiar to his fellow Americans. Although he had been speaking publicly since 1921, when Hamilton College invited him to lead off the Myers (for Bristol-Myers) Lectures, the small honorarium hardly paid the price of transportation. Now that he had become a nationally known radio star, Aleck decided that no longer would he speak for a pittance. Cross-country lecture tours would be booked, and Woollcott the Great would speak before audiences that could afford to hear him.

Accompanying him generally were either his secretary, Leggett Brown, or his general manager and friend, Jo Hennessey. Now and then a valet would be added, and more frequently one or two of his dogs.

Although the airplane had come a long way from Kitty Hawk, most travelers in the early and mid-Thirties went by train. The Pennsylvania. The New York Central. The Chicago & Northwestern. The Santa Fe. The Union Pacific. The Southern Pacific. The Great Northern. Names that are remembered mostly in folk songs today were then railways with engines and coal and mail

219

cars, conductors, brakemen, baggage handlers called redcaps, porters called George, roadbeds, ties, tracks, rights-of-way, bridges, signals, water towers, the works! People moved from one coast to another in something like five days and five nights of constant traveling.

In the Thirties, when Woollcott lectured to America, Pullman cars were still citadels of luxury, ranging from upper and lower berths to compartments and drawing rooms. Aleck preferred the latter. Almost all passenger trains carried dining cars where white linen, heavy silver, bud vases, perfect service, and delicious food abounded.

It was, to be sure, a distinct contrast to the style in which he had traveled from Hamilton to New York in 1909. Drawing rooms pleased Aleck's patrician tastes. He would waddle down the aisles of Pullman cars, squeeze between the tables of the diner, and consume meals that made chefs beam and waiters roll their eyes. Then back to the privacy of his drawing room, where he would answer mail sacks full of letters and dictate and correct material for his next broadcast or future books.

The sound of his own voice always had a soothing effect on Aleck, and at $750 a lecture the result was positively glorious. He loved to speak and not be interrupted. He loved even more to speak and be applauded.

The early lectures he delivered at Hamilton, Columbia University, and the Bread Loaf Writers' Conference at Middlebury, Vermont, dealt with journalism or past luminaries of the English-speaking theater. As soon as he tried them out on the lecture circuit he knew he had to be more selective. Alexander Woollcott, who had been so strict a critic of others, decided to apply the same criteria to himself.

What the ticket buyers wished to see was the Town Crier in person. What they wished to hear were his thoughts and opinions salted with his reminiscences and a possible whiff of gossip. As a platform performer Woollcott proved to be a wizard.

He would stand in the wings as eager as a thoroughbred race-horse awaiting the signal to run. He wasn't nervous but he felt restrained until his introductions were over. Then he would dash to the lectern, smile beatifically, and proceed to enchant, entice, or, if need be, startle the bloomers off his audience.

"All of the things I like to do," he would frequently say, "are either illegal, immoral, or fattening."

The titters and the giggles demonstrated at the outset that he had captured his listeners' attention and affection completely.

From there on, using no visible notes, he spoke for whatever time was allotted him on whatever subjects came to his mind.

Generally, the forty-five minutes plus fifteen minutes of questions were given over to talk of books, movies, plays, and the people who wrote or appeared in them.

A delicious lecture-platform story dealt with Aleck's close friend, the actor Alfred Lunt, who was appearing in the new Robert E. Sherwood comedy *Reunion in Vienna*.

"At one point when Helen Westley faced upstage and her behind was aimed toward the footlights," Aleck would say, "Mr. Lunt was to lift her skirt to see if she was still wearing her old red flannel drawers.

"I know you're ahead of me," Aleck always told his audiences, "because sure enough, there was that one night when Miss Westley forgot to put on her red flannel drawers. Lunt raised her skirt and heard the patrons of the theater gasp.

"He pulled down her skirt and managed to deliver his next line which read, 'Well, thank God, there is one thing in Vienna that hasn't changed!'"

Another opening line at Woollcott lectures concerned the marriage in London of Lord Reading to a woman some forty years younger than himself.

"The London *Times* account of the wedding was most unfortunate," Aleck said. "It ended with the following sentence: 'The bridegroom's gift to the bride was an antique pendant.'"

Katharine White, his editor at *The New Yorker*, constantly cut such stories from Aleck's column, "Shouts and Murmurs." When she wasn't about to do it, Wolcott Gibbs did. The commercial editors on radio also blue-penciled these mildly prurient tales. On the lecture platform, however, Aleck felt free to indulge himself. The result was immediate. His price went to $1,500 per talk plus traveling expenses.

Mrs. White sometimes became difficult for Aleck to take because she edited his column, and he didn't like to have anyone messing about in his prose. The two remained friends, however, and were friends at the time of his death. When Aleck returned to Manhattan from the road, he sometimes gave huge "Welcome to New York" cocktail parties for himself. E. B. White, who wrote the "Notes and Comment" page for *The New Yorker*, once attended one of these affairs. After a single drink White, who genuinely hated large social gatherings, fled out the back door. From then on he graciously refused invitations to Woollcott's soirées.

One day while Mrs. White and Aleck were going over proof, Woollcott asked irritably, "What's the matter with your husband? Has he taken the veil?"

When Woollcott left Wit's End, he took up residence at 10 Gracie Square. Close by lived Cornelia Otis Skinner.

By now the actress-author was the properly married Mrs. Alden Blodgett. As socially accepted as she was professionally acclaimed, Mrs. Blodgett had joined the exclusive Colony Club in New York City at the urging of her husband. Shortly after she became a member, the program committee urged her to write a note to that darling Mr. Woollcott and ask him if he would address the ladies of the Colony Club on such-and-such a date. Hoping to please her fashionable club members, Miss Skinner whipped off an appropriate note to Woollcott. He hurled back his reply in the very next mail.

"Dear Cornelia," he wrote, and the paper almost crackled, "You can tell the ladies of your club that my price for attending anything as repulsive as what you're asking me to do would be $5,000 with a certified check in advance."

The certified check phrase may have read as a joke. The truth is that Woollcott's fame as a lecturer grew so rapidly and so impressively that he made it a point not to step before an audience until a guaranteed check had been placed in the hands of Jo Hennessey.

Evidently, the right check had been placed in the right hands when Kathleen Norris, the novelist and sometimes-on, sometimes-off friend of his, rose in the Opera House in San Francisco to introduce Aleck. Instead of the usual long and flowery tribute to him, Mrs. Norris spoke of the day when a niece told her that Charlotte was coming to the house to play. "And who is Charlotte, dear?" Mrs. Norris asked. "Oh," her niece answered dreamily, "she's that friend that I hate."

No angry rejoinder came from Aleck. Instead he complimented her on the story and launched into his lecture.

Luncheons and dinner parties are as much a part of the lecture circuit as the speaker's fees. Woollcott pretended to abhor such functions. Actually, he enjoyed the company of women and delighted in eating, but every now and again he reared back and feigned horror, disdain, or disgust at such gatherings.

He pouted, snorted, insulted people, or plunged into periods of sulking silence, so that the ladies at the next twenty-five stops would feel flattered if Alexander Woollcott had three orders of the main course and a double helping of dessert. It appeared to them that they had been singled out and favored while women all over America had been scorned and disgraced.

"I only pose in public," Woollcott lied to Dan Golenpaul, the radio producer.

When he went to Kansas City he never missed looking up his first-grade teacher, Miss Sophie Rosenberger, with whom he kept up a lifelong correspondence.

In Cincinnati he stayed with Dr. Gustav Eckstein, an M.D. whose abiding interest in canaries and other creatures made him into one of the nation's prime naturalists.

When he spoke in Indianapolis he made it a point to call up the author Booth Tarkington.

Visits weren't always arranged far in advance. Once, just before he stepped out onto the podium in San Diego, he received a note from a woman who had appeared with him in the Shakespearean play when he was four years old. Quickly he scribbled an answer to her. "I won't forgive you if you don't have your wheelchair brought around to the stage door after my gibberish is completed."

Very often he planned his lecture dates the way a chess master plans his moves on the board.

"Keep me off the road at Thanksgiving," Aleck used to instruct his manager. "I always have the Harrimans to dinner at their little place in the country."

Arden House is the ninety-six-room country residence erected by the railroad magnate Edward Henry Harriman. The house is located on top of Mount Orana on the more than seven thousand acres that comprise Harriman, New York. The estate always seemed too large to Edward's son, W. Averell Harriman, chairman of the board of the Union Pacific Railway and later governor of New York and ambassador to the Soviet Union and Great Britain.

Averell Harriman closed off most of the house and lived with his family in the smaller East Wing. Woollcott, invited to Arden House one weekend in the Thirties, envisioned the entire residence filled with his friends on the Thanksgiving weekend. Enlisting the aid of Marie Harriman, Averell's wife, Aleck pored over lists of guests to be invited.

At least forty bedrooms were available each year, and until the war began in Europe, Marie Harriman and Alexander Woollcott labored diligently to select occupants for those rooms: Helen Hayes and Charlie MacArthur, Ben and Rose Hecht, George and Beatrice Kaufman, Bennett and Phyllis Cerf, Robert and Madeline

Sherwood, Marc Connelly, the Harold Rosses, the Herbert Bayard Swopes, the Heywood Brouns, Ralph and Peggy Pulitzer, Oscar Levant—all these and many more attended the Thanksgiving weekend at Arden House.

Viewing the magnificence of the house and the distinguished guest list, a wag suggested, "What a play this would make."

"Yes," George Kaufman spoke up. "The appropriate title would be *The Upper Depths.*"

The marble-floored music room, cleared of all pianos, harps, and benches, became a badminton court. Croquet was played on one or two of the several thousand acres. What annoyed Aleck, Governor Harriman recollected, was the bowling alley.

Following dinner each evening, a large group of guests adjourned to the room that held the hardwood and the tenpins, and the thunder of bowling balls went on for two hours or more.

"Not only did the sound bother him," Governor Harriman said, "but Aleck was a hearts player, and seven is the precise number of players to make up an ideal hearts game. Very often only Aleck and George Kaufman remained at the hearts table. The others had gone into the bowling alley."

One evening, as Woollcott and Kaufman approached their gaming area, they noticed that a vase of autumn blossoms had been moved from a sideboard to the center of the card table.

"It's hearts-and-flowers time for you, Aleck," Kaufman commented.

"Watch out for the arrows, George," Woollcott answered. "Robin Hood and his band still roam the wing you're quartered in."

Aleck planned a pre-Christmas stopover at the Harrimans' Sun Valley ski lodge. While watching the skiers leap and tumble on the hardened snow, twisting ankles and breaking legs as they fell, Aleck reached into a pocket and withdrew one of the many notebooks he had carried with him since he was a reporter.

Averell Harriman's daughter Kathleen Harriman Mortimer

watched with fascination as Woollcott wrote a note and read it aloud:

"Remind self never to go skiing."

En route to lecture in St. Louis, Woollcott received a letter from an old friend who insisted that he meet her elderly aunt in the city in which he was to speak. "A dear, delightful lady who is an admirer of your writing," the letter read.

Aleck, tired from the strain of overnight sleeper jumps, hissed back an answer as soon as he arrived in St. Louis.

"I already know too many people," he wrote in reply.

Lines such as that caused James Thurber to measure him correctly when he called Woollcott "Old Vitriol and Violets."

While Woollcott had been a highly respected journalist during his days at the city desk of *The New York Times,* he never became a really great reporter. That was because of a slight failing in his nature. It can be summed up in a single word that his successor as the *Times* drama critic Brooks Atkinson kept pasted on the wall over his typewriter. The word was ACCURASY.

Woollcott's tendency to bend the facts of a story rather than stick to the truth caused Carr Van Anda more distress than satisfaction. Still, that very quality made him into a great lecturer.

There was a story that he relished telling on the circuit. A stage-hand, smitten by the lure of the greasepaint, constantly muttered how good he would be on the boards if only he had the chance to step out of the wings and appear before the audience. He would not, he continually told everyone who would listen, throw away his lines and mumble. No, given the opportunity, he would speak clearly so that everyone in the theater would hear the words of the playwright.

Then that evening arrived when one of the bit players failed to appear at the theater. The manager of the stock company, who doubled as the director, looked about for someone to play the part of a page in Shakespeare's *King John.* The eager face, the pleading eyes of the stagehand struck him. More importantly, he saw something else.

"You," he said to the stagehand, "you'll fit into the costume just fine."

The chosen one was properly grateful.

"But what are my lines?" he persisted. "What do I say?"

The manager-director glanced at the text. Shakespeare had written no lines for the page, but Shakespeare was dead; and in the manner of so many directors of repertory, the manager improvised.

And for that performance only, the audience heard, very clearly, the page proclaim, "Here comes Philip the Bastard!"

While some of the ladies blushed and some laughed, Woollcott would invariably stare at the ceiling for a few seconds, take a sip of water, and murmur almost to himself, "I'll have to admit, it *is* a most difficult line to deliver."

Between lecture dates in the mid-Thirties Woollcott returned to New York to see new shows and old friends. His radio producer's sister, who had played the role of Huey Long's daughter to rave notices in Bomoseen, came up with a fresh challenge to Aleck's assorted talents. Shortly after she turned eighteen, Pratt Williams had married a naval flier. Before she was nineteen, her husband was killed in a crash. Pratt went into mourning.

Aleck did not approve of widow's weeds. "Grief is private," he was quick to tell her. "Why advertise it?" After a year of widowhood Pratt decided to shed her black raiment in favor of what she claimed was one of the first short evening dresses ever shown in New York. It was of midcalf length, hand-painted, and made in France. Pratt was so pleased she telephoned Woollcott.

"Aleck, I'm going to a party and I'm not wearing mourning anymore," she said excitedly. "I want you to see my dress."

"Okay, toots," he yawned, "come up and I'll take a look at it."

Pratt raced to 10 Gracie Square to find Woollcott and Noel Coward deep in both conversation and a bottle of gin.

"In I came, pirouetting," Pratt recalled. "Never did an entrance lay such an egg. They both looked at me and shook their heads."

"That's the worst-looking frock I've ever seen," Noel Coward pronounced.

"You can't wear it, toots," Woollcott added. "What you need is someone to design your clothes."

Crestfallen but still endowed with the audacity of the young, the widow answered, "Okay, buster, see you at Bergdorf's tomorrow—in the custom department, not the ready-mades."

"I'll be there," Aleck snorted. And he was. This was not his first try at dress designing. In 1932, he had created an entire collection and shown it, utilizing as models the famous women who were close to him. There had been a four-page program with words of introduction by M. Alexandre and each ensemble was named by him with bland jokes in French and English. "The high bustline has entirely disappeared, the left hip is lower, and by a clever use of rubber, the waistline enters a happy compromise between Victoria and Ming," wrote Woollcott in the brief introduction. A few of his creations were named *"Pour le Brothel,"* *"Mlle. Est Enceinte,"* and "Let Us Lie Down." His first and only fashion show had been considered a great success.

The next day at the appointed hour, Aleck marched into Bergdorf's. Pratt arrived and Woollcott, quite professionally, began to examine the fabrics. At that point Emmy Ives entered. Emmy, with her husband, Raymond, had been one of the founders of the Neshobe Club on Lake Bomoseen. She was also the editor of *Vogue.* Sensing a story for her magazine, Mrs. Ives promised to pay for the material and labor if *Vogue* could have an exclusive.

Aleck agreed. He worked rapidly and, Pratt remembered, with much enthusiasm and great personal satisfaction. He liked the feel of the materials and the lines of the gown itself.

"There!" he exclaimed when it was completed. "Pity I don't have the figure to wear it."

That he had designed a dress worthy of attention was seen in the two-page layout in America's foremost fashion monthly.

It took Aleck just a few days to display his creativity in *haute couture* and then it was time to get out of New York and back onto the lecture platform.

Francis Robinson, now a high official with the Metropolitan Opera Company of New York, booked Woollcott's first transcontinental tour.

"He was fascinating," Mr. Robinson said. "Woollcott was a one-man show. He had a handful of set lectures—'The Confessions of a Dying Newspaperman,' 'The Stream of Folklore,' or 'Opening Nights in the Theater'—and he could and did throw anything he wanted into these talks. He gave a sensational performance, this pudgy, not-too-attractive character. He had them spellbound. He had them laughing. He had them on the verge of tears. And he took to it all like a cat to cream."

Sellout audiences were often treated to Woollcott on the topic of theatrical premieres. He had written an article for *Collier's* magazine in 1929 on that subject and made constant use of it while lecturing.

"The cry of 'Author, author' is almost invariably heard somewhere in the tumult of the first performance," Aleck would say. "If the first-nighters like the play he has written, they have a good-humored impulse to tell him so. If they don't like it, they have a morbid curiosity to see what manner of creature could ever have written it.

"George Bernard Shaw, making a curtain speech, was interrupted by a bellicose voice from the gallery.

" 'Shut up, Shaw. Your play is rotten!'

" 'You and I know that,' " Woollcott claimed Shaw replied, " 'but who are we among so many?' "

He retold the story of the slim, lovely actress Hope Williams on an opening night. Before making her first entrance, Miss Williams balked.

"I'm paralyzed with nervousness," she confided to her manager.

"Nonsense," he answered. "You're not nervous at all. You can walk, can't you? Why, we had to *carry* Nazimova from her dressing room to the wings."

For a moment this seemed to reassure her, but suddenly a new fear clutched at her heart.

"Perhaps," she said, "I'm not nervous enough."

Separated by an ocean and a six-hour time difference, an English playwright paced anxiously in his London club while his play opened in New York. Unable to stand the tension any longer, he sent a cable to his American producer.

"How is it going?" the cablegram read.

Charles Frohman, the producer, walked a block up Broadway, turned in at the telegraph office there, and, while the third act was still faltering dismally to its close, dispatched the following succinct reply.

"It's gone."

Although he spoke with as much ease before men's audiences, providing the fee was the same, Woollcott had a double standard when it came to young people. Colleges and universities were special areas where the price of a Woollcott lecture was drastically reduced or waived completely.

He addressed the Nieman Fellows in journalism at Harvard. He gave a literature course for a time at the New School for Social Research in New York City. His fees were always negligible. After his talks he enjoyed sitting with the collegiate audience and listening to their views on a variety of subjects. To those who thought him irascible, Aleck was indeed a paradox, for as he grew older he became gentler and more tolerant of the undergraduates.

The private Aleck did not object to his close friends' having knowledge of his earlier escapades. Publicly, he would not permit discussion of them. It was a highly intolerant Woollcott that the students of the State College for Teachers in Albany, New York, saw when the man introducing Woollcott began describing Aleck's fondness for playing feminine leads in his college days.

With his eyes glaring and his face turning ever-increasing shades of red, Woollcott rushed forward and interrupted the speaker.

"Look at me, boys and girls," he bristled, "half god, half woman!"

He poured himself a glass of water from the pitcher. The cold water cooled his temper, and he launched into his lecture.

"I have been asked here to discuss the high state of present-day journalism," he began. "I must tell you that it recalls to mind George Ade's line about the man who was kicked in the head by a mule and thereafter believed everything he read in the papers."

Loneliness is the lot of the itinerant salesman, preacher, and lecturer. He may be surrounded by hundreds of people during the day, but at night those people go back to their homes and the wanderer is generally left alone in an unfamiliar hotel and city.

When Hennessey could not accompany Woollcott or when Richard Carver Wood was unable to drive the car and snap pictures, Aleck felt the loneliness acutely. Flicking on the light switch in a darkened hotel room and finding no one there often proved unbearable to Woollcott.

Fortunately for him, it was at this period in his life that he met a remarkably beautiful and completely fascinating woman. Her name was Eleanora von Mendelsohn.

Woollcott always lived in a world overpopulated with women. He enjoyed talking about their work and their clothes, listening to their gossip and contributing to it; he liked nothing better than to discuss the plays in which they were appearing, the servants they hired or fired. Above all, he did not have to compete with them as women or with their husbands or lovers as a male figure. Women knew they had nothing to fear from Woollcott except an occasional remark.

His coterie of female friends included Beatrice Kaufman, Ruth Gordon, Helen Hayes, Neysa McMein, Lynn Fontanne, Katharine Cornell, Lilly Bonner, Gertrude Lawrence, and Beatrice Lillie, but Eleanora was something different.

Born in Germany, the daughter of one of the great banking

families of Berlin, Eleanora had her own castle, four husbands, and regiments of lovers. Kissed by Caruso at the age of fourteen, Eleanora fainted dead away. Her preference for men of talent continued throughout her life. People said that Jean Gabin, the French movie idol, had been one of her lovers. Her affair with the Italian maestro Arturo Toscanini lasted twenty years. In pre-Hitler Germany she had sold her emeralds to finance Max Reinhardt's earliest theatrical productions. With the rise of Hitler, Eleanora, who was one-fourth Jewish, fled her homeland for America. Before the war began she returned to her *Schloss* to get Reinhardt out of the Reich. To her dismay she found the castle occupied by the Gestapo. Secreting herself on the grounds, she managed to make arrangements for Reinhardt's escape as well as her own. She succeeded in both.

To women she was a mystery. To men she was a magnifying glass. "She made everybody, no matter how great, feel greater," Leo Lerman, the writer and editor, said. "She made you feel larger than life."

She had met Aleck in Europe. In New York their friendship deepened.

Both were long-range talkers. Mercifully, both were also first-rate listeners. Woollcott gave her a select education in the history of America. She gave Aleck a history of her affairs. Aleck reveled in them. He could never hear enough.

He invited her to Bomoseen to meet his friends. He sent for her when he felt lonely on the lecture circuit.

She would be among the chosen few to sit in the client's booth at Aleck's radio programs and blow kisses to him through three thicknesses of glass. She would sit in the audiences at lecture after lecture and laugh at the same stories.

Eleanora often invited Woollcott to Toscanini's concerts at NBC. Generally, he went to 8H, the huge studio from which the maestro broadcast. He would arrive early enough to be seated in the reserved section. Once he was late. Arriving at NBC with his new press agent, a young man just out of college named Irving Mansfield, later to become known as a television and film producer,

Aleck found the elevator area thronged with people waiting behind the velour restraining ropes. All held general-admission tickets for the concert.

"There's another way, Mr. Woollcott," Mansfield suggested.
"The back elevator."

"By all means," Aleck responded and waved his hand for Mansfield to lead the way.

Over the doorway to the back elevator the sign read: "NBC
ORCHESTRA ONLY."

Mansfield rang the bell.

As the elevator door opened, Woollcott started to enter, only
to be stopped by the operator wearing the deep blue of NBC.

"I'm sorry, sir," the man in uniform said, "this car is for musicians."

"That's perfectly all right," Aleck answered as he and Mansfield
stepped in. "I have my organ with me."

Mansfield remembered the puzzled look on the elevator operator's face as he obediently closed the door and whisked them up
to the eighth floor.

Eleanora knew all about Aleck. She understood his weaknesses,
she forgave his petty cruelties, and she appreciated his finer points.

"He is on my genius list," she told her close friend Leo Lerman.

"Have you gone to bed with him, too?" Lerman asked. She
laughed a light, frothy laugh.

"Oh, darling," she said.

Lecturing across the face of America provided Woollcott with
more than money, continued fame, the opportunity to travel, and
the heady sound of applause. It was while he was lecturing that
Aleck developed his own public character. Long before George S.
Kaufman and Moss Hart wrote their last smash hit, which was in
fact a theatrical biography of Woollcott, Aleck played the eccentric
throughout the country.

In Shreveport, Louisiana, a lady recollects that Woollcott stayed in her home as a guest, that he allowed his two poodles to race through the cotton fields each morning, and that each afternoon the cream of Shreveport society gathered in her home to pick the cotton burrs off the fluffy hides of the two animals.

In Dallas, Texas, a hostess remembers that when Woollcott came to lecture he not only fired her cook, but had her telephone number changed so that he could make long-distance calls without being interrupted by her friends.

In Evanston, Illinois, Woollcott switched the date of the wedding of the daughter of the house so that it would be more convenient for him to attend the festivities.

The outrageous character Woollcott drew for himself did not appear on the New York stage for several seasons, but audiences throughout the country were savoring it for years before its Broadway debut. Woollcott himself enjoyed it. In fact, he took much pleasure in the entire experience of lecturing. He loved traveling around America almost as much as he loved America itself. New and smiling faces, always eager to hear his latest round of stories, pleased him nearly as much as the tedium of traveling wore him down.

In the end, the one-night stands, the cold creamed chicken, the hours of waiting for the train to take him to the next town exhausted Woollcott, and he began to realize that there were other ways of winning the applause he received at the end of his lectures. Speaking before audiences was a single step from performing. The lecture platform, he came to realize, was a barren stage swept clean but with no actors to support him, no scenery, and no costumes, and certainly no surefire laugh lines.

When he began to explore another way to gain acceptance, he gave serious consideration to combining the theater with the rostrum. Woollcott had always been part show-off. The time now arrived for him to put this trait to work as a talent.

17 Legitimate

AS FOR PERFORMING IN FRONT OF AN AUDIENCE, Aleck was very much like most people: he began at an early age and was really quite bad at it.

"I played Puck when I was four years old and everyone thought I was enchanting," Woollcott, the objective drama critic, said of himself. If his notices of the Kansas City debut are to be believed, Woollcott's portrayal of the mischievous, gossamer-winged sprite marked the high point in his acting career. Everything for the next fifty years went downhill.

Stuart Scheftel, a friend of Woollcott's, remembered the promising actor telling him that he appeared a few years later in another play. The stage directions called for him to blow a trumpet for ten or fifteen seconds. Rehearsals went brilliantly, and on opening night Woollcott entered on cue. Placing the trumpet to his lips, Aleck blew. Not a sound came forth. He tried a second time. Still no sound. To the uproar of the audience, Aleck made his way off-stage embarrassed and angry. He never played Kansas City again.

Of a single performance in Germantown there was not much one could say to recommend him to the casting agents of Broadway or the talent scouts who would be riding out of Hollywood.

At Hamilton his work as founder of the Charlatans secured him his choice of roles—always leading ladies. Those who saw him had a unanimous comment: he camped too much.

His Broadway debut was nothing short of a disaster. Appearing in an all-star benefit performance with Madge Kennedy in 1920, Woollcott played a scene from *Henry VIII*. In the audience were Helen Hayes, Mrs. Fiske, Lynn Fontanne, Alfred Lunt, and Irving Berlin. Upon Woollcott's exit the audience hissed and booed loudly.

As he fled into the wings, Aleck mumbled with mock seriousness, "I had no idea how unpopular Madge Kennedy was."

Undaunted by his reception, he made his next appearance in 1922 at the Forty-ninth Street Theatre. The vehicle was *No Siree!* "An Anonymous Entertainment by the Vicious Circle of the Hotel Algonquin." Woollcott, by reason of his power on the *Times*, received first billing, and appeared with no dire results in the opening chorus along with John Peter Toohey, George S. Kaufman, Marc Connelly, Robert Benchley, and Franklin P. Adams.

In a sketch called *The Greasy Hag*, a spoof of O'Neill's success about the waterfront prostitute, *Anna Christie*, Woollcott found his own level. He took the part of the Second Agitated Seaman, with Kaufman playing the First Agitated Seaman and Connelly portraying the Third Agitated Seaman.

Aleck also performed as a butler in another sketch, as a Precisionist in a third sketch, and participated in the finale.

Rather than review the presentation himself, Woollcott unwisely allowed the gifted actress Laurette Taylor to serve as the *Times* drama critic for one night.

"They all gathered to show how it should be done," Miss Taylor wrote, "and being a constructive critic I would advise a course of voice culture for Marc Connelly, a new vest and pants that meet for Heywood Broun, a course with Yvette Guilbert * for Alexander Woollcott, and I would advise them all to leave the stage before they take it up. A pen in their hands is mightier than God's most majestic words in their mouths."

Despite the devastating notice from the temporary *Times* person, the cast of *No Siree!* reveled in the fun they had had and

---

* A tall, red-haired French chanteuse whom Toulouse-Lautrec captured for posterity in many of his posters.

seven months later brought forth another revue called *The Forty-Niners*. Woollcott, who could not endure the rejection of a bad review, stayed out of *The Forty-Niners*.

For a while it seemed that Aleck's activities in the legitimate theater would be confined to that of a member of the audience. In 1929, the almost inevitable step took place. The next best thing to acting is playwrighting.

George S. Kaufman, the number-two man on the *Times* when Woollcott served as critic, had become the most consistent and successful collaborator in the American theater. Not only were Woollcott and Kaufman old friends, but Kaufman's wife, Beatrice, had become one of Woollcott's darlings. There was much talk, none of it hidden, of course, and none of it serious, that Woollcott should murder Kaufman and marry his widow. Instead of committing homicide, he collaborated with Kaufman on a flop.

The Channel Road was taken from a short story by Guy de Maupassant and turned into a play that very few critics and even fewer ticket buyers liked. It concerned itself with that traditional stock character, the whore with the heart of gold. In this version she had to deal with the Germans who were occupying France. Kaufman, who always sought perfection in his collaborators, still remembered that Woollcott had been his boss. What Woollcott wrote, Kaufman hesitated changing. The result, unfortunately, was that the play opened and closed at the Plymouth Theatre in New York in November.

"We got mixed notices," George Kaufman said in summing up the reaction. "They were good and rotten."

Woollcott wrote a profile of Kaufman for *The New Yorker* called "The Deep, Tangled Kaufman," a takeoff on the Kaufman-Connelly play *The Deep-Tangled Wildwood*. Kaufman was pleased by the profile and Woollcott was paid for it.

Born in Worcester, Massachusetts, Samuel Nathaniel Behrman first attended Clark University and then was graduated from Harvard University. He received a master's degree from Columbia

University. A writer of great polish and sophistication, Behrman devoted his professional life to comedies of elegance. Although he wrote some of Hollywood's most distinguished screenplays— *Queen Christina, Anna Karenina, Cavalcade,* and *Quo Vadis*—he was best known for his work in the New York theater. *The Second Man, Biography, Amphitryon 38, No Time for Comedy* are classics of American comedy in the Twenties, Thirties, and Forties. His published works included two biographies, *Duveen,* about the British art dealer, and *Portrait of Max,* a study of the English author and caricaturist Max Beerbohm. For these achievements he received an honorary doctorate from Clark and the Brandeis University Creative Arts Award.

Behrman, as all playwrights do, occasionally leapt from his pedestal and landed on his face. *Brief Moment* must be listed among his less fortunate attempts. A conversation on the problem of marriage, *Brief Moment* succeeded only in brevity. As though he had preordained it himself, Behrman brought on his own demise. His opening stage direction reads as follows:

"At rise: we discover Roderick Dean and his friend, Harold Sigrift, familiarly known as Sig. Sigrift is very fat; about thirty years old, he lies down whenever possible, spouting acrid remarks. He somewhat resembles Alexander Woollcott, who conceivably might play him."

Although in his splendid autobiography, *People in a Diary,* Behrman denies his intention to engage Woollcott for *Brief Moment,* his own stage direction says otherwise.

"I've got our Sig," producer-director Guthrie McClintic told Behrman over the phone.

"Oh, good," the playwright answered. He and McClintic had been discussing a well-known comedian to play the role. "You've signed him, have you? He'll be fine."

"Didn't give it to him," the producer-director said. "Woollcott's going to play it."

Behrman claimed he was sure McClintic had been drinking.

"You're not serious?"

"I certainly am. So is Woollcott."

Behrman considered Woollcott one of the busiest nonactors in the country. Writing "Shouts and Murmurs" for *The New Yorker* and emoting as the Town Crier, Woollcott had made himself into a national figure. Let Behrman illustrate:

"I had been, sometime before, in a hospital in Baltimore for a checkup. Woollcott was in Baltimore. He telephoned the hospital to tell them that he would be up to see me at three in the afternoon.

"About an hour after this portentous announcement, a nurse came in with a basket full of magnificent apples. I asked who on earth had sent them.

"'Mrs. Kimberly,' the nurse said.

"I said I knew no Mrs. Kimberly.

"'She told me she didn't know you, but that she heard that Mr. Woollcott is coming up to see you and she says that any friend of Alexander Woollcott can have all the apples she's got.'"

At the first rehearsal, Aleck, in wonderful spirits, took over. He congratulated McClintic on keeping up the appearance of "that vintage boyishness of yours." He made a dedicated effort to keep the star of the show, Francine Larrimore, as an equal. This gallantry did not endure for long.

Miss Larrimore, in her program biography, gave her birthplace as Verdun.

Aleck took to referring to her as "The Miracle of Verdun."

The cast of *Brief Moment* included Louis Calhern. Woollcott loved him from the moment he heard that Calhern had said after a failure, "Well, we got good notices, but word of mouth killed us."

Rehearsals went along smoothly until one afternoon when Miss Larrimore delivered a line as Behrman had written it. "Oh, Sig, Sig," she said to Woollcott, "if you were a woman, what a bitch you would have made!"

Aleck put his script down and looked Miss Larrimore right in the eye.

"Opening night in New York," he said knowingly, "you'll get a big hand for that."

The cast of a play that is going to fail in New York seems as psychic as a clairvoyant. The actors in *Brief Moment* sensed their fate during rehearsal. Despite it all, *Brief Moment* had its premiere in Cleveland in the spring of 1931.

"I went out to see the opening," Margalo Gillmore, the popular actress, recollected. "Woollcott didn't know how to put on makeup so I made him up. He took off his glasses and he wouldn't wear them onstage. The result was that his strong and dominating personality suffered completely. Instead, a miserable little fellow crept on the stage and couldn't see any of the people he was playing with. He lost all his confidence, all his bravado. I went backstage after it was over."

"How was I?" Woollcott inquired hopefully.

"Put on your glasses," Miss Gillmore told him firmly.

Thereafter, he did.

"He wasn't an actor," the highly professional Miss Gillmore commented. "He was an ego having a lovely time."

At a later performance Behrman entered Woollcott's dressing room and found him covered with galley sheets. Busy on the telephone with Robert Maynard Hutchins, president of the University of Chicago, Woollcott was trying desperately to persuade Hutchins to give up the job as president of that freshwater university and take over as president of that most prestigious eastern college, Hamilton.

When Woollcott finished his telephone call, Behrman remarked that he'd known few actors in his plays who spoke with such poise to university presidents.

"You're damn right," Woollcott retorted. "And you've had mighty few actors in your plays who correct *Atlantic Monthly* proofs with an eyebrow pencil!"

His devotion to Louis Calhern was strained when Woollcott decided to adopt the acting technique of the Lunts. During most of *Brief Moment* Woollcott lay on a couch and delivered his lines with elegance and grandeur. But after seeing a Sunday-night performance of *Reunion in Vienna,* in which the Lunts were starred, he suddenly decided to change his style.

"I see everything now," he told Calhern. "I've been working too hard. God, you ought to see the Lunts work. Never raise their voices. Just throw away their lines. They're marvelous."

After the next performance Calhern raged, "Goddam it, Aleck is throwing it away so much that I can't hear *my* cues. He just lies there and mutters!"

In his biography of the Lunts, Maurice Zolotow revealed what happened next. Behrman, Zolotow wrote, asked Woollcott if he had laryngitis. Oh, not at all, explained Aleck with an air of triumph. He now realized he had been overplaying his part, shouting his lines. He was speaking quietly on purpose. The experience of watching Lunt and Fontanne the previous night had enlightened him.

"Behrman diplomatically explained that the Lunts gave the illusion of underplaying," Zolotow wrote, "of speaking in conversational tones, but were really enunciating loudly and clearly and could be heard in the last row of the balcony, whereas Aleck had been inaudible at the previous performance. Woollcott at once ceased imitating the Lunts."

He laughed at himself when describing the episode to Katharine Cornell. "A sort of lunacy takes over theater people who are trying out a play on the road. I had as much chance of acting like the Lunts as I had of satisfying a nymphomaniac during a hot summer night."

Brief Moment managed to open in New York City, where the critics with few exceptions were hardly kind. Business at the Belasco box office sagged. The only reason the public had for buying tickets was to see Alexander Woollcott on the stage.

Unfortunately, Woollcott knew it. *The New York Times* sent the eighteen-year-old artist Irma Selz to sketch him for the Sunday drama section. He had expected at the very least Albert Hirschfeld. The sight of a young woman infuriated him.

"What the devil does *The New York Times* mean, sending a green kid over to sketch!" he told Miss Selz. "I've been sketched by the greatest artists in Europe. I've been caricatured by famous people."

There was nothing Irma Selz could say. To one of the foremost celebrities of that time she was new, and so while he thundered, she began to sketch away at her first assignment.

Woollcott walked about, flailing his arms in the air for so long that Miss Selz had time to do two drawings of him. One the Woollcott she had seen serenely reclining in the play, the other the much crueler Woollcott whom she visited that day.

The *Times* chose the serene sketch for the front page of the Sunday drama section, and despite all of his threats Aleck never called to complain.

What was the other sketch like? Miss Selz recalled: "He wore crumpled pajama bottoms and a great big dressing gown which sort of floated around him like a tent, and he loomed—quite vast and bulbous with very tiny hands and feet. When Harpo Marx spoke in his book, he described him well. Harpo said he looked like something that had gotten loose from Macy's Thanksgiving Day parade. He had fierce eyes that glinted beyond thick spectacles and a little moustache he twitched back and forth. The overall impression was that of the great ruffled owl."

Brief Moment opened in November, 1931, and ran haltingly into the summer of 1932. When the play moved from the Belasco to another theater, everyone, including the producer, the author, and the stars, took a 25 percent cut in salary to keep it open. Woollcott, realizing that he alone kept the play going, refused to accept a cut. In fact, he demanded more than his four hundred dollars a week. When he received the increase in salary, his joy became boundless. If the critics didn't take much to his acting, the public did. The extra cash from Guthrie McClintic proved that Alexander Woollcott, in print, on the air, on the lecture platform, and on the stage, was definitely a draw.

✿   ✿   ✿

A misprint in the *Times* gave Aleck almost as much enjoyment as any comedy of the season.

"Arch Selwyn presents *Cora Potts* without Francine Larrimore," the *Times* ad read.

"What a cast!" exclaimed the composer Howard Dietz.

After the resounding success of Woollcott's book *While Rome Burns*, the publisher Harold Guinzburg began spurring Aleck to put together an anthology. By 1935 Aleck had done so, and Guinzburg's Viking Press brought it out under the title *The Woollcott Reader*.

By now the name of the anthologist had been so well advertised and broadcast and introduced from lecture platforms that the book became an immediate best seller. The seventeen selections it contained ranged from J. M. Barrie to Evelyn Waugh.

Woollcott catered to this radio audiences. He never thought of them as the intelligentsia. The telegram he sent to Orson Welles after "The War of the Worlds" broadcast in 1938 (a program that had millions of Americans seeing men from Mars) best illustrated his attitude:

DEAR ORSON THIS ONLY GOES TO PROVE MY CONTENTION THAT ALL INTELLIGENT PEOPLE LISTEN TO CHARLIE MCCARTHY.

ALEXANDER WOOLLCOTT

Aleck chose many works of his friends and authors he had long admired for the anthology. He made no pretense that he wanted to turn out anything other than a popular book, and that's what he did.

Woollcott's Second Reader, published in 1937, did not sell quite as well as the first. But it, too, made the best-seller list. Both books were well accepted by the critics. A few referred to his choices as "hokum" and "corn." The "corn" that his detractors recognized has not died during the last forty years. It has grown taller and sturdier. Woollcott almost always exaggerated his literary infatuations, but while no one was looking some became classics.

Among them are: "The Happy Journey to Trenton and Camden"

by Thornton Wilder, William Allen White's journalistic obituary of his daughter Mary, "The Schartz-Metterklume Method" by H. H. Munro, and "God and My Father" by Clarence Day.

"I think too many people overlook his ability as an anthologist," John Hutchens, the critic and author, said. "He had a special gift for selecting readable material. He was a man who had the greatest catholicity of taste."

Woollcott summed it up when he said, "I may not be able to do it myself, but I damn well know a good piece of writing."

Now that he was no longer a critic but a playwright and an actor, Aleck began to discover facets of the theater that had eluded him during the many years he had sat on the aisle. He couldn't wait to tell Walter Slezak about Arthur Hopkins' misadventure in Lancaster, Pennsylvania. Hopkins, one of the most prominent producers of his day, had made the mistake of putting his name over the title of *Deep River*, an opera in English. Jules Bledsoe was in the cast. Throughout rehearsals Hopkins did his best to keep the company from the histrionics of grand opera.

On opening night in Lancaster, a horrified Hopkins watched Bledsoe come down to the footlights, ignore the direction of weeks, face the audience, and sing with all the gestures he had been instructed not to use. Hopkins involuntarily stood up.

"You son of a bitch!" Hopkins said aloud to the actor.

A woman sitting in front of him turned about and spoke furiously, "If you don't like it, you can get your money back!"

"I wish to God I could," Hopkins said and left the theater.

Woollcott chortled when he told Slezak that the woman was mistaken by a cool $120,000.

The story reminded Aleck of the time during the Depression when a Broadway producer approached a Wall Street broker.

"There's a lot of money in the theater," the producer told the would-be angel.

"I know it," the broker said sadly, "and four hundred thousand of it used to be mine."

The legitimate theater held such enchantment for Aleck that in 1933 he chose to collaborate again with Kaufman on a mystery play called *The Dark Tower.*

The same Margalo Gillmore who had made him up for his opening in Cleveland was playing stock in Denver. To her Woollcott sent the following telegram:

BEFORE YOU SIGN UP WITH WEE AND LEVENTHAL * GEORGE AND I HAVE WRITTEN A PART FOR YOU. TWELVE CHANGES OF CLOTHES.

He had learned the ways of the theatre quickly. To lure an actress into a play, tell her how many costume changes she has. The beautiful Margalo Gillmore signed as the leading lady, the handsome Basil Sydney was chosen to be the leading man, and Margaret Hamilton, the remarkably gifted character actress who later would play the Wicked Witch of the West in the film version of *The Wizard of Oz,* was signed to play the maid, Hattie.

Woollcott wished to try his hand at directing. He and Kaufman were to be not only co-authors but co-directors. Miss Hamilton, one of the hundreds of actors who benefited from Kaufman's direction, found herself unnerved by his pacing in the aisle of the theater during rehearsals. When he began shaking his head she decided to muster up the courage to approach one of the playwright-directors.

"After lunch, I went up to him and said, 'Mr. Kaufman, may I speak to you for a moment?' "

"Of course," Kaufman replied.

"Am I doing anything very wrong that you don't like, or am I not coming through in the part, or would you like me to leave?"

"What are you talking about? I chose you, didn't I?"

"Well, yes," Miss Hamilton persisted, "but why is it that every time I'm on, you shake your head and I think I'm simply awful in the part."

* A pair of fly-by-night stock producers.

"You're just fine in it," Kaufman told the actress. "You're just exactly what I want. I'm simply listening to the rhythm of the words. I write with a sense of rhythm, and when I hear that rhythm is wrong, I shake my head. I shake my head at what Aleck and I have done and what we've written and not anything that you've done."

As for Woollcott's direction: "He would come down to the footlights and call you over and tell you some little thing," Miss Hamilton remembered, "and then Mr. Kaufman would wander over and ask, 'Is there a problem?' and Mr. Woollcott would say, "'I just thought in that speech . . .' and Mr. Kaufman would listen and say, 'Yes, Aleck, you're absolutely right. We'll do that,' and of course we never did."

At a rehearsal of the play, an actor spoke of someone having a broad beam.

"Mr. X," Kaufman called out, "I want you to know that in making that remark you have insulted Mr. Woollcott grossly—and therefore you shall have a gold medal."

"You will note," Aleck commented drily to the cast, "that Mr. Kaufman is careful to treat me like everyone else—just like dirt."

So much was wrong with *The Dark Tower* and so many people came to the early performances and afterward offered so many suggestions that Kaufman could not bear it.

"You know, Aleck," he told Woollcott, "everyone is such an authority on the theater that the telephone directory should be rewritten. It should read:

"Brown, Albert, milkman and playwright.
"Jones, Walter, dentist and playwright.
"Smith, John, plumber and playwright."

For opening nights on Broadway, some plays rise to the occasion, others fall. *The Dark Tower,* the Woollcott-Kaufman collaboration, belongs in the latter category. Woollcott, who knew how capricious opening-night audiences could be, decided not to have the usual crowd. Instead, he selected 250 of his personal friends to fill the better part of the orchestra floor at the Morosco Theatre. Two pairs of seats went to his old pal Edna Ferber. Escorted that night by the millionaire diplomat Stanton Griffis, Miss Ferber had as guests the Hollywood motion-picture star Gary Cooper and his wife. At curtain time Miss Ferber and party had not arrived at the theater, and the house lights went down on four choice but empty seats.

Woollcott barely had time to become enraged. Shortly after the curtain went up, the leading man, Basil Sydney, was about to make his entrance. The cue had been thrown by the proper actor and Mr. Sydney did indeed attempt to get onto the stage. His means of entrance was a door and that door suddenly stuck.

Mr. Sydney tried valiantly to open it, but the door would not budge. Without Mr. Sydney on the set, the rest of the cast simply stood around, stammered, coughed, and attempted to ad-lib. The audience, sensing something was amiss, grew restless. George Kaufman was seen running into the night.

Not as nimble of foot as Kaufman, Aleck waddled into the lobby only to find Ferber and her party standing there while Gary Cooper gave autographs to movie fans.

"Into your seats! Into your seats!" he hissed. Then, when they looked at him, he roared, "One of my autographs is worth ten of his!"

There are many explanations of the feud between Aleck and Edna Ferber. None has the ring of truth. The truth is, no playwright can ever forgive anyone for arriving late for his opening night. Nothing else mattered, not even the fact that Stanton Griffis gave a dinner party that ran a bit long, that Edna Ferber, given her choice, would never in her life have been late for a play, that Gary Cooper felt professionally bound to sign his name on the small books or pieces of paper thrust before him. Aleck herded and shooed the Ferber party into the theater and sent them toward their seats just as a stagehand managed to free the door for Basil Sydney's entrance. This brought unexpected and unwanted laughter and applause from the audience. Mr. Cooper, thinking the applause was for him, modestly nodded his head from side to side as he sat down.

Woollcott was apoplectic.

"Afterward, they all converged in my dressing room," Margalo Gillmore said. "Woollcott, Ferber, Stanton Griffis, poor Beatrice Kaufman. Woollcott glared and glared and his eyes through those thick glasses he wore seemed as big as the ends of the old telephone receivers. Ice dripped everywhere." Finally, Miss Ferber and her party began to move out of Miss Gillmore's dressing room. Before they left, Aleck, who felt the greatest gift he could bestow was his own presence, gave his ultimatum.

"I'll never go on the Griffis yacht again," he snapped.

The issue had been joined. A short time after that, Miss Ferber referred to Woollcott as "That New Jersey Nero who thinks his pinafore is a toga."

Less than a year later Aleck repaid his former friend.

"I don't see why anyone should call a dog a bitch when there's Edna Ferber around."

They never spoke after that.

The Dark Tower barely made it through the Christmas holidays, and then, as they do every year, ticket sales to legitimate attractions dropped drastically. The play at the Morosco closed quietly on a Saturday night after fifty-seven performances.

Aleck appeared to take his second panning from his former colleagues with much grace. He claimed that *The Dark Tower*, while slightly inferior to *Macbeth*, "was a tremendous success except for the minor detail that people wouldn't come to see it."

That was the public Woollcott. The private Woollcott suffered intensely from his two failures as a playwright. No mention of *The Channel Road* or *The Dark Tower* was ever listed under Woollcott's name in *Who's Who in America*. The fact that he refused to acknowledge them gives a glimpse into the depth and bitterness of his feelings.

When *The Dark Tower* was published, Margaret Hamilton was

about to purchase a copy because she really thought it was a fine play. Instead, Woollcott called her and said, "Don't buy it, I'll get it for you."

True to his word, he sent Miss Hamilton a copy inscribed, "To the incomparable Hattie, with the compliments of a fractional but grateful playwright, Alexander Woollcott."

That season he wrote the Lunts, "I could tell you how Master Charles Lederer was evicted from the Warwick (Alas, poor Warwick!) for non-payment of room rent and how, when the manager went around to throw him out, he was peculiarly annoyed by a message that the defaulter was even then shopping at Cartier's. Oddly enough, this was true. He was designing a Christmas present for Alice Miller; a breast-pin in the form of a scarlet letter A."

Ben Hecht and Charles MacArthur were a pair of Chicago newspaper reporters trapped by the wiles of the legitimate theater. Each had tried writing plays in collaboration with other playwrights, and great success had eluded them. They finally made it big when they teamed up together and wrote about what they knew best, the sleazy, exciting, harsh world of the press room in the Criminal Court Building in Chicago.

In 1928, *The Front Page* rocked the New York theatrical season. Audiences labeled it a "blockbuster," a "bombshell," everything every press agent always wanted to put on the window cards and three sheets that advertised plays on Broadway.

They followed this hit with the riotous and hysterical *Twentieth Century*, a play adapted from a work by Charles B. Milholland. It took place on the train of the same name en route from Chicago to New York. With their two such enormous and ribald successes, Hollywood predictably summoned them. Hecht and MacArthur refused to budge. Only when they were given carte blanche and a million dollars to write, direct, and produce four films in Astoria, Long Island, did they go to work as moviemakers.

Their first film, *Crime Without Passion*, turned out well. The story of a great criminal lawyer who committed a murder, it starred a seventeen-year-old dancer named Margo and a stage actor, Claude Rains. Their second picture caused people to wonder. *The Scoundrel* starred Noel Coward playing a dissolute publisher who dies but is given a second chance at redemption. It featured Julie Haydon, Stanley Ridges, and Alexander Woollcott.

Hecht and MacArthur's experience as screenwriters, their skill as film directors, and their knowledge of production could have been put on a single frame of 35-millimeter raw stock. Woollcott seemed aware of this when he wrote Dorothy Parker:

> After I had said one line ninety-seven times and begun to forget what it was, Charlie [MacArthur] walked past me and ventured a criticism out of the corner of his mouth. What he said was that he thought my reading of the line was "just a bit too violet." But in consideration for my some-what exaggerated sensitivity, he spoke so softly I thought he said my reading was "a bit too violent." In subsequent renditions therefore I tried to subdue somewhat my too virile manner and, as I watched him out of the corner of my eye, he did look a bit frustrated.

Noel Coward did not escape Aleck's pen pricks. Coward's name in Astoria, Aleck told his friends, was "Czar of all the Rushes."

Like *Crime Without Passion*, *The Scoundrel* came in for under $200,000, a ridiculously low amount in terms of most motion-picture production budgets. Where *The Scoundrel* differed from its predecessor was at the box office. Exhibitors throughout the country complained bitterly of its "artsy" concept and execution and of its lack of name value and drawing power. So few tickets were sold that Hecht and MacArthur felt obligated to write amusing letters to local movie-house operators. An exhibitor in Iron Mountain, Michigan, replied. "Messrs. Hecht and MacArthur, I have received your letter, framed it, and hung it in the lobby of my theater, where it is attracting a great deal more attention than did your motion picture." When Academy Awards were handed out, however, *The Scoundrel* won an Oscar, and Woollcott was at last part of a genuine artistic success.

For years the braves of the movie tribe had been cautiously sending smoke signals in Woollcott's direction. It was the chiefs who were reluctant about him, principally because they didn't know precisely what he was.

A New York drama critic? What can he do for us? This was back in the days when Aleck was the man on the aisle for the *Times* and the Shuberts had given him a national press.

A celebrity? Yes. An actor? No. A writer? Could be. Despite the fact that the medicine men of Hollywood were ideologically in complete agreement with the moguls of Broadway, they still sent a courier to sound out the critic. Hector Turnbull of *The New York Sun* lunched with Aleck in New York. He had just returned from the land of milk and money, and during coffee he urged Aleck to try working on the Coast.

"Why don't you come out to California?" he asked.

Aleck sniffed and ordered more coffee.

"What's the *Times* giving you?" Turnbull demanded.

"A hundred a week."

"Chicken feed," Turnbull told him. "Anyone could get five hundred on the Coast. You could get a thousand."

"When I take up streetwalking," Aleck answered disdainfully, "the street will be Broadway, not Hollywood Boulevard."

That attitude got Aleck four thousand dollars for three days' work in Hollywood in 1935. He wrote and acted in a short entitled *Mr. W.'s Little Game.* Its thin plot dealt with Woollcott, an attractive blonde, a headwaiter, and the ability of each to think of words that began with the letter *L.* Surprisingly, it was well received, but Woollcott's opinion of Hollywood did not change. With the exception of Walt Disney and Charlie Chaplin, whose joint praises he sang on the air, on lecture platforms, in magazine articles, and over the luncheon and dinner tables, Woollcott sneered at Hollywood. He made· it a point to insult everyone worth insulting and behaved charmingly only to Charlie Lederer and to the Marx Brothers, whom he still considered his dear friends and personal protégés. Also highly acceptable to Woollcott were the former members of the Algonquin Round Table, its poker game now transferred to the Hillcrest Country Club.

Although he was quick to endorse the checks Hollywood gave him, Aleck could not abide the hot lights, the countless retakes, and the thought that many of his friends were actually working and prospering there. He considered them slaves, indentured servants, or dupes. He not only pitied them but told them so to their faces or through the mails. He felt personally humiliated by Hollywood and his "foolhardy attempts to act." As soon as he got there, he longed to get out. His first visit to Los Angeles lasted less than a week. Luckily, he received a greater number of offers from outside the movie capital. Accepting them quickly, he returned to the East. In 1937, Hollywood beckoned again, but an irresistible offer came from The Theatre Guild and S. N. Behrman.

Apparently, Sam Behrman was a man who simply didn't know when to let bad enough alone. Having gone through the turmoil of using Woollcott as Sig in *Brief Moment,* he decided seven years later to create practically the same character. Instead of Sig, Behrman named him Binkie. Instead of a bit player, Behrman featured him. A comedy of manners about the chic Long Island set, *Wine of Choice* showed Woollcott as the suave, witty philosopher.

The Theatre Guild, which produced Behrman's latest play, had little to say about the decision to employ Aleck. To begin with, Behrman had become so prominent and successful as an author that Lawrence Langner and Theresa Helburn, the Guild's co-producers, would not challenge his selection. Secondly, Woollcott had been one of The Theatre Guild's earliest and staunchest friends. To reject him now would appear to be not only an act of ingratitude, but also a mindless defiance of the future in light of Woollcott's power in the theater.

Aside from Aleck, the cast included some of the best stage actors in New York: Claudia Morgan, who replaced Miriam Hopkins. Further members of the cast were Donald Cook, Paul Stewart, Leslie Banks, and others.

"Woollcott considered us all his supporting players," Paul Stewart said, "but only in fun. He spoke every word of the play at the Philadelphia opening and it was twenty minutes long because he spoke so slowly."

The cast and the critics felt the trouble with the play lay with Woollcott, but Woollcott believed the play at fault. He merrily began rewriting his old friend's lines "because Behrman's dialogue simply cannot be spoken."

For those who never spent a Sunday in Philadelphia before the abolition of the blue laws, a word must be written here. Most restaurants were closed, no drinks were served; no plays, movies, baseball games, dancing, or music were allowed; and the streets were empty and silent. Philadelphia on Sunday became the largest ghost town on the Eastern Seaboard.

Anyone who appeared in a play in Philadelphia did his best to get out of town on the sabbath.

Following the opening, Alexander Woollcott played the required number of performances and then, on a Sunday morning in January, 1938, had himself driven into Bucks County, Pennsylvania, seat of the country palace of Moss Hart, the brilliant playwright.

Immediately upon entering the Hart household, Woollcott took to insulting his host, his host's guests, and his host's taste in architecture, household furnishings, and social acquaintances. He then demanded and was shown the master bedroom, where he disrobed, got into bed, ordered the heat turned off throughout the entire house, asked for and received a frosted milk shake and a large chocolate cake. Next he embarked upon a loud and unprintable discourse on the dishonesty of the Hart servants.

Woollcott retired for the night, but not before he wrote in the guest book, "I wish to say that on my first visit to Moss Hart's house, I had one of the most unpleasant evenings I can ever recall having spent."

The next day he insisted that Hart drive to Philadelphia and see him act in *Wine of Choice*.

"I would have gone to Alaska to get him out of the house," Hart said later, "so that I was perfectly willing to settle for Philadelphia, and that night I saw Mr. Woollcott act for the first time."

Hart blundered after the play by telling Woollcott he liked his performance. Aleck led Moss to his hotel suite and there confided that he should wish nothing more than to have a play written in which he played the central character. Foolishly, Hart promised he would speak to George Kaufman about such a play, and then quickly made his escape to Bucks County.

The Theatre Guild, recognizing that it had problems with *Wine of Choice*, closed the play for repairs in Philadelphia, fired the director, and engaged Herman Shumlin to take over. A dichotomy existed because while Woollcott may have been the problem with the play, the public bought tickets to see Woollcott. No question about it, the featured player had to be retained.

"He had no acting skills," Shumlin commented, "but he had an immaculate taste as to what he should not do and what he should do and he did everything with a flair. He was very observant of the problems of the stage, that he had to learn his lines; he knew them immediately. He was crisp on the cue, always alive and ready for each moment he was on the stage. When he moved from one part of the stage to another, he possessed the stage; he had authority. You didn't see an experienced actor up there but you saw somebody who was quite a person."

Did Woollcott take direction even from as great a director as Herman Shumlin?

"Very easily," Shumlin replied. "I knew there was not much I could do to teach him about acting, to be something different than he was, and what he was was perfectly fine for the play and he did it very well.

"At one time, I remember, I had a kind of sharp discussion with Leslie Banks. I wanted Leslie to do a certain thing and had a problem getting him to accept what I said. Banks began to tremble. The next day, Woollcott said to me, 'Please go easy on Banks. You know he was shell-shocked in the World War.'"

Throughout his life, the Great War and the men who fought it affected Woollcott's emotions deeply. Perhaps because he remained a romantic at heart, he could never forget what he had seen and heard during 1917 and 1918.

Banks repaid him almost at once by telling him the story of his encounter with the difficult and ambitious Broadway star Jane Cowl. In a letter to Rebecca West, Aleck related the tale with zest.

It was during that heady interlude when Jane, having got hold of a bank-roll, was going in for repertory in a big way. Banks was one of the many actors she sent for and at the end of a long day gave him a few minutes of her exhausted attention, explaining that they would all be a simple troupe of players together. She herself might be a stellar one night and play merely a bit the next. "Yes, Mr. Banks," she said, "On Monday I may be Lady Macbeth and on Tuesday carry on a tray."

Leslie went home considerably impressed but Mrs. Banks proved more skeptical. "You watch out for that woman," she said. "I know that tray. It's got John the Baptist's head on it."

In 1935, Lunt and Fontanne talked an English actor, Graham Robertson, into giving them a cape he had purchased in Madrid so that they might make a present of it to Woollcott. The cape, black on the outside and lined in red and green, delighted Aleck. He decided to wear it during one of the scenes in *Wine of Choice*. Not a happy bit of costuming.

"Every time he comes on," Claudia Morgan said, "I think, My

God, it's Bela Lugosi!" The cape from the play remained in Aleck's wardrobe and as Wolcott Gibbs wrote in *The New Yorker*, "was frequently mistaken for an advertisement."

Wine of Choice reopened on January 28 in Baltimore and toured in triumph for a month. Many reviewers showed a lively interest while the audiences waxed rapturous over it. Consequently, The Theatre Guild decided to bring the play into New York City, where it was soundly trounced by the critics.

In his autobiography, Behrman mentioned nothing about Woollcott and *Wine of Choice*. Instead he wrote, "Our friendship cooled."

Woollcott's friendship with Hart and Kaufman, however, was becoming warmer. Aleck bombarded Hart with letters, phone calls, and telegrams inquiring about the play the young author and his collaborator had promised to write for him.

In the summer of 1938, Moss began to feel the heat, not of the season but of Aleck's attentions. They dined at "21," and Moss confessed that no progress had been made on the project for Woollcott.

Although their intentions toward Aleck were the best, Moss explained that another play would have to come first on their schedule—a dramatic history of the American theater called *The Fabulous Invalid*.

After that unfortunate show closed, Woollcott's patience grew short. He issued a royal command for them to appear at Bomoseen. He first had them served a full-course meal and while they were trying to digest it, Woollcott employed some harsh words.

'The two of you disgust me," Aleck snarled. "Kaufman, you're a second-rate hack with the ethics of a Storm Trooper. Hart, you're a groveling slum gutter with the instincts of Gyp the Blood. Together you have prostituted your little talents in the most cheap and vulgar way imaginable. Collectively, you remind me of a Bruno Hauptmann without charm."

Kaufman winced and Hart cringed.

"The warden at Alcatraz is kinder, Aleck," Moss said.

"Consider me the Dowager Empress of China," Woollcott replied as he dismissed them, "and consider yourselves a couple of coolies. Go to work."

Instead, anticipating World War II, Kaufman and Hart wrote a flattering dramatic history of the United States that ended on an anti-Nazi theme.

As Hart wrote, they brought their newest property, *The American Way,* starring Fredric March and Florence Eldridge, into Radio City's Center Theatre, thus being "the first people, I believe, to guarantee the Rockefellers against loss."

The year was 1939, two theatrical seasons had passed, and *still* the most facile collaborators since Beaumont and Fletcher had yet to write a line for Alexander Woollcott.

If Woollcott was dissatisfied, so were Kaufman and Hart. *The American Way* ran a scant eighty performances. During the previous season, *The Fabulous Invalid* had run an even fewer sixty-five performances. What all playwrights seek is acceptance. Kaufman and Hart had not received it from either of their last two plays.

But would anyone care for a play revolving about Alexander Woollcott? What sort of role could they write for him? Could he capture and sustain the attention of the critics and audience? What was there to say about him that Sam Behrman hadn't already written?

Moss recalled Woollcott's visit to his home in Bucks County, how Aleck had taken over, how happy Moss had been to have him leave the house.

"But suppose he'd broken his leg on the way out," Moss suggested, "and I had to keep him there?"

Kaufman peered over the rims of his glasses staring at Hart. Then he took off his medium-distance glasses and put on the pair he wore for typing. Whipping a single sheet of paper into the machine, he rolled it through. His long fingers suddenly flashed across the keyboard of the typewriter.

"Act One, Scene One," he wrote.

18 Enter Sheridan Whiteside

"*T*HIS CAN BE A VERY FUNNY PLAY," HART KEPT AS-suring Kaufman.

"All we have to have now are three very funny acts," Kaufman replied.

Throughout the spring of 1939, Hart and Kaufman worked on the vehicle for Woollcott. By summer they had enough pages for a first draft. They had written a masterful comedy that caught the daffiness of their cronies. Not only was Aleck their central character, even Aleck's friends were part of it. The role called Banjo was Harpo Marx, thinly disguised. Metz, the mad naturalist, was an imitation of Dr. Gustav Eckstein of Cincinnati. In the play, cockroaches replaced canaries. The leading lady was patterned after Gertrude Lawrence. Almost everyone who saw the show recognized the takeoff of Noel Coward and other assorted Woollcott chums. Apparently only Hart and Kaufman had been spared, and that was entirely due to the fact that they had written the play.

A play *for* Aleck was one matter. A play *about* him brought up a host of personal problems and possible legal complications. As senior partner in the playwriting firm, Kaufman decided not to face Woollcott. Instead, he selected Hart to make the trip to Bomoseen and read the script for Aleck.

"Moss is used to being insulted by Woollcott. I've outgrown it," Kaufman said.

With a freshly typed copy of the first draft in his overnight bag, Hart made the journey to Vermont. Captain Bull's son ferried him across the lake to the island. There, after many greetings, a game of croquet, and lunch, Hart tentatively broached a reading of the script.

"By all means, by all means," Woollcott said heartily. "I've been waiting for this for two years. I will not wait another moment." With an elated Aleck leading the way, an assemblage consisting of Hart, his radio producer, Herschel Williams, his manager, Jo Hennessey, and his secretary, Leggett Brown, proceeded to a pine grove. When they were comfortably seated, Hart began.

Drawing upon his earlier skills as a social director in the Catskills, his gift as a playwright, and his talent as a stage director, Hart read the play from start to finish.

"This was the funniest performance ever and Woollcott screamed with laughter," Herschel Williams recalled. "He was beside himself with delight."

Pleased that he had done so well and that his host evidently had not taken umbrage at the character of Sheridan Whiteside, Hart took up the second step of his diplomatically charged mission.

"Aleck," Hart asked, "would it amuse you to play Whiteside?"

"Amuse me? It will amuse everyone."

"I mean," Hart persisted, "is this the play you want to appear in?"

"A very difficult decision," Woollcott hedged.

Hart put it to him flatly. "Yes or no, Aleck?"

"It would be a great piece of personal effrontery on my part to act in this play. It's so completely identified with me," Woollcott replied.

His radio producer could see that Aleck's reactions were two-fold: pleasure at the size of the role and fright at the prospect of appearing onstage for most of the evening.

"I'll let you know in a week," he promised Hart.

And then, just as Hart began to tuck the manuscript under his arm, Aleck asked, "May I have a copy?"

"We'll send one to you," Hart promised.

"Before you put it away, Mossie," Aleck concluded, "what are you calling the play?"

"*The Man Who Came to Dinner*," Hart answered.

During his long career as a playwright, Kaufman followed a single rule for billing: if *he* thought of the idea for a play, he took first billing. If his collaborator came up with it, Kaufman took second billing. Thus:

THE MAN WHO CAME TO DINNER
a comedy
by
Moss Hart and George S. Kaufman

Hart's report to Kaufman had elements of a personal triumph. With voice and gesture he described every nuance of Woollcott's reaction to the first draft. Hart was certain they had a hit.

Kaufman was certain only that they had to rewrite. He remembered that Woollcott could be a savage drama critic and he wanted the second draft of the script to be in better shape before he faced him.

Let Thornton Wilder describe it:

There was an evening set aside in Bucks County in which the play was read to Aleck. George and Moss played all the characters. When the reading was over, Aleck complimented them. He thought it was a fascinating play. But suddenly he turned to Kaufman.

"Now, George," Woollcott said, "there's no line in Whiteside's part that I couldn't imagine saying myself except those in which he talks to the paid underlings. George, you talk that way to waiters and servants. I am well-known for having a sharp and biting tongue but I only use it on those who can defend themselves. You use it all the time to make yourself twelve feet tall. Now keep your goddam dungforks out of my characterization!"

The reading took place at George's home. He was the host. "George had a good tongue himself but he didn't answer back. Instead, he got up and wandered along the gravel path to the swimming pool. That's when Moss and I became worried. We knew George couldn't swim."

Aleck asked for another cup of coffee and a copy of the play to take back to New York with him. He allowed a few of his friends to see it.

"Do you think that's really you, Aleck?" Ned Sheldon, a prominent playwright, asked after reading it. "Do you really think so little of yourself?"

"I'm not always that rude and I'm not always that funny," Aleck told Harpo Marx. "What the boys have done is bring out the worst and the best in me."

The next meeting between Hart, Kaufman, and Woollcott took place at the Gotham Hotel. Aleck, ready for his final answer on the casting of Sheridan Whiteside, said it would not be played by Alexander Woollcott. He explained reluctantly, "I'll have no mask to hide behind. That's me or a reasonable facsimile of me. If the play's a flop, I'd be embarrassed. If it turns out to be a hit, I'll have to spend the next two years in New York and I'll have none of that."

The Messrs. Hart and Kaufman took him at his word.

Any suggestions? they inquired.

"John Barrymore," Aleck answered promptly, "but I don't believe he can remember his lines anymore."

Hart and Kaufman looked at each other. It was not their custom to hire actors for their comedies who were paid the kind of money Barrymore demanded.

"Who else?"

"Robert Morley," Aleck stated.

Hart and Kaufman looked at each other again. Still too high.

They agreed to look around. Woollcott returned to Bomoseen. Hart and Kaufman took the train to their respective estates in Bucks County.

"There is this drama professor I met up at Yale," Kaufman began after the train pulled out of Newark. "He's got a full white beard and a white moustache and he might just be what we're looking for. He's been playing Aleck for years in New Haven. Might as well bring him in."

Monty Woolley was a dissatisfied teacher of drama. It had been his belief that he should have been named head of the Yale School of Drama. Unfortunately, the trustees thought otherwise. When George Pierce Baker's 47 Workshop moved from Harvard to Yale in the mid-Twenties, Baker became dean of the School of Drama. Woolley had played a few bit parts on Broadway and had appeared briefly in a Hollywood picture or two, but his ambitions at Yale were dashed.

But not forever.

In the mail one day came an envelope with a playscript. A single sheet of Kaufman's richly engraved stationery accompanied the script. On it were typed the words, "If Professor Woolley likes this play, will he consider reading for it?"

Rehearsals began in the first week of September, 1939, at the Music Box Theatre on West Forty-fifth Street. Aleck pretended to take no notice of them, but when *The Man Who Came to Dinner* company arrived in Boston, Woollcott had already registered in the Ritz Hotel.

Ensconced in a corner suite overlooking Arlington Street and the Boston Common, Aleck restlessly waited while the scenery for the play was hung and the actors got into the set to rehearse. If a single hotel on the Eastern Seaboard matched Aleck's personality, it must have been the Ritz. Its hallways were wide, its chambers were spacious, and room service was available twenty-four hours a day at the touch of a button. Into its elevators was pumped a subtle fragrance supplied by Charles of the Ritz. The bar was just inside the front entrance; the main dining room was on the second floor. Among the many *spécialités de la maison* was the most delectable chocolate sauce in the Western Hemisphere.

"I gained five unneeded damn pounds simply sitting in the Ritz, stuffing myself to get rid of an acute case of nerves until that wretched play opened," Woollcott declared later.

He had his photograph taken with Hart, with Kaufman, with Hart *and* Kaufman, with numerous well-wishers and admirers. Before the opening Aleck was beside himself with anxiety. Woollcott, the best man at so many weddings, was now more wretched than any bridegroom.

"Suppose they don't laugh?" he worried. "Suppose they don't know it's me? Suppose they *do* know it's me and they *hate* me? Suppose I turn out to be the villain and not the hero?"

Ever so gently his friends led him away from the rehearsals and back to the Ritz. He was not, they pointed out, either one of the playwrights, the director, the producer, or even an actor.

"But that's me up on that stage, damnit, me."

Someone pushed a button on the wall and the floor waiter brought in enough steaks and potatoes to occupy even Aleck.

He refused to be seated on opening night, remaining in the rear of the house with Moss Hart, George and Beatrice Kaufman, and Sam H. Harris, the producer of the play.

A few moments after the curtain went up, the first laugh of the play boomed into the hushed theater. Kaufman grimaced. Hart grinned. Harris smiled. Aleck beamed. By the end of the first act he was radiant. By the end of the second act he was transported with joy. When the curtain came down on the third act, Woollcott was convinced that he and not Monty Woolley should play the role of Sheridan Whiteside.

To the very proper Bostonians *The Man Who Came to Dinner* proved a very amusing comedy. To those who knew better, the play presented a wildly funny cartoon of Aleck and his friends. Shortly after the production opened, the Boston correspondent of the *Times* filed a story alerting New Yorkers that the Man in *The Man Who Came to Dinner* was in reality the distinguished and debonair Alexander Woollcott.

The news traveled fast along Broadway. As usual, ticket brokers got the word early; their runners were sent out with hard cash to be exchanged at the box office for choice seats. Habitual first-nighters mailed in their checks for $3.30 a seat on the orchestra floor. The advance sale at the Music Box was brisk.

Then, shortly after nine o'clock on the evening of October 16, 1939, the curtain rose on that single set, the living room of Mr. and Mrs. Ernest W. Stanley, people of means, in a small town somewhere in Ohio. Through the dramatic device of action and exposition the audience learned that the great critic, lecturer, and radio personality Sheridan Whiteside had fallen and broken his hip some time ago and remained quarantined in the Stanley dining room through the period of recuperation.

Whiteside turned the Stanley home into a bedlam of his own. Telephone calls and telegrams were sent and received at all hours of the day and night. Among those persons of stature actually mentioned by name during the first few moments of the evening were H. G. Wells, Felix Frankfurter, Jascha Heifetz, Katharine Cornell, Schiaparelli, the Lunts, Anthony Eden, Sacha Guitry, Arturo Toscanini, Sam Goldwyn, Louella Parsons, Ethel Barrymore, and Ginger Rogers. More were to follow.

Seated in a wheelchair for the better part of two and a half hours, Whiteside ruthlessly ruled the Stanleys themselves. At the same time he arranged for his secretary to marry the local journalist, and issued a stream of orders, suggestions, and imperious requests to the great and near-great who made up the long list of his friends.

At the end of the play Whiteside left the Stanley home, only to slip on a piece of ice, fracture his other hip, and be carried into the house for another period of convalescence.

The curtain came down. The audience cheered the cast for fourteen curtain calls. Then came that period between hand shaking, backslapping, and cheek kissing in the actors' dressing rooms and the first words of the drama critics' reviews.

Brooks Atkinson, bellwether of the critical fraternity, led the cheers. The first advertisement Sam H. Harris ran was headed: " 'The funniest comedy of this season'—Atkinson, *Times*."

For the most part, his fellow critics were in complete agreement.

Writing in a more carefully considered and less hurried fashion in the Sunday *Times*, Atkinson raised higher his banner of admiration for the current work of Hart and Kaufman.

"After doing their bit for democracy last season," Atkinson wrote, "Moss Hart and George S. Kaufman have turned to the more relaxing task of doing one of their friends. In *The Man Who Came to Dinner*, which brought out the Fire Department on Monday evening, he is dubbed Sheridan Whiteside, popular lecturer, critic, and radio sage. But even the despot of Lake Bomeseen, brooding over his island acres, is not disposed to deny that Alexander Woollcott is their model. Taking him in his malicious phase as a spiteful-tongued tyrant with literary overtones, Mr. Hart and Mr. Kaufman have translated him into the first comic phenomenon of the season. It ranks with *You Can't Take It with You* and *Once in a Lifetime*."

The Music Box Theatre was one of New York City's loveliest and most intimate playhouses. Built especially for Irving Berlin, it was considered a jewel both inside and out. It had but one single flaw. The theater's architect, Herbert Krapp, in designing a perfect oval lobby, forgot to include a box office. To his aesthetic disappointment, the contractors had to break the fresh plaster on the left side of that perfect lobby, and they installed the tiniest box office on Broadway. But during the fall, winter, and spring of 1939–1940, it was the busiest box office in town. And Broadway had quite a season that year.

William Saroyan's *The Time of Your Life* opened then. So did Lillian Hellman's *The Little Foxes*, starring Tallulah Bankhead. Howard Lindsay and Russel Crouse brought in the play that eventually set the longest run in the history of the New York theater,

Life with Father. Mr. Lindsay and his wife, Dorothy Stickney, played the leads in the original production.

Katharine Hepburn starred in Philip Barry's *The Philadelphia Story*. Helen Hayes was billed above *Ladies and Gentlemen*. Gertrude Lawrence took similar billing over *Skylark*. Katharine Cornell brought in *No Time for Comedy*, featuring a young leading man named Laurence Olivier. *Key Largo* starred Paul Muni. Ethel Waters appeared in her first play without music, *Mamba's Daughters*. William Gaxton, Victor Moore, and Sophie Tucker starred in *Leave It to Me*, a musical in which a youngster named Mary Martin simulated a striptease while singing "My Heart Belongs to Daddy." Walter Huston sang "September Song" in *Knickerbocker Holiday*. Vera Zorina played the title role in *I Married an Angel*, costarring Walter Slezak and Vivienne Segal. Eddie Albert and Jimmy Savo were *The Boys from Syracuse*. *The Corn Is Green* starred Ethel Barrymore.

Other players seen that season were James Barton, Eva Le Gallienne, Frank Fay, Gene Kelly, Nancy Hamilton, Carmen Miranda, Bill Robinson, Alfred Drake, Joseph Cotten, Maurice Evans, Lillian Gish, Luther Adler, Frances Farmer, Judith Anderson, Sam Levene, Otto Preminger, Julie Haydon, and Eddie Dowling.

It was an enormously successful year. Perhaps because it arrived early, *The Man Who Came to Dinner* was the "hottest ticket" on Broadway.

Aleck took bows at countless luncheons and dinner parties. The authors were too busy to socialize. They were being sued by a Boston lawyer for plagiarism. The judge threw the case out of court, but not before Kaufman wrote Aleck, "It seems we stole the character of Woollcott from the play *Sticks and Stones*. It will probably turn out that you got it from there, too."

Woollcott, pleased and delighted with the attention he received from the new comedy, told Hart and Kaufman that he would reverse his earlier decision not to play himself.

While not completely satisfied with Woolley's interpretation of Woollcott, Aleck was willing to follow the rule of thumb that forbids any tampering with a Broadway hit. However, he hinted strongly that he would be content to play a second company in Chicago.

"I'm perfect for the part," he told Kaufman. "I'm the only man you know who can strut sitting down."

To his dismay and disgust, the role was given to the actor he had once dubbed "a general futility man," Clifton Webb. Webb— thin, steely, brilliantly effective—received fine reviews, and when they arrived from Chicago, Aleck left New York in a huff for an extended lecture tour of the United States and Canada.

When word reached an ecstatic Woollcott in British Vancouver that he could head a third company, he completed the lecture tour and arrived in Los Angeles for rehearsal in January, 1940.

Although Aleck enjoyed traveling and meeting people, a single set of circumstances pleased him particularly. He enjoyed most living in a replica of the Red Bank commune. Bomoseen was his own personal fiefdom, but Bomoseen was, for the most part, a summertime way of life.

Whenever he journeyed to the West Coast, Woollcott invariably settled in The Garden of Allah. Originally, it had been an estate purchased by the Russian actress Alla Nazimova. During one of her downs after a spectacular series of ups, Nazimova was advised that if she built cottages on her three and a half acres and established a hotel, she would be financially secure for the rest of her life.

So of course she did and of course she lost it and of course the new owners promised her it would remain her monument forever and of course the bulldozers finished it off at the end of 1959.

What Aleck liked about The Garden of Allah was that so many of his friends lived there at the same time he did.

"Hart, Kaufman, and Alice Duer Miller are here," he mentioned happily. "Rachmaninoff has the next bungalow and begins practicing every morning at dawn. Beyond him are the Charles Laughtons. Beyond them Robert Benchley. Beyond him is Dorothy Parker. Across the way, Dame May Whitty, rehearsing as the Nurse to the Juliet of Vivien Leigh and the Romeo of Laurence Olivier. It's the kind of village you might look for down the rabbit hole."

Kaufman cast the Pacific Coast company of *The Man Who Came to Dinner* with his usual expertise. Rex O'Malley, the English-born actor-director and a favorite of Woollcott's, came out from the New York company to do the Noel Coward role. Claudia Morgan, with whom Aleck had gotten on famously in *Wine of Choice*, was engaged as the leading lady.

On the first day of rehearsal, Aleck, to use his own word, was "ebullient." Nothing stimulated him more than the opportunity to play Sheridan Whiteside. Before the first reading of the play he even ventured a question to Kaufman. Gossip was spice to Aleck and he tried a frontal assault on George.

"What's this buzzing I hear about your Bea and a Mr. Martin?"

"His name is Charles and he's one of her young protégés like Oscar Levant."

"Oh? Anything else I should be told?"

"You know," Kaufman replied with just the faintest trace of irritability, "Beatrice is always picking up these sensitive, ambitious young Jewish boys."

"Sometimes," Aleck smiled, "she marries them."

George gave Aleck a long look over his glasses and then told the stage manager to call the company together.

Woollcott wasn't much good during rehearsals and he knew it. Kaufman knew it, too. He worked gently and constructively with Aleck, never embarrassing him before the cast. Kaufman was the professional and Woollcott was the highly paid amateur. In the Behrman plays he had one bit part and one supporting role. Now it was Woollcott's job to carry the production.

No actor tried harder than Aleck. But then no actor had ever had an entire play written about him. In the second act he kept throwing the cast into unwanted laughter.

"At Christmas," Aleck invariably said, "I always feel the needy."

"The word is 'feed,'" Kaufman admonished him quietly. "That's something you aren't going to be able to do for yourself if you don't get your lines straight."

They opened in Santa Barbara in February, and Aleck acknowledged that he acted like a third-company Woollcott. Most of it he blamed on laryngitis. The rest he put down to the great number of parties given in his honor.

After a two-week stand in Los Angeles, Woollcott and his company played a week in Pasadena. Following the almost twenty-four-hour-a-day festivities in the south, life on the road took on a bucolic quality. Woollcott gave eight performances a week, acted as host at long, talkative suppers after the show, and rose early to answer the mounds of daily mail. Rehearsals continued at Aleck's insistence, because if there was one thing he now wished to do it was to play Woollcott better than Woolley or Webb.

After the play opened in Los Angeles, he said, "You can take it from me, I was pretty lousy."

Hard work and determination to succeed made his performance improve. Audiences started to respond favorably to him. When they did, Woollcott was prepared. He stepped out after the curtain calls, waited for the patrons to quiet down, and then addressed them.

"It's not true that this role of the obnoxious Sheridan Whiteside was patterned after me. Whiteside is merely a composite of the better qualities of the play's two authors."

Then he retreated behind the house curtain and was seen no more.

On the night the comedy closed in Pasadena, Woollcott the critic considered Woollcott the actor to have progressed sufficiently to allow Woollcott the man a little relaxation.

Rex O'Malley, the actor who played the part based on Noel Coward, answered the telephone in his hotel room in Pasadena. Woollcott's voice came out of the other end of the line.

"Come on, Puss, gather your shabby little belongings, we're going to Fresno."

"It's one o'clock, Aleck. The company isn't leaving until tomorrow morning."

"I've rented a car and a driver. Are you going to let me go to Fresno alone?" There was the slightest pause and Woollcott, the gentle bully, snapped, "I'll pick you up in twenty minutes."

With Woollcott and the driver in the front seat, the back door of a limousine opened at the entrance of the hotel and the dapper O'Malley got in. Off they drove to Fresno.

Irked that his sleep had been interrupted, O'Malley sat silently while Woollcott went on mile after mile, offering a seemingly endless dissertation on radio.

"Radio is a one-dimensional medium. The audience can only hear. Further dimension must be supplied by the imagination of the individual listener. That's why the voice is so all-important," Woollcott pronounced.

"Orson Welles, the greatest voice on the airwaves, plays entirely to the minds of his listeners. And you, Rex, with your voice, it would require music perhaps swelling behind it to be fully effective."

The actor in the back seat bristled. He roused himself.

"My own voice," Woollcott went on, "has the quality of swelling and singing and soaring."

"I've heard your voice many times," the infuriated O'Malley said, "and all I hear is a faint homosexual mosquito."

There was a heavy silence in the front seat. Slowly, Aleck managed to turn around.

"I see what you mean, I see what you mean," he sputtered. And then came his revenge. "By the way, Puss," he asked, "how would you like to take a good suck of my lizzie?"

The chauffeur involuntarily turned the wheels of the car onto the shoulder of the road. However, he avoided disaster by spinning the wheel to the left and they were back on the hard surface heading for Fresno.

For the rest of the drive they sat in silence.

Believing that he had offended Aleck, O'Malley was quite unprepared when they arrived in Fresno to see Woollcott spring out of the car—as much as Aleck *could* spring out of a car. Putting his arm around O'Malley's shoulder, he addressed the chauffeur.

"You may take the car away, driver," he said grandly. "Mr. O'Malley and I are going out to get humped!"

O'Malley's eyes were drooping from lack of sleep. They snapped open.

"Good exits are necessary for actors," Aleck explained. And with that they made their way to the hotel.

Aleck's arrival in San Francisco had many of the elements of a victory celebration. The theater was sold out for all six weeks. Aleck's calendar, which he kept, in Gibbs's phrase, "as precisely calculated as a dentist's," was booked solid with breakfast appointments, luncheons, dinners, and after-theater suppers.

The closest hotel in San Francisco to Boston's Ritz was the Fairmont. Aleck Woollcott occupied a three-room suite with a view of the bay.

Once the jitters of opening night were behind him, Aleck began to socialize. Jo Hennessey, who had been with him for six months through the entire lecture tour and the rehearsals and tryouts of the play, was now permitted to return east aboard a Norwegian freighter, steam through the Canal Zone, and catch a Grace Line ship bound for New York by way of Havana.

"No one has ever been such a blessing to me as Jo," Woollcott said.

With Hennessey gone, he required Rex O'Malley and Claudia Morgan to keep him company. Miss Morgan held Woollcott's interest not only because of her beauty and her fine acting but because Woollcott believed he had ferreted out a secret in her life. Her father and uncle were both named Morgan. Ralph and Frank Morgan had been successful in the theater and in films, but the family name was not Morgan. It was Wuppermann. And as Wuppermanns, they were the multimillionaire inheritors of Worcestershire sauce.

271

None of the Morgans hid any of these facts, but Aleck, titillated by the knowledge of their name and fortune, said, "Every time you spread that sauce on your steak, you are putting a few shiny coppers into this young thing's purse."

Friends flocked to San Francisco to see Woollcott: Dorothy Parker and her husband, Alan Campbell, Margaret Webster, the renowned stage director, H. R. Knickerbocker, the foreign correspondent, Olivier, Leigh, and Levant.

"Oscar came and went like a tornado, accompanied by his pregnant bride, and staying here at the Fairmont because I had suggested it," Aleck wrote Charlie Lederer.

> As it is extremely expensive, he grew more bitter with every check he had to sign. My major triumph was seeing that his phone call to Harpo, which he made from my room, was charged to him. At the concert, his performance was truly incandescent. After he had finished the "Rhapsody," Claudia Morgan and I joined him backstage and through the peep-hole we watched Monteux conduct the final Sibelius and Ravel numbers. With the concert over Oscar and I, heading for the green room, debouched into a corridor where a comely Miss with an autograph book was lying in wait. "Oh, Mr. Woollcott," she said, "may I have your autograph?" With a bellow of pain, Oscar left for New York.

A few weeks later, Woollcott bellowed with pain. Not a fanciful or imagined pain, either.

Although he felt better in San Francisco than he had in a dozen years, the food, the pace, the acting made him a candidate for a white-cotton hospital gown. After a Sunday dinner at the Palo Alto home of Charles G. Norris, the writer, and his wife, Kathleen, "the friend who hated him," Aleck suffered what was thought to be an acute attack of indigestion. By the time he arrived back at the Fairmont, the house physician realized that the fifty-three-year-old Woollcott had symptoms of a coronary occlusion.

Doctors were summoned, diagnoses compared. The conclusion was that Aleck had sustained a severe heart attack, and the play had to be closed.

Drugged and frightened, Woollcott sent for Jo Hennessey. His anxiety lessened when he learned that his good friend would arrive momentarily.

By May 4, 1940, Aleck was well enough to dictate an entire letter from his bed in the Fairmont Hotel.

My dear George [S. Kaufman]:

This evening I am being shipped, in care of Hennessey, to Al Getman in Syracuse, whence, after inspection, I expect to be sent on to the island with orders to rest madly. The expedition will be a pretty picture, being a succession of stretchers, wheelchairs, ambulances and trains. . . .

For the first eight or ten days after I cracked up, I was so steadily dosed with morphine that I had only the vaguest notion of what had happened or what was going on. When this cleared, my thoughts, as you might well imagine, were poor company, and it is still my strong recommendation that one's first heart attack should also be one's last.

I gather that this man Bloomfield from Leland Stanford is supposed to be the crack heart man this side of the Mississippi, and he tells me that in another month I will be as good as ever, which, if you ask me, is not good enough. Even if he may be putting it all a little rosily to me, he will certainly talk turkey to Getman who in turn will talk turkey to me. In any event, it seems to be agreed among them that before the end of June they will be able to tell me whether I must spend the remainder of my life on the shelf (which, let me assure you privately, I have no intention of doing). . . .

In Syracuse, Dr. Getman ordered Woollcott to remain in bed, to cut his caloric intake. The doctors also prohibited the use of coffee, tobacco, and alcohol.

By late May the patient had recovered sufficiently to be discharged from the hospital and was remanded to his own care at Bomoseen.

His weight dropped as rapidly as his spirits. Cut off from his work and his friends, Aleck dipped into an emotional depression. He pugnaciously and not too secretly vowed not to lead the life of an invalid. Soon after his release from the hospital he began to drink coffee. Smoking came next and then white wine. None of it appeared to restore his state of mind. He grew cranky and started to view his many friends with increasing hostility. Companionships that had lasted from his college days began to snap off like tree branches breaking after a heavy ice storm. He quarreled or tried to quarrel with Booth Tarkington, Harold Ross, Herbert Bayard Swope, and Neysa McMein. Additional moodiness took a different and surprising turn.

He was genuinely distressed that his illness had put an entire company of actors out of work. Woollcott, who for years had professionally closed play after play with bad reviews, now felt guilty that his own failing health was the sole reason for posting the closing notice for the third company of the Hart-Kaufman comedy.

Each time he started to reminisce about the good old days, he remembered what Franklin P. Adams had told him: "Nothing is more responsible for the good old days than a bad memory."

The war that had begun in Europe in the late summer of 1939 was a second source of anguish to Woollcott. He was rabidly anti-Hitler. He believed passionately in American intervention and he wished fervently to do whatever he could for England and France. Any action he might have taken was halted by his illness.

The death of the man who had been supervising his recovery, Al Getman, intensified his discouragement.

"I know from my only previous experience that I am a delayed-reaction boy," he said later, "and if some months from now you hear me howling like a dog you will know it is grief for the loss of my friend."

His recuperation took much longer than he anticipated. The breezes of summer gave way to the winds of autumn and Woollcott remained on his island. He went to Manhattan only to campaign for Franklin Roosevelt's third term as President, but it was long enough to break openly with his beloved *New York Times.* The *Times* supported Wendell Willkie, and Aleck criticized it for backing a "mountebank."

Its publisher, Arthur Hays Sulzberger, asked, "Where is the excellent, objective drama critic I used to know?"

In reply, Aleck attacked Sulzberger, the *Times,* and Willkie so sharply that his old comrade-in-arms Adolph Shelby Ochs, cousin of Sulzberger's wife, wrote to him from Chattanooga:

> I don't know how this election will turn out, but I do know that Alexander Woollcott . . . did not enhance his reputation as the leading man of American letters.
>
> Your crack at Arthur Sulzberger was cheap and unworthy of you.
>
> I hereby submit my resignation as your faithful leftenant. You might take on Elliott Roosevelt.
>
> Please give my regards to Coca-Cola *—or whatever your dog's name is. He is not such a brilliant stylist, but he has better manners than his master.

Obviously tempers ran high before that election. After Roosevelt beat Willkie, Aleck wrote from Bomoseen to Arthur Hays Sulzberger in New York and patched the rift.

> Perhaps you realize that I am incurably romantic about the newspaper business and feel for the *Times* something of the sentiment which any grateful person feels for the school at which he was happy. . . . I have long given you credit for the fact that the *Times* is, all told, a better paper than it was in my day, more expertly produced and more

* Recently Aleck had named one of his French poodles Cocaud.

interesting. I even think the drama department is better, which is saying a good deal.

Being romantic I am always thrown for a loop when I come upon disconcerting reminders that a great newspaper is not only a public institution, like the Rockefeller Institute or Harvard University, but also a piece of private property in somebody's pocket.

Whether, after a year's reflection, my judgement will still approve the course I took I cannot tell. I wonder if you yourself, a year from now, will think that the *Times* did well in the past election. If after that interval you are willing to tell me I shall regard the communication as confidential.

In the meantime, I should like to say that I envy you your job and think for the most part you have done it magnificently.

By December, 1940, after an absence of eight months, Woollcott received his doctor's permission to return to the stage. He had recovered as much as he could. Although his heart had suffered lasting damage (he would continue to have attacks of angina pectoris for the rest of his life), nothing could keep Aleck on the permanently disabled list. Rather than that, he chose to risk what was left of his life.

Two months later the West Coast company of *The Man Who Came to Dinner* reassembled in Philadelphia to become the East Coast company. Woollcott played Philadelphia, Hershey, Pennsylvania, Richmond, Virginia, and then, at last, Washington, D.C.

When Woollcott appeared in the capital he always stayed at what he referred to as "the best boardinghouse in Washington." The address pleased him—1600 Pennsylvania Avenue—and so did his accommodations, the Lincoln Room. He had met the President when Mr. Roosevelt was governor of New York, although his social connections had been with "the out-of-season Roosevelts" of Oyster Bay. Aleck never gave up his friendship with the Republican Roosevelts; but with the election of Franklin Delano Roosevelt to the Presidency, he gave his allegiance to the New Deal. His visit to Russia in the early Thirties was arranged through the White House.

What caught him in the Roosevelt net were the invitations to dinners at the White House, the circumstances in which he could meet the powerful friends and perceptive advisers. He also enjoyed the opportunity of speaking with a fellow radio star, the President himself.

His eyes, always large behind the thick spectacles, grew even bigger as he watched Franklin Roosevelt mixing predinner cocktails himself.

"The President pours whiskey for his friends," he told Guthrie McClintic, the producer, "the way he might pour it for voters the night before election day: heavily. His drinks are always too strong."

At the beginning of his relationship with the Roosevelts, Aleck devoted himself only to Franklin. In the 1936 campaign, Woollcott actually believed there was a serious challenge from the governor of Kansas, Alf Landon. Aleck spoke convincingly in favor of FDR. He thought the election would be a squeaker. The fact that President Roosevelt carried all forty-eight states except for Maine and Vermont apparently had little or no influence on Aleck's understanding of the political scene.

When he wrote of Roosevelt he used much the same style as when he wrote of Maude Adams, Mrs. Patrick Campbell, Helen Hayes, Katharine Cornell, the Lunts, and the Barrymores. Superlatives abounded in his text.

Woollcott campaigned actively for Roosevelt in 1940. "I want to put my two cents in," Aleck advised the Democratic National Committee. Purchasing a quarter-hour of national radio time cost him $3,544.18 more than the two cents he originally wished to invest, but Woollcott paid for it and spoke on thirty-three CBS stations across the country in favor of the incumbent.

Roosevelt thought his speech extremely effective and sent him a silver-mounted ruler in appreciation of his efforts.

Relations between the two men, while cordial, were not as Aleck would have liked. With the President it was quite impossible to dominate the conversation in the manner in which Woollcott had been doing for years. Besides being the President of the United States, Mr. Roosevelt not only had his own store of anecdotes, but he was almost as good a raconteur as Aleck.

In the family dining room on the second floor of the White House, the President, his immediate staff, what members of his family were in Washington, and Aleck sat chatting over a late supper. Aleck, as he told George and Beatrice Kaufman, had just finished complimenting FDR on the Willkie campaign when Roosevelt picked up the cue.

"I like to think of myself as a polished campaigner," the President said. "I heard Willkie's speech to organized labor in Pittsburgh over the radio. He said all the right things. 'I will appoint a Secretary of Labor directly from the ranks of organized labor.' Very good. Lots of applause. Willkie obviously loved it so he tried for a second hand. 'And it will not be a woman either,' he told them.

"That was a boner!" Roosevelt went on. "He not only took a swipe at my Labor Secretary, Frances Perkins, but at every woman in the United States. Why insult American women? They vote, too. I knew right then that if we didn't do anything to break the spell, Wendell would talk himself out of enough votes to reelect me. It was a close race, but as an old politician, I considered that a turning point."

When he was in Mr. Roosevelt's company, Aleck behaved rather like a small child; either he maintained a pouting silence or he spoke too eagerly, too pleasingly, and too loudly. Beneath his outer sophistication, Aleck reacted exactly the way any middle-class American would have behaved in the presence of the Chief Executive of the United States. Even though they shared common interests—mystery books, Dickens—he was still intimidated by Franklin D. Roosevelt.

Slowly, he began to maneuver his friendship to the more accessible, the more understanding, and the more tolerant wife of the President. It is questionable whether Eleanor became his pet or he became hers. This much is certain: he became more and more attentive to her.

One day Woollcott invited the wife of the President to tea at his hotel in New York, and she accepted. Requests to join them came from Harpo Marx and Charlie Lederer. It was a stern and highly proper Woollcott who turned them down.

Infuriated at what they considered the stuffiness of their friend, Marx and Lederer went to Abercrombie & Fitch, the sporting goods store, and bought a croquet set. After taking the elevator to the nineteenth floor of the Gotham Hotel, they set up a wicket in front of Aleck's door and began to slam those large wooden balls around the wide corridors.

Outside, a secret service man watched with some wonder. Inside, Mrs. Roosevelt began to notice a banging at the door. Determined not to have his tea with the First Lady spoiled, Woollcott doggedly ignored the commotion. At last the sounds became so insistent that Mrs. Roosevelt inquired if someone was trying to get in.

Imperiously, Woollcott arose from his chair, strode to the front door, and pulled it open.

"Is it someone for you, Aleck?" Mrs. Roosevelt asked.

Woollcott viewed the croquet players and their equipment with contempt and disdain.

"There is no one here," he said between clenched teeth, "absolutely no one." With that he closed the door and returned to his guest, while the properly chastised Harpo Marx and Charlie Lederer packed up the croquet set, slunk down the hall, and rang for the elevator.

As small boys love circuses, Aleck loved staying at the White House. To sleep in the bed Lincoln had used almost made him feel a part of history. To write letters, as he did with great frequency, on stationery that read simply but effectively "The White House" always achieved the dramatic effect Aleck sought.

When the Roosevelts learned that Aleck would be appearing in *The Man Who Came to Dinner* in Washington, a buff-colored card under the gold seal of the President arrived, inviting him to stay at the White House. Aleck accepted promptly.

The opening night in the capital brought enough important members of the government and Washington society to fill the orchestra floor. The second night brought the President and Mrs. Roosevelt. They occupied what Aleck termed the royal box. Following the performance, the entire company was invited to supper by the Roosevelts at the Executive Mansion. Janet Fox, Edna Ferber's niece, and an accomplished actress in her own right, played the role of the nurse, Miss Preen, in the East Coast company.

"Supper was served in the State Dining Room," Miss Fox recalled. "It was marvelous and we all enjoyed ourselves thoroughly. But Aleck continued the habit of midnight suppers at the White House, and word began to trickle back to us that the Roosevelts were getting a bit upset by these carryings-on. The White House chef gave his notice saying, 'I've served an awful lot of people, but at two in the morning . . . ?' "

As a guest of the First Family, Aleck had the finest quarters in the Executive Mansion. He told Beatrice Kaufman, "This time I have the big Pink Room that was occupied by Queen Elizabeth, so that the small and rather chilly bedroom adjoining gives Hennessey the status of lady-in-waiting which he seems to enjoy."

While appearing in Washington, Woollcott spent an evening after his performance with two friends, Thornton Wilder and the son of the man with whom Aleck had had such a difficult experience while he was broadcasting for Cream of Wheat, Paul C. Harper, Jr. Young Harper, now a lieutenant in the U. S. Marines, suddenly realized that they had talked so much he had missed the last train back to his barracks. Prewar Washington was so filled with defense personnel that hotel rooms were impossible to obtain.

"Don't worry about me," Harper said. "I'll spend the night in the Union Station waiting room."

"Ridiculous," Aleck snorted. "I have two rooms. You take one."

"Great," the Marine answered. "Where're you staying?"

"The White House."

Thornton Wilder heard Harper whistle softly and then begin to protest that he could not stay at the home of the Commander in Chief, but Aleck overrode his objections. Half an hour later, Lieutenant Harper was bedded down in the room recently occupied by Winston Churchill.

The next day Woollcott wrote Mrs. Roosevelt in Hyde Park, New York.

"I wish to deny in advance," his letter read, "the rumor that I quartered an entire regiment of Marines in the White House during your absence. It was only one Marine."

By return mail Mrs. Roosevelt answered.

"Any time there is an empty bed in the White House it could not be better filled than by a United States Marine."

Aleck, who had been writing to his college classmates, "You ought to see me. I'm really good," received a letter while he was in Washington from a Hamilton man. T. D. Martin had become a social worker, and his letter read critically:

Dear Aleck:

I saw you and your play yesterday and enjoyed both thoroughly except for three unnecessary "God Damns" and half a dozen unnecessarily vulgar "wisecracks." If these were deleted, "The Man Who Came To Dinner" would be a rollicking good comedy which I would be glad to recommend to all of my friends without qualification.

Stung by what he considered to be pettiness, Woollcott cracked back:

My dear Martin:

This is to acknowledge your letter of March 6th, which really shocked me.

When you speak of "three unnecessary God damns" you imply that there is such a thing as a necessary God damn.

This, of course, is nonsense. A God damn is never a necessity. It is always a luxury.

Yours very sincerely,
Alexander Woollcott

The Roosevelts did not have the problem that faced the Stanleys, those people of means who lived in that small town somewhere in Ohio. Unlike Sheridan Whiteside, Woollcott fractured nothing during his stay in Washington, and at the end of two weeks the road booking called for the show to move on to Baltimore.

Miss Fox was summoned to the star's dressing room. Woollcott was seated at his dressing table in a silken robe that hung open to a startling degree in the front. Miss Fox asked why she had been called.

"There," said Woollcott, flinging an arm in the direction of an object hanging from the wall. It was a framed needlepoint portrait of Aleck. "What do you think of it?" he demanded.

Miss Fox allowed as how it was interesting.

"You bet your sweet ass it's interesting," Woollcott replied with a trace of a smile, "especially when you know that the little old lady who made it is in San Quentin doing twenty years for second-degree murder." *

A typical Woollcott foray, a two-pronged assault on the senses, it utilized one shocking statement after another. In Woollcott's day, profanity such as "You bet your sweet ass" had not been in use since Hogarth's time. That the artisan who made the portrait turned out to be a murderess proved the second shocker. Woollcott reveled in profanity and homicide. Miss Fox, although not as shocked as Woollcott would have liked, retired to her own dressing room, never forgetting the needlepoint portrait or the words that accompanied her introduction to it.

In a postscript attached to a letter written to Margaret Leech Pulitzer in May, 1941, Woollcott employed an even stronger example of his startling use of words: "P.S. You tempt me beyond my

---

* Another of Woollcott's exaggerations. San Quentin was a correctional facility for men.

strength when, in your letter, you say 'Let me know your pleasure.' I cannot resist answering as follows: 'Buggery, self-abuse, and flagellation.'"

Peg Pulitzer, though worldly and sophisticated, would not allow anyone to see that letter for thirty years.

The tour of the third company of *The Man Who Came to Dinner* took Woollcott up and down the East Coast, with incursions into Canada and the Middle West. Business had been excellent, so had the notices, but because of the usual lack of air conditioning, the production closed in May.

When the published version of the play appeared, Aleck took great joy in Hart and Kaufman's cryptic dedication to it. At last the authors conceded to the world that Sheridan Whiteside came to the stage by way of their friendship for the man whom they found to be a cross between Nero and St. Francis of Assisi. It read:

TO
ALEXANDER WOOLLCOTT
FOR REASONS
THAT ARE NOBODY'S BUSINESS
THE AUTHORS

Though pleased by the dedication, Woollcott began to fret the moment negotiations began for the movie sale of the play.

"How do I know what Warner Brothers will do to me?" he inquired of George Kaufman. "Suppose they decide to have Mr. Whiteside turn out to be a pansy?"

The chance of his image being damaged decreased when he learned that Hart and Kaufman had "the right of approval" in the film version.

Placated by telegrams and letters, he finally capitulated. "I find myself in complete agreement with the late Mrs. Patrick Campbell, the great English actress who said: 'I'm not a moralist. I really don't care what people do. They can do it on the street as far as I'm concerned as long as they don't scare the horses.'"

19 The Bundle for Britain

NANCY LEWIS, DAUGHTER OF LLOYD LEWIS, THE
Chicago drama critic and Civil War historian, had once been taken
to a military review by her father. Many questions arose. What
were soldiers? How were they used? Why? As young Nancy understood it, soldiers were men who killed other men in battle, and
battles made up wars.

Pondering this thought, Nancy arrived at a conclusion.

"Well," she said, "I'll tell you. I'll bet you that someday they'll
have a war and nobody'll come."

"Oh, Nancy," Woollcott said, as he told the story on the air,
"I hope you're right, but I'm afraid your day is far off."

Regrettably, Aleck proved more accurate than little Nancy
Lewis.

While Woollcott recuperated, the conflict started by Adolf Hitler
turned his thoughts from himself to the blitzkrieg in Europe. Many
of those people dearest to Aleck lived in London, and he could
hardly bear to dictate letters to them. He was like a child at night
who couldn't look into the shadows of his room without seeing
the dragons of war.

Aleck expressed his feelings of the 1940 disasters the way he
had always handled misfortune: he camouflaged his distress with
anger and humor. He tried to escape reality by making light of a

284

grave situation. Here is one of the stories he told Harpo Marx:

> The Poles have surrendered. The Danes have been con-
> quered. So have the Norwegians and the Dutch. The Bel-
> gians have given up. The French have capitulated, and the
> British have retreated from Dunkirk. A woman in Scotland
> had received these tiding over the wireless. "Well," she
> sighed, "I suppose the English will give up next. In that
> case, it will be a long war."

Following World War I, Aleck claimed to be a pacifist, but as
the power of fascism increased, his sympathies went toward the
English and he became a strong interventionist. Fight For Freedom, the more militant group of Anglophiles, secured air time
on American radio. Among this group were Fiorello LaGuardia,
mayor of New York, and Aleck's political foe of last year, Wendell
Willkie. Woollcott joined them, and in the spring of 1941 he broadcast:

> This is Woollcott speaking. All over this country there is a
> great murmur of voices. Confabs from countless cracker
> barrels. Talk under many an evening lamp. Men and
> women, old and young, rich and poor, wise and foolish, all
> talking freely about the war. How long will it last? How
> will it turn out? Are we in it now? Can we stay out of it?
> Listen and you will hear something as unmistakable as the
> footfalls of fate. The historic sound of the American people
> making up its mind. . . .
>
> It is my guess that most people in this country have it
> quite clear what this war is about. The people of Germany,
> always strong in their conviction that they are a master
> race, are now in the grip of an armed gang, headed by an
> able and tricky and murderous adventurer named Adolf
> Hitler, have set out to take command of the world. The war
> is being fought to decide whether or not they will get away
> with it. . . .

In this world today there is no such thing as neutrality. You are either for Hitler or you are against him. You either fight him or you help him.

A man who wrote words such as those had to get into the fray. Reaching England became Woollcott's immediate goal. The British Ministry of Information invited the Town Crier to fly to London. His doctors were of the unanimous opinion that owing to the severe damage suffered by his heart the risk was too great.

"I risk my life every time I walk through Shubert Alley," Woollcott protested. The doctors remained adamant. A flight to London would be out of the question.

In the fall of 1941, a British battleship, H.M.S. *Resolution*, put into the U. S. Navy Yard at Philadelphia for reprovisioning. Upon receiving a phone call that he could, if he wished, become a passenger on the journey back to England, Aleck and his secretary, Leggett Brown, joined the ship as quickly as they could.

No bosun piped Woollcott aboard with full naval honors, but the British Ministry of Information had made the proper signal to the Admiralty. Aleck was received with the warmest of personal welcomes. The captain himself greeted Mr. Woollcott and ordered his distinguished passenger to be shown to an officer's cabin.

The sight of the warship, her decks cleared for action, her guns loaded with live ammunition, excited Aleck to such a degree that he was unable to sleep the first night aboard. When at last he did, he awoke only to peer out of a porthole and realize to his disappointment that the ship was still tied to the pier at Philadelphia.

Aleck knew all about the "hurry up and wait" tactics from being in the Army in the First World War. He was not at all surprised that the same unofficial orders held true in the Royal Navy in the Second World War. Rather than become irked while the ship was being provisioned, he did some provisioning himself.

He discovered Wanamaker's department store, filled with articles that could not be found in England: razor blades, silk stockings, canned bacon, cheese, lipsticks, face powder, rouge, pipe tobacco, cigarettes, tea, coffee, hairpins, bobby pins, and shaving soap. He bought as much as the capain of the *Resolution* and the Woollcott checkbook would allow and brought his loot aboard.

"There you have my life in a nutshell," he told Leggett Brown. "Crossing the perilous seas at the age of fifty-five, carrying a box of chocolates to Lady Astor."

The seas were not really perilous on the first leg of the journey, although German submarines would frequently lie quite close to the American shore. With her running lights turned out at night, the battleship zigged and zagged without incident to Bermuda. There she remained for a week before putting to sea again.

Two days out of Bermuda, the captain stopped by Aleck's cabin and inquired if his passenger was enjoying the voyage. Aleck, wiping the perspiration off his forehead, used a line that Charlie MacArthur had given him three years before.

"I can't get over the feeling," he told the captain, "that I'm on a boat."

H.M.S. *Resolution* made port at Glasgow on October 6, 1941. The crossing had taken twenty-one days. Woollcott left immediately for London.

The sight of the devastated capital horrified him. He had visited London almost annually from the first year he had become a drama critic. Until now he had always thought of it as a city of parties and plays.

He was stunned to find nearly half of London destroyed by German bombs. Fifty-seven straight nights of attack by 200 to 250 Nazi planes left the English capital charred and ruined. The House of Commons had been hit and burned out, but St. Paul's Cathedral stood and the red double-decker buses still ran and Londoners sang "Roll Out the Barrel."

The countless blocks of rubble reduced Woollcott to melancholy. But the gallantry of the British people lifted his spirits to the point of sharp anger and defiance. He requested to see everything and talk with everyone, which was exactly what the Ministry of Information wanted.

From his suite at the Dorchester that gave him a surprisingly pleasant view of the park and gardens, Aleck went forth on daily excursions to visit old friends and make new acquaintances. First he wished to see the fighter pilots, that handful of young men to whom "so many owed so much." A Royal Air Force staff car drove him to the airfields around London: Dover, Southampton, Plymouth, and Bristol. He watched them "scramble" into the sky at the first alarm of German raiders.

Next, he asked to be taken to the bomber commands in the middle of England. He talked with the young men who were now carrying the war to Germany. He sat and joked with them on many subjects, frequently about his rank in the American Army in the First War.

"I was a sergeant," he told them, "but if it hadn't been for the Armistice I would have been made a corporal."

In England in 1941, Aleck was the same partisan and emotional reporter he had been in France in 1917 and 1918. "Courage is the only quality that makes me weep," Woollcott said. He saw more than enough courage displayed in England during the Blitz. When he returned to America, he would be filled with countless tales of the valor of the British people and the heroism of the RAF. And he would tell those tales as only Woollcott, the master raconteur, could tell them.

Sandwiched between his trips to the fighter squadrons and the bomber commands were visits with his old chums. The soaps and tobacco and lipsticks that he bought at Wanamaker's in Philadelphia Aleck brought out in London and gave away at luncheons and dinners to friends he had known for years.

Rebecca West, whom Aleck had befriended in New York in the early Twenties, received a visit from him. So did Noel Coward, Evelyn Waugh, and Lady (Sybil) Colefax, one of London's great social arbiters, who turned her salon into a canteen with the coming of war.

Bearing gifts, Woollcott had himself driven down to Surrey, where he spent a night with Graham Robertson, the actor who had sacrificed his Spanish cape to the Lunts so that Aleck could wear it in New York.

He made further journeys to see George Bernard Shaw, H. G. Wells, and Lady Astor. Woollcott grabbed the last two items remaining from his purchases in Philadelphia and hurried to Ayot St. Lawrence in Hertfordshire, where Shaw lived. Placing his gifts on a table before Shaw, Aleck realized at once what a colossal blunder he had made.

He had brought the bearded vegetarian a package of razor blades and a tin can filled with bacon.

Shaw looked at the two offerings balefully.

"I'm terribly sorry," Aleck started to apologize. As he raised his hands to remove the bacon and the razor blades, Shaw pounced on them and whisked them off the table.

"Quite satisfactory—under present-day circumstances," Shaw concluded.

As Woollcott's car left the driveway, he turned and saw the tall Irish playwright wildly waving his arms and running after him. Shaw caught up with Woollcott and breathlessly explained they were taking the wrong road. He then gave detailed instructions on the best way back to London. The Cockney chauffeur listened, sniffed, put the car into gear, and drove off on the road he had originally planned to take.

"Typical!" Shaw shouted. "No one *ever* follows my directions!"

The next night Aleck dined with H. G. Wells and related the story of the bacon and the razor blades.

"Shaw has an open-door policy as far as meat is concerned," Wells told Aleck. "I've long suspected he nibbles a rind or two now and again. As for the razor blades, I'm quite sure that by now he's traded them for half a dozen cucumbers and a healthy squash."

Lady Astor, born in Virginia and at the time of Woollcott's visit the Member of Parliament for Plymouth, coaxed Aleck into her constituency for a look at the average Englishman at war. Lady

Astor and her guest disagreed violently on every subject, but she did take him on a tour of Plymouth. At the end of two days he was happy to get back to London.

"My God," Aleck said of his hostess, "what energy and no brains can do for you!"

Woollcott saw some of his favorite Americans in London, too—Thornton Wilder, representing P.E.N., the writers' organization, and Averell Harriman, representing President Roosevelt in the Lend-Lease negotiations. Upon meeting Harriman in the lobby of the Dorchester he paraphrased Browning and exclaimed, "Oh, to be in England now that Averell's here." Wilder dined with Aleck at the Savoy Grill.

"Food in England these days," grumbled Woollcott, "is good for the diet but bad for the palate."

"The hotels had leather curtains in front of their windows," Wilder recalled, "so that no light would leak out. Traffic moved slowly on the streets. Cars were allowed little purple or blue lights so that the German bombers would have no visible target.

"I remember Aleck pushed aside one of those leather curtains, looked out at the night, and said sadly, 'Oh, this mother darkness.' "

Among his fellow employees at CBS was a young reporter whom Aleck admired enormously. Edward R. Murrow broadcast to America each night from London during the fateful hours of the Battle of Britain. As Spitfires outfought Messerschmitts, Murrow recorded and broadcast their deeds to his countrymen. Aleck saw him as frequently as their mutually hectic schedules allowed.

Murrow and Helen Kirkpatrick, the London correspondent for the Chicago *Daily News,* took turns in serving as Aleck's unofficial guides. At his request and to their pleasure they took him repeatedly to the Tilbury air-raid shelter in the predominantly Jewish East End of London to visit Goldberg and Bubbly. The shelter was under a series of railway arches. It had become a well-organized community with Goldberg as its elected head. Bubbly was a nine-month-old baby who had been born there during the height of the Blitz.

Lord Haw Haw, the renegade Englishman who broadcast nightly to Britain from Berlin, boasted constantly over the air that German bombers, under direct orders from Hitler, paid special attention to the Jews in the East End. Before the V-I and V-II rockets that were sent over toward the end of the war, the Tilbury docks actually took the worst beating from the Germans.

In the Tilbury shelter, families had regularly reserved spaces night after night with their own cots, blankets, and pillows. It contained its own infirmary, canteen, and other underground amenities.

This could not compare with the arrangements provided by the Savoy and the Dorchester. These two hotels provided private air-raid shelters for their patrons, with mattresses and other conveniences such as hot breakfasts to begin the day.

Aleck scorned the deep shelter at the Dorchester.

"I'm a smaller target now than I used to be," he said serenely, and spent every night he was in London in his own bed.

Ostensibly, Woollcott's reason for being in Great Britain was to speak to both the English and the American people. That he broadcast seven times to the Americans and five times to the English tipped the scales slightly. The scales were tilted even more when the Town Crier's fee came under consideration. In America he received $3,500 for a broadcast. In England, he accepted $100.

An even greater tilt appears when the contents of Woollcott's talks are examined. To America, he pounded hard on the destruction and havoc created by the merciless Germans. He reported vividly how the British with their bulldog grit managed to survive and fight back. The British Ministry of Information knew what it had in Alexander Woollcott: a superb propagandist for the English cause.

To England, he spun little tales of harmless fluff that somehow ended with an encouraging lift: the differences between British and American speech, the life of Mr. Justice Holmes, the small matter of the revolt of the American colonies from the mother country.

By far the most successful of these broadcasts was about the ninety-odd-year-old Associate Justice of the U. S. Supreme Court. The fifteen-minute talk included a number of memorable stories of Oliver Wendell Holmes the Younger.

Reaching back to the Civil War, in which Holmes served as a lieutenant colonel in the Twentieth Massachusetts Volunteers, Woollcott recalled the apocryphal story of Holmes's behavior during Jubal Early's raid on Washington. It was as close as the armed might of the Confederacy had ever penetrated the Union lines. Federal troops were rushed into the outer perimeter of the capital's defenses to check the anticipated Confederate advance. President Lincoln inspected the Northern positions personally.

"Where are the rebels?" Lincoln supposedly asked his guide, Colonel Holmes.

The colonel pointed to the foot of the wooded ravine at the foot of the slope. Standing on a parapet, wearing his stovepipe hat, Lincoln drew a volley of musketry.

"Get down, you fool," Holmes cried as he pulled the Commander in Chief to safety. Before he left, Lincoln approached the young officer and held out his hand.

"Good-bye, Colonel Holmes," he said. "I'm glad you know how to talk to a civilian."

Woollcott's final Holmes story jumped from July, 1864, to March, 1933. Franklin Roosevelt had been in office only four days.

. . . and I must take off just one moment to remind you of the state of chaos in which he found the nation when he took office. The whole visible machinery of life in America had run down like an unwound clock. The consequences of a heedless, devil-take-the-hindmost economy had come home to roost. The wheels of industry had stopped revolving and a great silence had fallen on the land—a silence broken during the last few days only by the crash, crash, crash of falling banks. Now all the banks were closed and the people were holding their breath. At this point the President decided to go calling—the first call he had made since he had been in office and, indeed, I think the only one he has made since he has been in Washington. You see, it was Mr. Justice Holmes's birthday and in the afternoon the President and Mrs. Roosevelt went around to see him where he lived all alone in his little house in I Street. At long last he had retired from the bench. This had happened only the year before. He had merely said to the man whose job it is to look after the robes of the nine Justices, "Won't be in tomorrow." And that was that.

Alone because his wife had died—Fannie Dixwell Holmes, whose epitaph you'll find in one of his letters to Pollock.* "She made my life poetry for more than half a century." Now he was ready for the end. In his desk his will distributed the considerable fortune his father had left him—a few bequests here and there but the bulk of it to one legatee—his country. And here, on his ninety-second birthday, was the new President coming to call. . . . As they settled down to tea—oh, yes, quite a lot of us drink tea in America—the tongues wagged gaily enough and in no time the old judge was addressing the President as "young feller." They talked of everything. Not shoes perhaps nor sealing wax but of ships certainly, deep-sea fish, they talked about prizefights— about everything indeed, except the paralysis which, beyond the walls of that quiet room, had seized upon the vitals of the country. But as the President was leaving, the tone changed. As he stood, hat in hand, to take his leave, he turned to the Judge and said, "Mr. Justice Holmes, you are the great American. You have lived the great life. You have seen everything and known everything. What is your advice to me?" The old Judge straightened up and this is what he

---

* Sir Frederick Pollock, the English jurist with whom Holmes enjoyed a lifelong friendship.

said. This was, I think, the last opinion he handed down. "Mr. President," he said, "you're in a war. I've been in a war. There's only one thing to do in a war. Form your battalions and carry the fight to the enemy."

Of course, that was in 1933—another kind of war—a war against folly and inequity and poverty and fear. Now, eight years later, as the President sits in the White House with good and bad counsel beating upon him like the surf upon the coast of Maine, when daily he must make decisions which may shape all the lives of kids now at play on the floors of countless American homes, I wonder if when he is alone at night, he ever hears that voice of the old Judge speaking to him. "Mr. President, you're at war. I've been in a war. There's only one thing to do in a war. Form your battalions and carry the fight to the enemy."

That was a speech for wartime England. Telephone messages and notes of congratulations poured into the Dorchester from all over the United Kingdom.

As Aleck was preparing to leave England after seven weeks, a telephone call was put in by the Minister of Information.

"Mr. Brendan Bracken wishes to speak with Mr. Alexander Woollcott," an impersonal voice announced.

"This is Leggett Brown, Mr. Woollcott's secretary. May I take a message?"

"Do hold on, please," the impersonal voice asked. A few moments later another voice was heard.

"Brendan Bracken here. We should like Mr. Woollcott for Sunday breakfast at a certain country house. Is he available?"

"I'm sorry," Leggett Brown answered, "but Mr. Woollcott unfortunately has made other plans for this coming Sunday."

"This is a matter of a command performance. Do I make myself clear?"

"Yes, sir," Brown replied, suspecting whose name and country place dared not be mentioned on an open telephone.

"Splendid. A motorcar will be in front of Mr. Woollcott's hotel at oh-seven hundred on that morning."

At precisely 7 A.M. Sunday, a Royal Navy staff car, chauffeured by a Wren, took Aleck to Chequers, the country seat of the British Prime Minister. A tall, serious-looking man ushered him into the breakfast room. Winston Churchill and his wife greeted him. Through the thick blue haze of cigar smoke, Mrs. Churchill apologized for her husband's appearance. Aleck expressed disappointment in not finding the Prime Minister in his much-described "jump suit." In place of the single-piece garment that zippered up the front, Winston Churchill wore a pair of crumpled pajamas and a loosely fitting robe.

"You look like I do in the morning," Woollcott said.

"Do you awake with a head that feels like a barrage balloon?" Churchill asked, and motioned Aleck into a chair at the table. Breakfast began, but not before Mrs. Churchill tried once more to excuse her husband's appearance.

Woollcott immediately recalled a lecture appearance of Heywood Broun back in the Twenties. The slovenly giant's dress brought protests from some members of the audience to his mother. Mrs. Broun reproached her son.

"Heywood," she said, "the buttons were off your shirt. Those women could see your chest and even some of your stomach when you bent over."

"Mother," Broun replied, "they only paid me fifteen dollars for that appearance. How much do those women expect to see for fifteen dollars?"

Although Mrs. Churchill suffered from a head cold, and her husband suffered from what Woollcott diagnosed as a hangover, both of them were greatly amused.

Toward the end of the meal, Mrs. Churchill developed a sneezing spell. After many "God bless you's" from both men, she made her regrets and left the room.

Aleck, realizing he could not take up much more of Churchill's time, wanted to give the Prime Minister one last message. Years ago, Churchill and Ethel Barrymore had been intimate friends. Aleck, who had recently seen her performance in the New York production of *The Corn Is Green,* leaned forward and lowered his voice.

"Miss Barrymore sends her best to you," he said.

Winston Churchill stopped as he lit a cigar and allowed the match to die. Reaching out, he rang a small crystal hand bell. A footman appeared immediately and the P.M. gave what seemed to be his famous V for Victory; the first two fingers of his right hand went up. A moment later the footman reappeared with a silver salver on which stood a bottle of cognac and a pair of glasses. The V for Victory sign in this case meant brandy and two snifters.

Churchill carefully poured out the liquor.

"I hope she is well," he said as he raised his glass.

"She hopes you are well," Aleck answered.

They drank.

The Prime Minister walked Woollcott to the front door of Chequers.

"Thank you for helping England," Churchill said.

Aleck, sentimentalist that he was, choked up. His eyes misted as he got into the car for the return trip to London. He rode back in silence.

As no more battleships were bound for the United States, and Woollcott playfully asserted that any other class of warship was beneath his dignity, he and his secretary flew from Bristol to Lisbon at the end of November, 1941. After spending a few days in that Portuguese capital, they sailed for New York aboard an American Export Line ship, arriving home on December 2, 1941.

Woollcott returned to the United States with high hopes for British victory and, as his doctors had feared, high blood pressure as well.

He gave little attention to his health, bragging that his weight was down from 195 to 160 pounds, ate as much steak and eggs as he could consume, and told everyone he met that his English experience had been exhilarating. The conclusions he arrived at were that all good, intelligent people must be in favor of England.

He was dismayed, therefore, to find his country even more firmly divided on the question of the war. Not only did Charles Lindbergh, Father Coughlin, and scores of newspapers and newspapermen firmly oppose intervention, but millions of Americans believed strongly in isolationism.

Countless Americans were of the opinion that they should remain behind their protective oceans and wait for the madness abroad to be settled.

Woollcott had made his position known. He had attacked isolationists at every opportunity, for he deeply believed that freedom and fascism could not coexist on the same planet.

A justification of his views came when the radio in his suite at the Gotham Hotel in New York announced early one Sunday afternoon in December that the Imperial Japanese Navy had bombed Pearl Harbor.

20 Tattoo

THE DAY AFTER PEARL HARBOR HAD BEEN AT-
tacked, New York City appeared to be in as much confusion as if
a major thunderstorm had broken suddenly and snarled traffic in
all directions. First, there was the President's ringing call for a
Declaration of War. Everyone stopped to listen as he addressed a
joint session of both houses of Congress.

Immediately following, New York went through its first air-raid
alarm. Fire trucks rolled into the streets, their sirens at full blast.
As there were no designated air-raid shelters, most New Yorkers
stood where they were and looked up.

On the nineteenth floor of his suite in the Gotham Hotel, Woollcott raced to the window for a sight of the German bombers. He
wasn't even treated to American fighter planes rising in the air to
intercept them. The alarm was false.

That night, however, the city began its "brownout." In no way
did it equal London's blackout, but people who had light pouring
through their windows were asked by hastily organized air-raid
wardens to cover the windows with thick blinds or lined draperies.
The amount of wattage in streetlights was reduced and ladies were
advised to wear white gloves or scarves or both so that taxicabs
and private cars would not run them down as they crossed the
street.

The rationing of meat, gasoline, and shoes began almost at once.

Woollcott remained in Manhattan for the second or third false air-raid alarm, and then, feeling like a veteran of London's Blitz, he left for a series of twelve lectures in the Middle West. His purpose was twofold: (1) he was in need of money because he had tremendous medical expenses and had done little work, and (2) he believed that the isolationist sentiment in that part of the United States had to be dispelled.

Although he was paid well for his lectures, his doubts as to the patriotism of the Corn Belt proved to be groundless. What the Japanese had done at Pearl Harbor was to unite the States into a single war machine. The Midwest, breadbasket of the nation, was already working three eight-hour shifts a day to become "the arsenal of democracy."

Satisfied that the American war effort was in shape, Woollcott returned to New York, where his slimmed-down silhouette caused much comment among the theatrical profession.

"Woollcott dropped fifty pounds," an actor announced at the Players' Club.

"On whom?" a cynic asked.

Over the years his jowls, chins, and stomach had grown to such vast proportions that his newly lost weight made little change. The immense amount of blubber perched atop his tiny feet still seemed an architectural incongruity. His pudgy little hands appeared out of character with a body, a head, and a pair of eyes so large. If he had changed, only Jo Hennessey and a few select members of the A.M.A. really knew it.

When DeWitt Wallace, editor of *The Reader's Digest*, first approached Woollcott to write for the magazine, Aleck contemptuously told a friend, "Mr. Wallace has destroyed the pleasure of reading; now he is about to destroy the pleasure of writing."

Still, by 1942 Woollcott agreed to an annual salary of $24,000 to serve as a roving editor and writer for the *Digest*. His monthly contributions were filed under the title of "Twice Told Tales." There was no nonsense here as there had been on *The New Yorker*. Aleck never attempted to use any of the suggestive stories that he had tried to slip by Katharine White. His copy read exactly as DeWitt Wallace wanted.

Next, he decided to compile an anthology for American servicemen to be titled *As You Were*. As Aleck saw it, he would accept no royalties from this volume. He was fond of quoting the newly appointed Captain Thornton Wilder of the Army Air Corps, who said, "Nothing so lifts a soldier's morale as getting a letter from home. And nothing so depresses him as reading it." *As You Were* was to provide the American servicemen with reading matter that did lift their morale.

Woollcott asked for suggestions from all of his noted friends. Typically, he accepted only those that pleased him personally. Included in the book were writings by Edgar Allan Poe, Mark Twain, Bret Harte, Stephen Vincent Benét, Dorothy Parker, Ring Lardner, and Carl Sandburg. Other authors were Eugene Field, Willa Cather, James Whitcomb Riley, Alice Duer Miller, William Allen White, and Woollcott himself. What all of these writers had in common, what the basis of the anthology rested upon was America—its glories, its wit, its pride—the land of the free served as both theme and inspiration for the men who left home to fight for its defense.

His appetite for work was still healthy.

"I've got an idea for a radio program," he told Cornelia Otis Skinner. "A family show. I'd like to do a series of husband and wife's quarrels. It should be about intelligent people, and not very bitter quarrels, but amusing, something that all married people can see in their own marriages."

"That should be easy," the actress replied.

"Don't be flip with me, my girl. You know all about being a wife, and you're used to writing dialogue. Suppose you write the first one? I'd like to call it 'William and Mary.'"

Because of Aleck's somewhat tremulous voice, Miss Skinner had the same doubts of his playing William as Helen Hayes had once had about Woollcott's playing Romeo to her Juliet. Still she agreed to write a draft of the first script.

William and his wife, Mary, were sitting quietly after dinner.

WILLIAM: My goodness, old Mr. So-And-So died.

MARY: You shouldn't frighten me like that.

WILLIAM: How would you have me do it?

MARY: You could say, "Guess who's dead?" (PAUSE) William, if I died, who would you marry?

WILLIAM: What a perfectly awful thing to say.

MARY: No, no, I mean who would you . . . if you *had* to, if it was the law?

WILLIAM: Well . . . Peg McFadden mightn't be so bad.

MARY: Peg McFadden!

The dramatic situation having been established, the script went on from there. Miss Skinner, in addition to being an eminent actress, was also the foremost monologist in America and a playwright of consequence. Knowing who had originated the idea for the program and realizing with whom she might be acting for thirty-nine weeks a year, she gave William the better role.

To her dismay, Woollcott read the script and sent it back at once.

"You bitch," he railed at her, "you gave yourself the best part and all the best lines." He refused to do the program, not out of anger, as Miss Skinner believed, but because he knew that at that point in his life he lacked the stamina to do a weekly program for an entire season. Rather than admit his infirmities, he hid his ailments behind his rascality.

When Cornelia Otis Skinner asked him if she might have the rights to the program he conceived, he immediately and generously gave them to her. "William and Mary" ran for three years as a successful radio series starring Miss Skinner and Roland Young.

Free of the encumbrances of a weekly show, Woollcott did more lectures, sold War Bonds for the U. S. Treasury, and attended the early days of the Stage Door Canteen. He began thinking about a third Woollcott reader, he worked every day in the week from seven in the morning until after midnight, and all of this labor so exhausted him that he and Jo Hennessey sought refuge and quiet on Neshobe Island in the middle of winter.

The stone house that Hennessey had constructed was weather-proof even against the harsh cold of Vermont in the early months of 1942. Sleeping a bit more than was usual for him, eating carefully, reading still in voluminous amounts, Aleck soon grew impatient with the silence that echoed through his home. At the age of fifty-five, he decided to learn to ice-skate. Katharine Cornell came to teach him.

"He wore a heavy coat, heavy mittens, and a cap worn down over his ears," she remembered.

"Kit, you've got to help me to skate," Woollcott told her.

"I was an old hockey player," Miss Cornell continued, "so I was able to hold him up when we got out onto the ice. I was quite strong and he kind of fluttered along, and we laughed and sat on the ice a great deal, and eventually he got strong enough so that he could skate by himself."

When Miss Cornell left, Aleck became increasingly worried about the war, the articles he had to write, and the speeches he had promised to make. Staying indoors offered no relief to his anxieties. Having learned to skate, he took to the ice on Bomoseen. Again and again he fell on the wet snow that covered the lake. One afternoon in March, sitting near the stone hearth, Aleck admitted to Jo that he felt chilled. A few hours later, Hennessey found Woollcott unconscious on the floor of the house. He called in a local doctor, who decided that Aleck had either suffered a stroke or a severe heart attack. Nothing could be done.

Hennessey immediately telephoned Frode Jensen in Syracuse. Jensen by then owned a pilot's license as well as a license to practice medicine. He promised to fly at Lake Bomoseen before sundown.

"Put a broom on the ice and point the handle into the wind," Jensen instructed Hennessey.

Hennessey did precisely as asked, but by the time Jensen was ready to land the light plane on the ice, the wind had shifted, and Jensen, his copilot, and the plane went off the lake onto the rocky shore.

"I got to the house and Aleck was still unconscious," Dr. Jensen recalled. "I gave him a respiratory stimulant, a cardiac stimulant, I gave him everything I had in the bag. In the course of the evening, he came around."

Finding that Woollcott's lungs were congested, Dr. Jensen made the diagnosis of pneumonia.

"Then Jo and I went through that miserable business of getting an ambulance," Jensen continued. "In those days in Vermont, hearses were convertible into ambulances. Jo knew someone in a town north of Bomoseen, Poultney, I believe it was, and this fellow had just gotten himself a fleet of new hearses and was looking for business.

"He wouldn't cross the ice, though, unless we put insurance on his vehicle. So Jo got hold of Aleck's agent in New York, who insured the hearse and the life of the driver, and we drove to the island, put Aleck into the hearse, and started back—the driver, Aleck, Jo, and I. And as we crossed the lake, the ice behind us cracked wide open. Oh, Jesus!"

After two weeks in the hospital in Syracuse, Woollcott was on his feet again.

"Please note that I am in no need of your God damned sympathy," he wrote Rex O'Malley. "I know that you are addicted to visiting the sick and have yourself vaguely confused with Florence Nightingale, but I ask only to be entertained by some of your grosser reminiscences."

Word of his recovery reached New York, and Neysa McMein,

the artist, who recently had undergone a back and spine operation, invited Aleck to share a mutual convalescence at her home in Manhattan. He accepted immediately.

Dr. Jensen took him to the railway station in a wheelchair. Just before he hoisted himself aboard, Woollcott turned to his friend and paid him an endearing tribute.

"Son," Aleck said affectionately to Frode Jensen, "I never would have forgiven myself if I had died on you."

As with so many ideas in the theater, the notion of a mutual convalescence should have been tried out and closed on the road. In New York it fared poorly. Neysa McMein's ability to attract visitors was a lifelong habit. Aleck's presence in her apartment compounded matters to the point where men and women were streaming in and out from early one morning until early the next. Neysa, who had married a handsome mining engineer, and Aleck hit a high score of entertaining twenty-seven callers in a single day. It proved to be too much for both of them. Woollcott collapsed and returned to the island with Hennessey. Neysa, whose husband fled to Cuba, was left to mend in comparative silence.

At Bomoseen, recovery started slowly. Aleck had been a vigorous man. Now he tenaciously clung to life. It was difficult to define the precise cause of his problems. He had functioned under the stress of twenty-minute deadlines for writing theater reviews, twenty-four lecture dates in twenty-three days, thirty-nine weeks of broadcasting year in and year out, all-night poker games, four Welsh rarebits at one sitting. The machinery that had made all this possible began to break down.

In the early 1930's, Woollcott had been told by a Viennese internist practicing in New York that he was one of those people who had a high threshold for pain. Accepting this observation at face value, Woollcott had gone bravely to the dentist's and had fallen asleep with his mouth open while having root canal work done.

He had informed Lynn Fontanne three years earlier, "Tell Alfred that I, too, have not been idle. I, too, have had a tooth out and would like to now find out how novocaine affects him. It affects me strangely. I rose from a painless extraction, strode majestically out of the office, stopped at Holliday's * and bought half his stock, went to Saks Fifth Avenue and made many injudicious purchases of sporting wear. These included a green straw hat. Through the fog I could hear the clerk protesting faintly, 'I advise against it, sir,' but I just brushed him aside. Then, before the effects wore off, I also bought a new Cadillac car and a French pup. The next time I need a tooth out I shall tie a string to it with the other end on the doorknob. It is more painful but less expensive."

Now, in the spring of 1942, Woollcott, with a genuine sense of outrage, experienced pain of a truly ferocious nature. His past medical history showed nothing of the hypochondriac about Aleck. His friends and physician therefore quickly realized that his complaints were real. Woollcott, who had been so proud all his life of his ability to withstand pain, suddenly found himself twinging and finally howling at his physical distress.

Wisely, Hennessey marked those portions of the Woollcott torso with crayon to show Jensen where the pains recurred most frequently. After studying the colored outlines traced across Woollcott's stomach, chest, and right shoulder, Dr. Jensen hazarded an opinion that his patient could be suffering from gall bladder attacks.

To ease the discomfort that kept him awake at night, Jensen first prescribed chloral hydrate, a mild liquid sleeping potion. As the pain grew more intense, barbiturates were administered. Finally, Jensen taught Hennessey how to inject Aleck with morphine.

Thus, in one way or another, Hennessey kept him comfortable enough so that in April, Woollcott began to invite others to convalesce on his island. Neysa McMein was the first to come. Her back was still in need of mending. George Backer, who had been

---

* A bookshop in Manhattan.

in Saranac, New York, came next. Alice Duer Miller was also ailing. She, too, received an invitation.

Because Frode Jensen was entering the U. S. Army Medical Corps, Aleck could not have his protégé attend him. He wanted to assure the presence of an on-island physician and invited an old comrade from Base Hospital #8 in World War I, Dr. Edmund Devol, to join him and his constant flow of guests.

It seemed as though better times might be ahead for all when suddenly Aleck's pain grew unbearable. By the second week of June, 1942, Hennessey convinced him to go into the Peter Bent Brigham Hospital in Boston.

If Hart and Kaufman had portrayed a Middle Western household turned upside down by Woollcott, Aleck did it himself to the Peter Bent Brigham Hospital. Entering that institution at nine o'clock in the evening, he spent only part of the night there. Then, despite the staff's protests, he put on his clothes, swept grandly out of the hospital, and checked into the Ritz.

Before noon the next day, he reentered the hospital. Dr. Samuel A. Levine, a cardiologist, examined him and suggested that a series of X-rays be taken. Wet prints of the Woollcott gall bladder showed "as pretty a set of stones" as the consulting physician could wish to find.

The decision to resort to surgery was made conditional by Aleck. He demanded and received three hours off on the day before the operation to see Charlie Chaplin's film *The Gold Rush*. Dr. Elliott Cutler, who was to perform the operation, inquired why it was so urgent for his patient to see the film.

"Because Chaplin's dedicated the picture to me, you fool," Aleck ranted, "and I'm going to see it if it kills me!"

Assured by his physicians that the visit to the movie theater would not kill him, Aleck rushed off. He returned, satisfied that his name in the billing was spelled correctly and in large enough print.

The next day the operation was performed without incident. Two days later Walter Winchell announced the successful outcome of the surgery in his column, and hundreds of telephone calls, telegrams, letters, cards, flowers, fruit, books, and other gifts poured into the hospital.

The bewildered staff had never seen anything like it. The nurses in particular were amazed that Woollcott didn't behave as the eccentric leading man did in *The Man Who Came to Dinner*. The visitors who came to see him dazzled the hospital personnel. Among the first to arrive was Irving Berlin. Then Ethel Barrymore put in an appearance. And the Lunts. They were followed in turn by Moss Hart, Louis Calhern, Dorothy Gish, a fair share of the Harvard faculty, public officials of the City of Boston and the Commonwealth of Massachusetts, and so many other persons of note that finally Dr. Cutler placed a limitation on his patient's visiting hours.

Acting as buffers for Woollcott, the personnel of the hospital was disrupted, overworked, and off schedule. Woollcott enjoyed it all immensely. The time limit on his visiting hours merely served as an opportunity for him to catch up on his correspondence. Three days before he was discharged from the hospital, he wrote to Charlie Lederer:

"Son of Heaven. Salutations! A group of variously witty specialists came into my bedroom at the Peter Bent Brigham Hospital in Boston, flung me on my face, and invaded my derriere with a proctoscope of such horrid dimensions that I was reminded that I wanted to write to you."

Discharged from the hospital after a three-week stay, Aleck returned to Bomoseen. His spirits vacillated between despair and elation. His behavior began to change slowly and subtly. He started to take off weight, not as a result of doctors' threats but because his interest in rich foods declined.

"The alarm of my friends changes to envy as I grow more sylph-like," he told Arthur Kober, the writer. "Time was when I danced like an overweight Fred Astaire. But the lower the arrow on the scale dips, the higher must grow the hopes of Ginger Rogers that she will find herself twinkling in the arms of a new partner."

As his body weight went down, the amount and length of his correspondence went up. The letters Woollcott dictated went on and on. An earlier Woollcott would have cut them drastically or at the very least edited them to some degree. The current occupant of his body and brain was content to allow them to stand as they were. He was beginning to expose more of his character.

"I came finally to the conclusion," he wrote a friend, "that I deeply regret nothing I have ever done. The several regrets which make me burst into cold sweat in the middle of the night are for the things I didn't do, failures of courage and generosity and even common decency, for which I can never atone. . . . I was denied the gift of faith and sometime I would like to ask some devout Catholic what comfort they can get out of being forgiven by God when they cannot forgive themselves."

He found a good Catholic in his old friend the actor Rex O'Malley.

"Aleck felt the need," O'Malley recounted. "He told me if he had a stroke he'd row out into the middle of the lake and end it all. He asked me if I was a practicing Catholic and I told him I was. He asked me all about it. There was no doubt in my mind as we talked after dinner at the island that Aleck felt the need and comfort of God and all He had to offer after this life here."

Later that night, O'Malley knocked at Aleck's door.

"Please leave, *whoever* you are," a strident Woollcott voice called out.

That ended Woollcott's questioning about the Church. It did not conclude his introspection.

"If, in the thirty-six years of our acquaintance," he wrote Samuel Hopkins Adams, "you had seen more of me you would have known that even in my most buoyant moments I never quite admitted that this business of living was worth the candle."

That was a shocking admission for the former world traveler who had loved life so dearly. It may very well have been brought about by the receipt of a letter from Alice Duer Miller in July, 1942. Mrs. Miller, writing calmly and thoughtfully, informed her old friend that she was a victim of cancer and did not expect to live much longer.

A month later she died. Others close to Woollcott had passed away earlier—Ring Lardner in 1933, Heywood Broun in 1939. Aleck grieved deeply for both men. When Otis Skinner's wife, Maud, died in 1936, Aleck had sent the actor a telegram: "YOU LUCKY BASTARD TO HAVE HAD ALL THOSE YEARS WITH THAT EXQUISITE PERSON."

Alice Miller's death shattered Woollcott. He went into the August heat of New York for her funeral. After it was over, he startled his friends by murmuring, "I'll see Alice before any of you do."

With that, he turned and had himself driven back to the island. Death had suddenly become a prime topic of Woollcott's conversation.

"One day I shall probably talk myself to death," Aleck said. "Those who live by the word shall perish by the word."

Abruptly, his letters began to complain of age, of having no children, of resigning himself to being fifty-five years old and facing a future of seeing his friends drop off one by one.

As the summer passed, Aleck's lugubriousness grew deeper. For the always loquacious Woollcott, a quiet despair set in. Summer had gone and with it went the visitors to the island. He was left with Hennessey, his books, the lake, and the sky. Aleck, about whom Hart and Kaufman had written *The Man Who Came to Dinner*, now resembled that earlier Kaufman and Hart play *The Fabulous Invalid.*

Only one invitation could lift him out of the depths of his depression: a visit to the wartime White House. That invitation came at the end of September, and Aleck was in Washington before either of the Roosevelts realized it.

On a late afternoon in October, Eleanor Roosevelt entered the living quarters on the second floor of the White House. "Come in, Mrs. Roosevelt, we are expecting you," Aleck said. Standing beside the open door, his hands held forward in welcome, was Woollcott. The First Lady giggled, the Secret Service men guffawed, and so did Aleck. Welcoming the President's wife into her own home seemed like the right thing to do.

The war maps in the Oval Office fascinated Aleck: the Pacific theater, the African theater, the European theater. The Navy had just won the battle of Cape Esperance in the Solomon Islands. The supply lines to Guadalcanal would be kept open. The Russians were engaged in what was to become the bloodiest battle on the European continent, Stalingrad.

Martha Gellhorn, the next to the last of Ernest Hemingway's wives, had occupied the room in which Woollcott had been put. This gave him the gossipy opportunity to write Dame Rebecca West, "I find comfort in the fact that women do not stay married to Hemingway."

Woollcott was in the White House when word came through that Montgomery and the British Eighth Army had turned from retreat and had gone over to the attack at El Alamein.

All of it was as dramatic as an ex-theatrical reviewer could have requested. Aleck was quite ready to stay on and help the President wage the war, but the next week Edna Ferber was coming and that got him out of town quickly.

He was invited back to the White House in November, 1942. "I was lucky to be there when word was released that the United States Army, under the command of General Eisenhower, sent our men ashore in North Africa," he told Peg Pulitzer. "The commander-in-chief predicts hard fighting but a quick end to the Nazis in Africa. It may please you to know that one year ago, General Eisenhower was a lieutenant colonel. When men of ability are needed the Army has always known how to bring them through the ranks. I, you might recall, was similarly promoted from private to sergeant in the last war and you know how well that came out."

A mid-December visit to the White House assured him that the war was progressing satisfactorily. He returned to New York for Christmas and the New Year. His breath came in shorter gulps. Walking was difficult, climbing stairs was impossible.

His love-hate feud with Harold Ross was almost at an end. Letters were exchanged. Ross was ill. Woollcott was worse. Convinced that his life would end soon, Aleck agreed to meet with his old comrade-in-arms and make peace. As soon as he recovered from a recurrent illness, Hennessey reminded him that he was to meet with Ross.

"Like hell I will!" Woollcott replied. "That lily-livered bastard just wants to see how terrible I look. Well, he's not going to get the chance." Ross and Woollcott never did see each other again.

It was his wish to celebrate his fifty-sixth birthday on January 19, 1943, with Eleanor Roosevelt, Helen Keller, and Mme. Chiang Kai-shek. All three ladies were in New York City and available for lunch, but Aleck was not strong enough. He was bitter that he was forced to forgo such a gathering. He was even more resentful that he had to carry nitroglycerin tablets for his ailing heart.

"Doctors want to keep me alive," he complained to Dorothy Gish. "I want to *live*."

21 Parker Was Right

ON SATURDAY, JANUARY 23, HE WAS ABLE TO LUNCH with Mr. and Mrs. DeWitt Wallace of *The Reader's Digest*. Following lunch, he sent a dozen yellow roses to Mrs. Wallace. Then he returned to the Gotham to rest. After a short nap, he felt good enough to tell Hennessey he could go to the theater that evening. Aleck was off to his old stamping ground, CBS.

Is Germany Incurable? was a book written by Dr. Richard Brickner. Discussing it on "The People's Platform" were Woollcott, Rex Stout, mystery writer and chairman of the Writers' War Board, Harry Gideonse, president of Brooklyn College, Marcia Davenport, novelist, and George Shuster, president of Hunter College.

Aleck opened by saying, "My answer to *Is Germany Incurable?* would be 'No.' Not by any human means, not by any of the physicians who are gathering for the purpose. I should say possibly she might be cured by the process of time as the Vikings were. . . .

"I do think it's a fallacy to think that Hitler was the cause of the world's present woes. Germany was the cause of Hitler."

His face flushed, he attempted to push himself away from the microphone, but his strength failed him.

Taking a pencil, he printed:

I AM SICK

on a single sheet of paper.

312

"I knew something was radically wrong with Aleck," Rex Stout recalled. "A healthier Woollcott would have printed:

I AM ILL."

Gideonse helped him out of the studio and onto a chair.

"I am dying," he told Gideonse.

A receptionist bent over Woollcott.

"Where are my tablets? Get my glycerin tablets," he managed to gasp.

What had started as a massive heart attack quickly developed into an even more serious condition. A major artery ruptured in his brain and a cerebral hemorrhage occurred. Suddenly the left side of his body became paralyzed. His vocal cords were unable to function. With the pencil he had been holding in the studio, he painfully managed to scratch on a pad the telephone number of Dr. Devol.

Devol, who had been listening to the program, became suspicious that something was amiss when he failed to hear Aleck's voice participating in the broadcast. His telephone rang as he was reaching to pick it up and call CBS. Upon hearing what had happened, the doctor directed that an ambulance be summoned and that Woollcott be taken to Roosevelt Hospital.

Police Emergency Squad Number 2 arrived on the scene and began administering oxygen.

A coronary specialist, Dr. T. Stewart Hart, who had been listening to the program in his home at 410 Park Avenue, just around the corner from CBS, rushed to the studio.

Woollcott, oxygen mask covering his face, was lifted onto a chair, placed in an elevator, and carried to the waiting stretcher of the ambulance. With sirens wailing he was rushed to Roosevelt Hospital.

It was all futile. The Town Crier had used up his last moment of time. He was off the air forever. Just as Frederick Birchall, his original night editor on *The New York Times*, had warned him when Aleck wrote his first obituary, "Not heart *failure*, Dearie, we all die of that."

Perhaps surprisingly for today, but not for 1943, Woollcott's obituary was carried on the front page of almost every newspaper in the country. Both *Timeses*, his own *New York Times* and the *Los Angeles Times*, eulogized him. Both Walters, Lippmann and Winchell, praised him.

"In the writing of criticism," Walter Lippmann declared, "it is much harder to express admiration than it is to find fault, it is much easier to be interesting and witty in the assault than it is in putting into words why the author's work is good, enjoyable, and worthy of praise. Only the best critics are able to write convincingly and persuasively when they praise. Woollcott had a sharp taste. He had a piercing eye for sham. He had an acid tongue. But he had gusto, he really liked what he praised, and he cared much more for the men and women he liked than he worried about those he did not like."

The other Walter of that day, Winchell, said, "I wish he was writing play reviews again. They were always more entertaining than any show he ever covered—even the hits."

The authors of "Notes and Comment" wrote in *The New Yorker*:

> Alexander Woollcott's unique contribution was his peculiar ability to infect one and all with the notion that they were at some sort of play, or masque. He always seemed to be at a play himself, whether he was in the bathtub, at the White House, or on a battleship. The whole aura of Woollcott was theatrical and delightful, and you approached him as you did the theatre—with misgiving but with vast fascination; and you left him as you left a matinée, with dread, at emerging from make-believe into a dull side street off Broadway. His famous ability to coil and strike was part of his infinite charm, and his quarrelsome and unwholesome tongue was a foil to his good deeds which were so many and which

he jealously kept secret while painstakingly publicizing his vices. We are glad we knew him well, for he was a most uncomfortable man to know slightly.

Woollcott's fellow reporter Frank Sullivan wrote: "In 1928, when he and I were on the staff of the *World*, a dear friend of mine died —Nora Bayes. Aleck asked me to write down some reminiscences of Nora that he could use in his drama column. I wrote a piece about that gay and exuberant girl so like Woollcott himself in rugged vitality and high spirits, but when I came to the end and tried to put down a goodbye to Nora it somehow wouldn't work.

"Aleck read what I had written, then said: 'Well, you don't seem to have ended it. How about this for a last sentence?'

"And at the end of my copy he wrote: 'I do not know where Nora Bayes is now, but I do know that whoever is with her is having a good time.'

"Well, Aleck, old friend, that goes for you today."

He died on Saturday night. His body was cremated on Tuesday. On Thursday a memorial to him was planned at the McMillin Academy Theatre at Columbia University.

It was snowing when Aleck was born in New Jersey, and it was snowing in New York on the day they were to honor him. There was such a blizzard that the Little Flower himself, Fiorello La Guardia, ninety-ninth mayor of New York, banned all vehicular traffic from the streets of the city.

Somehow, five hundred persons fought their way through mounds of drifting snow to reach McMillin Theatre. The room was filled to capacity.

The services were largely nonreligious. George Backer presided. Those three who were introduced spoke only of Aleck.

Lloyd Paul Stryker, the prominent attorney who had been Woollcott's classmate at Hamilton, called Aleck "a passionate defender of good causes, the enemy of whited sepulchers, of hypocrisy and sham, who died with his boots on, fighting."

Carl Ackerman, dean of the Columbia School of Journalism, said of Aleck, "He was a leader because he had an exacting sense of responsibility for the use men made of words."

But it was Ruth Gordon, actress and writer, who walked off with the show. Miss Gordon, diminutive, standing with hands clasped and head bowed, brought both tears and laughter to the audience.

"You know, I was Aleck's dearest friend," Miss Gordon stated softly, and eyebrows throughout the auditorium were lifted, "and so, I expect, were all of you. It is said that Aleck had nine hundred and ninety-nine dearest friends . . .

"Right about now I can see Aleck, absolutely convulsed at the thought of me standing here and trying to tell you what I feel. We do not mourn for him. We mourn for ourselves. It may be a terrible thing to say, but I'm not sure he would approve of all this. Can you imagine what he'd say to me, up here trying to explain him? 'Why, you withered ingenue, what do you think you're doing? Sit down, Blemish, this is Woollcott speaking.' "

Then Paul Robeson read the Twenty-third Psalm, a minute of silent prayer was called for, and Aleck's friends began to file out of McMillin into the still-mounting January snow. Out they came: Hawley Truax, who had been through four years of Hamilton with him; Harold Ross, whom he had first met during World War I in Paris at the start of *Stars and Stripes*; Katharine Cornell, whom he touted to stardom; Jo Hennessey, who had been his friend, confidant, and manager from the end of the First War until the last days of Aleck's life; Herman Shumlin, who Aleck believed had produced more plays of stature than anyone else to date in the American theater; Rex O'Malley, Frank Sullivan, Mrs. Irving Berlin —hundreds on whose cheeks tears mingled with melting snowflakes.

The Round Table gang adjourned to the Algonquin—Harpo Marx, looking solemn without his fright wig, wearing a dark-blue suit, and saying nothing, back in character again; Beatrice Kaufman, red-eyed from crying; George Kaufman, always relieved to be away from anything that had to do with death, silently staring at the whiskey in the glass before him; Dorothy Parker, quipless but knowing exactly what to do with her drink; Neysa McMein, agonized with her own pain and that of Aleck's loss. Moss Hart, always an organizer, had no taste that day for anything more than to ask for the check.

They rose, as if by common consent, realizing that no meeting of the Round Table could ever be happy again without Aleck. Slowly, they walked from the dining room to the front of the hotel. At the newsstand a leftover edition of the *World-Telegram* was sagging against the wires. Kaufman thumbed through it until he came to the book-review column written by Harry Hansen. The entire piece was a tribute to Woollcott.

From force of habit Kaufman glanced to the last few lines—— in the theater, the critic makes or breaks you in those lines. He read Harry Hansen's closing words aloud to what was left of the Round Table, and they agreed that Aleck would have approved of what Hansen wrote.

"The writing world is always beset by owlish men who demand uniformity," Hansen had written. "Woollcott's whole career contradicted them. When he told a good story mathematicians chuckled, watchmakers forgot the time and engineers put aside their blue prints. Now the landscape seems a bit grayer and more cheerless. It can't all be the fault of bituminous coal."

Dorothy Parker, a writer with as much critical ability as Woollcott, as much wit as Kaufman, as much insight as Sherwood, came up with a line in the heyday of the Round Table.

"When Aleck dies, he'll go to Hamilton."

Twenty years later, one day in June when the sunlight danced through the leaves of the trees on the Hamilton campus, Woollcott's ashes were placed in the rich soil of the hillside overlooking the Oriskany Valley.

After not too many years, Aleck had returned to what he himself had once facetiously called "The Last Dormitory."

Today the graveyard at Hamilton College is set in a sylvan slope surrounded by a high hedge. Many of the trees that grew when Woollcott was an undergraduate are now stumps, and several have survived time and blight and still tower over his final resting place.

It is a matter of pure chance rather than significance that the graveyard is directly behind the theater. Gray granite headstones mark the burial areas of Hamilton's favorite sons and their families.

Always different, always outstanding from his college days to the present, Aleck's headstone is not of that gray rock. Instead, it is white and shining. On a cold cloudy day, on a warm summery day, it glistens, just as Woollcott himself glistened in life.

Bibliography

Abbott, George, "*Mr. Abbott*," Random House, New York, 1963.

Adams, Franklin P., *The Diary of Our Own Samuel Pepys*, 2 vols., Simon & Schuster, New York, 1935.

Adams, Samuel Hopkins, *A. Woollcott*, Reynal & Hitchcock, New York, 1945.

Adamson, Joe, *Groucho, Harpo, Chico and Sometimes Zeppo*, Simon & Schuster, New York, 1973.

Amory, Cleveland, and Frederick Bradlee, editors, *Vanity Fair*, Viking Press, New York, 1960.

Atkinson, Brooks, *Broadway*, Macmillan, New York, 1970.

————, *Broadway Scrapbook*, Theatre Arts, Inc., New York, 1947.

Backer, George, *Appearance of a Man*, Random House, New York, 1966.

Baldridge, C. Le Roy, "*I Was There*," G. P. Putnam's Sons (Knickerbocker Press), New York, 1919.

Baragwanath, John, *A Good Time Was Had*, Appleton-Century-Crofts, Inc., New York, 1962.

Barnett, Lincoln, *Writing on Life: Sixteen Close-Ups*, William Sloane Associates, New York, 1951.

Barrett, James Wyman, *Joseph Pulitzer and His World*, Vanguard Press, New York, 1941.

Behrman, S. N., *People in a Diary*, Little, Brown & Company, Boston, 1972.

Benchley, Nathaniel, *Robert Benchley, A Biography*, McGraw-Hill Book Co., Inc., New York, 1955.

Bergsma, Daniel, M.D., *Birth Defects Atlas and Compendium*, Williams and Wilkins Co., Baltimore, 1973.

Brackett, Charles, *Entirely Surrounded*, Alfred A. Knopf, New York, 1934.

Broun, Heywood, George S. Chappell [and others] . . . edited by G. P. P., *Nonsenseorship*, G. P. Putnam's Sons (Knickerbocker Press), New York, 1922.

Brown, Catherine Hayes, *Letters to Mary,* Random House, New York, 1940.

Brown, John Mason, *Broadway in Review,* W. W. Norton & Co., Inc., New York, 1940.

————, *Two on the Aisle,* W. W. Norton & Co., Inc., New York, 1938.

————, *The Worlds of Robert E. Sherwood,* Harper & Row, New York, 1962.

———— and The Editors of the Ladies' Home Journal, editors, *The Ladies' Home Journal Treasury,* Simon & Schuster, New York, 1956.

Case, Frank, *Do Not Disturb,* Frederick A. Stokes Company, New York, 1940.

————, *Feeding the Lions,* The Greystone Press, New York, 1942.

————, *Tales of a Wayward Inn,* Frederick A. Stokes Company, New York, 1938.

Cerf, Bennett, *Try and Stop Me,* Simon & Schuster, New York, 1944.

Cornell, Katharine (as told to Ruth Woodbury Sedgwick), *I Wanted to Be an Actress,* Random House, New York, 1938.

Coward, Noel, *Present Indicative,* Doubleday, Doran & Company, Inc., Garden City, New York, 1937.

Dietz, Howard, *Dancing in the Dark,* Quadrangle/The New York Times Book Co., New York, 1974.

Drennan, Robert, editor, *The Algonquin Wits,* Citadel Press, New York, 1968.

Durhan, Robert H., M.D., *Encyclopedia of Medical Syndromes,* Harper & Row, New York, 1960.

Earley, Mary Dawn, *Stars of the Twenties,* Viking Press, New York, 1975.

Eells, George, *The Life That Late He Led,* G. P. Putnam's Sons, New York, 1967.

Ewen, David, *Richard Rodgers,* Henry Holt & Company, New York, 1957.

Ferber, Edna, *A Peculiar Treasure,* Doubleday & Co., Inc., Garden City, New York, 1960.

Frohman, Daniel, *Daniel Frohman Presents,* Claude Kendall & Welloughby Sharp, New York, 1935.

Gardner, Lytt I., M.D., *Endrocrine and Genetic Diseases of Childhood,* W. B. Saunders Co., Philadelphia, 1969.

Gibbs, Wolcott, "Big Nemo—I," *The New Yorker,* March 18, 1939.

————, "Big Nemo—II," *The New Yorker,* March 25, 1939.

————, "Big Nemo—III," *The New Yorker,* April 1, 1939.

Gill, Brendan, *Here at the New Yorker,* Random House, New York, 1975.

————, *Tallulah,* Holt, Rinehart & Winston, New York, 1972.

Gordon, Ruth, *Myself Among Others,* Atheneum, New York, 1970.

Gottlieb, Polly Rose, *The Nine Lives of Billy Rose,* Crown Publishers, Inc., New York, 1968.

Bibliography

Graham, Sheilah, *The Garden of Allah*, Crown Publishers, Inc., New York, 1970.

Grant, Jane, *Ross, The New Yorker and Me*, Reynal, in association with William Morrow, New York, 1968.

Griffis, Stanton, *Lying in State*, Doubleday & Co., Inc., Garden City, New York, 1952.

Griffith, Richard, and Arthur Mayer, *The Movies*, Simon & Schuster, New York, 1957.

Harriman, Margaret Case, *Blessed Are the Debonair*, Rinehart & Company, Inc., New York, 1956.

————, *The Vicious Circle*, Rinehart & Company, Inc., New York, 1951.

Hart, Moss, *Act One*, Random House, New York, 1959.

Hayes, Helen, *On Reflection*, M. Evans & Company, New York, 1968.

Hecht, Ben, *Charlie*, Harper & Brothers, New York, 1957.

Hellman, Lillian, *Pentimento*, Little, Brown & Company, Boston, 1973.

Hennessey, Joseph, selected by, *The Portable Woollcott*, Viking Press, New York, 1946.

Hewitt, Barnard, *Theatre U.S.A. 1668 to 1957*, McGraw-Hill Book Co., Inc., New York, 1959.

Higham, Charles, *Ziegfeld*, Henry Regnery Company, Chicago, 1972.

Hirschfeld, Al, *The World of Hirschfeld*, Harry N. Abrams, New York, 1971.

Holmes, Charles S., *The Clocks of Columbus*, Atheneum, New York, 1972.

Hoyt, Edwin P., *Alexander Woollcott: The Man Who Came to Dinner*, Abelard-Schuman, New York, 1968.

Hutchens, John K., and George Oppenheimer, editors, *The Best in the World*, Viking Press, New York, 1973.

Jessel, George, *So Help Me*, Random House, New York, 1943.

Johnson, Gerald W., *An Honorable Titan*, Harper & Brothers, New York, 1946.

Kahn, E. J., Jr., *The World of Swope: A Biography of Herbert Swope*, Simon & Schuster, New York, 1965.

Kaufman, Beatrice, and Joseph Hennessey, editors, *The Letters of Alexander Woollcott*, Viking Press, New York, 1944.

Kaufman, George S., and Moss Hart, *Six Plays*, Modern Library, New York, 1958.

Keats, John, *You Might as Well Live*, Simon & Schuster, New York, 1970.

Kramer, Dale, *Heywood Broun*, Current Books, Inc., A. A. Wyn, Publisher, New York, 1949.

————, *Ross and The New Yorker*, Doubleday & Co., Inc., Garden City, New York, 1951.

Leavenworth, Clarence E., editor, *The Hamiltonian*, George William Browning, Clinton, New York, 1908.

Levant, Oscar, *A Smattering of Ignorance,* Doubleday, Doran & Company, New York, 1940.

———, *The Unimportance of Being Oscar,* G. P. Putnam's Sons, New York, 1968.

Lewis, Emory, *Stages,* Prentice-Hall, Inc., Englewood Cliffs, New Jersey, 1969.

Little, Stuart W., and Arthur Cantor, *The Playmakers,* W. W. Norton & Co., Inc., New York, 1970.

Loos, Anita, *A Girl Like I,* Viking Press, New York, 1966.

McClintic, Guthrie, *Me and Kit,* Little, Brown & Company, Boston, 1955.

Malvern, Gladys, *Curtain Going Up!,* Julian Messner, Inc., New York, 1943.

Maney, Richard, *Fanfare,* Harper & Brothers, New York, 1957.

Marx, Groucho, and Richard T. Anobile, *The Marx Bros. Scrapbook,* W. W. Norton & Co., Inc., New York, 1973.

Marx, Harpo (with Rowland Barber), *Harpo Speaks!,* Bernard Geis, New York, 1961.

Matz, Mary Jane, *The Many Lives of Otto Kahn,* Macmillan, New York, 1963.

Miller, Henry Wise, *All Our Lives,* Coward-McCann, Inc., New York, 1945.

Moore, Grace, *You're Only Human Once,* Doubleday, Doran & Company, Inc., Garden City, New York, 1944.

Morehouse, Ward, *Matinee Tomorrow,* McGraw-Hill Book Co., Inc., New York, 1949.

Morley, Sheridan, *A Talent to Amuse,* Doubleday & Co., Inc., Garden City, New York, 1969.

Morse, Flo, *Yankee Communes,* Harcourt Brace Jovanovich, Inc., New York, 1971.

Mussey, J. B., editor, *The Cream of the Jesters,* Albert & Charles Boni, Inc., New York, 1931.

Nadel, Norman, *A Pictorial History of the Theatre Guild,* Crown Publishers, Inc., New York, 1969.

Nelson, Waldo E., M.D., editor, *Ninth Edition Text Book of Pediatrics,* W. B. Saunders Co., Philadelphia, 1969.

O'Connor, Richard, *Heywood Broun,* G. P. Putnam's Sons, New York, 1975.

Oppenheimer, George, *The Passionate Playgoer,* Viking Press, New York, 1958.

———, editor, *Well, There's No Harm in Laughing: The Collected Pieces and Letters of Frank Sullivan,* Doubleday & Co., Inc., Garden City, New York, 1972.

Perkins, Frances, *The Roosevelt I Knew,* Viking Press, New York, 1946.

Philistina, *Alec the Great,* Avalon Press, Inc., New York, 1943.

Bibliography

Phillips, Cabell, *From the Crash to the Blitz, 1929–1939*, Macmillan, New York, 1969.

Rice, Elmer, *The Living Theatre*, Harper & Brothers, New York, 1959.

Rogers, Agnes, and Frederick Lewis Allen, *I Remember Distinctly*, Harper & Brothers, New York, 1947.

Sanders, Marion K., *Dorothy Thompson: A Legend in Her Time*, Houghton Mifflin, Boston, 1973.

Sayler, Oliver, *Our American Theatre*, Brentano's, New York, 1923.

Seldes, Gilbert, "That Was Woollcott Speaking," *Esquire*, July, 1937.

Shadegg, Stephen, *Clare Boothe Luce*, Simon & Schuster, New York, 1970.

Sheean, Vincent, *Dorothy and Red*, Houghton Mifflin, Boston, 1963.

Sillman, Leonard, *Here Lies Leonard Sillman*, Citadel Press, New York, 1959.

Swan, Norma Lippincot, "The North American Phalanx," *Monmouth County Historical Association Bulletin*, Vol. I, No. 1, Freehold, New Jersey, May, 1935.

"The Talk of the Town: Notes and Comment," *The New Yorker*, January 30, 1943.

Taylor, Dwight, *Blood-and-Thunder*, Atheneum, New York, 1962.

Teichmann, Howard, *George S. Kaufman*, Atheneum, New York, 1972.

Thurber, James, *The Years with Ross*, Little, Brown & Company, Boston, 1959.

Tomkins, Calvin, *Living Well Is the Best Revenge*, Viking Press, New York, 1971.

Webster, Margaret, *Don't Put Your Daughter on the Stage*, Alfred A. Knopf, New York, 1972.

Weissman, Philip, *Creativity in the Theatre*, Basic Books, Inc., New York, 1965.

West, J. B., and Mary Lynn Kotz, *Upstairs at the White House*, Coward, McCann & Geoghegan, Inc., New York, 1973.

Wilk, Max, editor, *The Wit and Wisdom of Hollywood*, Atheneum, New York, 1971.

Wilson, Edmund, *The Twenties*, Farrar, Straus, & Giroux, New York, 1975.

Winterich, John T., editor, *Squads Write!*, Harper & Brothers, New York, 1931.

Wood, Peggy, *How Young You Look*, Farrar & Rinehart, Inc., New York, 1941.

Woodward, W. E., *The Gift of Life*, E. P. Dutton & Co., New York, 1947.

Woollcott, Alexander, "After June 30, the Deluge," *The New Yorker*, June 20, 1925.

———, *Enchanted Aisles*, G. P. Putnam's Sons, New York, 1924 (originally in *Vanity Fair, Scribner's, The North American Review, Life, The New York Times,* and *The New York Herald*).

————, "General Utility," *The New Yorker,* April 28, 1928.

————, *Going to Pieces,* G. P. Putnam's Sons, New York, 1928.

————, "The Great Camera Mysteries," *The New Yorker,* November 12, 1927.

————, "Heureux Noel," *The New Yorker,* January 1, 1929.

————, "The House That Jack Built," *The New Yorker,* December 26, 1936.

————, "Knight With the Rueful Countenance," *The New Yorker,* January 1, 1939.

————, *Long, Long Ago,* Viking Press, New York, 1943 (original copyright registration each year 1930–1943, inclusive).

————, "The Man Who Ruined Paris," *The New Yorker,* October 2, 1926.

————, *Mr. Dickens Goes to the Play,* G. P. Putnam's Sons (Knickerbocker Press), New York, 1922.

————, "The Mysteries of Rudolfo," *The New Yorker,* March 18, 1933.

————, "Office-boy of Destiny," *The New Yorker,* October 13, 1928.

————, "Open-Letter Department," *The New Yorker,* December 19, 1936.

————, "The Owner of Ben Finney," *The New Yorker,* May 12, 1928.

————, "Portrait of a Man with Red Hair," *The New Yorker,* December 1, 1928.

————, "The Prodigal Father," *The New Yorker,* July 19, 1930.

————, "The Revival of Ruth Draper," *The New Yorker,* December 29, 1928.

————, *Shouts and Murmurs,* The Century Co., New York, 1922.

————, *The Story of Irving Berlin,* G. P. Putnam's Sons, New York, 1925.

————, "Trips on the Magic Carpet," *Cosmopolitan,* July, 1932.

————, "Two-eyed Connelly," *The New Yorker,* April 12, 1930.

————, *While Rome Burns,* Grosset & Dunlap, New York, 1934.

————, editor, *The Woollcott Reader,* Viking Press, New York, 1935.

————, editor, *Woollcott's Second Reader,* Viking Press, New York, 1937.

————, "V.A.," *The New Yorker,* March 7, 1925.

————, "The Young Monk of Siberia," *The New Yorker,* March 9, 1929.

————, and George S. Kaufman, *The Dark Tower,* Random House, New York, 1934.

Woollcott, Barbara, *None But a Mule,* Viking Press, New York, 1944.

Woollcott, Sergeant Alexander, *The Command Is Forward,* The Century Co., New York, 1919.

Zolotow, Maurice, *Stagestruck,* Harcourt, Brace & World, Inc., New York, 1964.

Index

Index

Index

Index

Index